100
Years of
Alabama
Football

A Century of Champions
1892 - Alabama Football - 1992
™

100 Years of Alabama Football

Gene Schoor

LONGSTREET PRESS
Atlanta, Georgia

This book is dedicated to
Paul "Bear" Bryant,
immortal Alabama coach

Published by
LONGSTREET PRESS, INC.
2150 Newmarket Parkway
Suite 102
Marietta, Georgia 30067

Printed in the United States of America

1st printing, 1991

Library of Congress Catalog Number 91-061928

ISBN 0-56352-007-9

This book was printed by R. R. Donnelley & Sons, Willard, Ohio. The text was set in ITC Clearface Regular by Typo-Repro Service, Inc., Atlanta, Georgia.
Jacket Design by Kim Glover.
Book Design by Jill Dible/Tonya Beach.

ACKNOWLEDGMENTS

I wish to thank the authors of the following books for the wonderful contribution their efforts have made to the story of 100 YEARS OF ALABAMA FOOTBALL: John Underwood and Bear Bryant, *BEAR, the Hard Life and Good Times of Alabama's Coach* (Little, Brown, 1974); Mickey Herskowitz, *The Legend of Bear Bryant* (McGraw-Hill, 1987); Clyde Bolton, *Crimson Tide: the Story of Alabama Football* (Strode, 1972); Naylor Stone, *Coach Tommy of the Crimson Tide* (1954); Benny Marshall, *Winning Isn't Everything* (Parthenon, 1965); James Peterson and Bill Cromartie, *Bear Bryant: Countdown to Glory* (Leisure Press, 1983); James Edson, *Alabama's Crimson Tide* (Paragon, 1946); Herb Michelson and Dave Newhouse, *Rose Bowl Football: Since 1902* (Scarborough House, 1977); Bart Starr, *STARR* (Morrow, 1988); Joe Willie Namath, *"I Can't Wait Till Tomorrow . . ."* (Random House, 1969); Ken Stabler, *Snake* (Doubleday, 1986); Edwin Pope, *Football's Greatest Coaches* (Tupper & Love, 1965); and George Sullivan, *Foootball's All-Time Greats* (Putnam, 1968).

I would also like to acknowledge the work of the following sportswriters: Dave Anderson, George Vecsy, Koe Marcin, Michael Wilbon, Tom Wheatley, Zipp Newman, Alf Van Hoose, Marvin West, Cecil Hurt, Ivy McLemore, Bob Mayes, Wayne Hester, Charles Hollis, Jeff Hand, Greg Bailey, Roscoe Nance, Bill Lumpkin, Al Browning, Steve Martin, Tom Siler, Mike Lupica, Jimmy Breslin, Phil Pepe, Jimmy Cannon, Dave Klein, Larry Fox, John Pruett, Geoffrey Norman, Malcolm Moran, Gordon White, Steve Weiberg, Gary Cartwright, Joe Durso, Peter Finney, Bob Farrell, Max Kanter, John Crittendon, Harold Stout, Glen Willoughby, Jim Johnston, Chris Hall, Ben Nolan, and many others too numerous to mention. I also acknowledge the following magazines and newspapers: *Sports Illustrated, The Sporting News, Sport Magazine, Inside Sports, New York News, New York Times, New York Post, Tuscaloosa News, Birmingham News, Birmingham Journal, Birmingham Times, Newark Star-Ledger, Los Angeles Times, Los Angeles Herald, Birmingham Post-Herald, Dothan Eagle, Huntsville News, Gadsden Times, Huntsville Times,* and *Montgomery Advertiser.*

I offer a special acknowledgment to the late Bear Bryant. As a sportscaster in New York City, it was my pleasure to interview Coach Bryant from the first year of his career at Alabama. I interviewed Coach Bryant approximately ten times on the air for my programs, and much of the material in this book is a result of these talks. I also appreciate having been able to interview such other Alabama greats as Joe Namath, Ken Stabler, Marty Lyons, Coach Gene Stallings, Coach Frank Thomas, Bart Starr, Ray Perkins, Don Hutson, an Paul Bryant, Jr.

I want to offer special heartfelt thanks to publisher Chuck Perry, who gave it his best shot, and editor John Yow of Longstreet Press.

I am also deeply grateful for the generous help and cooperation of many people at the University of Alabama, especially Rob Davis of Host Communications/Alabama Sports Network; Brenda Burnette, Larry White; Ann Barron; the University of Alabama Sports Information Department; Steve Townsend of the University of Alabama Athletic Department; Athletic Director Cecil "Hootie" Ingram; and head football coach Gene Stallings.

I want especially to thank those two ladies at the Bryant Museum, Jan Adams and Debbie Turpin, and, finally, my All-American literary agent Julian Bach.

Photo credits: Cliff Byrd, Kent Gidley, the Athletic Department, and the Sports Information Office of the University of Alabama.

FOREWORD: ALABAMA MEMORIES

BOBBY HUMPHREY, '88

Playing football at the University of Alabama meant a lot to me. Several times I worked at the Legion Field stadium selling Cokes, and I always visualized myself down there on the field playing football for the Crimson and White.

One of my best memories was the first time I hit the 200-yard mark; I rushed for 250 yards against the University of Tennessee and scored three touchdowns. That really made me proud. That was one of my biggest and most exciting moments right there.

CORNELIUS BENNETT, '86

The University of Alabama has a tremendous football tradition, and the people in the athletic department give you a chance to prove yourself both on and off the field.

The game that really sticks out in my mind is the Auburn game my sophomore year (1984). We were 4–6 going into the game, and nobody gave us a chance to win, but we went out and laid our guts on the line and won the game, 17–15. And of course I'll never forget that hit on (Notre Dame quarterback) Steve Buerlein in 1986. The momentum totally shifted in our direction, and we dominated both offensively and defensively the rest of the game.

OZZIE NEWSOME, '77

Tradition and winning were very important, but Alabama didn't just recruit athletes; they recruited student athletes. When a student signed on and stepped on campus, he became part of the big University of Alabama family.

I'll always remember the Notre Dame game in 1976. Coach Bryant had given us such a great talk at the pre-game meal that I was ready to run through a wall for him, and then we went out and got behind 21–7 at the half. Coach came back to say that evidently some people didn't believe what he said before the game, and he would have something to say to those people after the game. I definitely saw a difference out there in the second half.

JOHN HANNAH, '72

Playing football was an education unto itself. Coach Bryant taught you a lot of things that weren't necessarily taught in the classroom.

One Saturday back in my sophomore year, we had such a rough practice that several guys were sent to the hospital with heat stroke and dehydration. The next day some of the guys had left, and we were wondering why we were still there. Coach Bryant said, "You learned an important lesson yesterday. You learned that you are going to push yourself and push yourself, and you aren't going to die. You will always pass out before you die." We all looked at him like he was crazy, but when we thought about it we saw that he was right. Most people never push themselves far enough to find out what they can do.

JOHNNY MUSSO, '71

Most practice sessions I wouldn't want to dredge up, but one session was memorable — the night before we traveled to play Southern Cal in the opening game of my senior year. Unknown to anyone outside the team — including students and sportswriters — we had switched to a wishbone offense and had closed all our practices. But that night, the students organized a pep rally in the Quad, and the rally moved over to the football field. They climbed the fence and pulled the curtain back and held the rally while we practiced. The students' excitement really built when they realized they were seeing something no one else had seen, and the whole thing was really emotional. I think the students played a big part in helping us win that game.

KENNY STABLER, '67

The education and the opportunity to play football that I received at Alabama just meant everything in the world. Coach Bryant always preached a tremendous team attitude and the importance of sacrificing yourself for the good of the team, and we were motivated by a man who was the best of all time.

My experiences at Alabama were a starting point for everything I have done since then, on and off the field. I was part of the National Championship team my sophomore year, 1965. In my junior year I was voted MVP when we beat Nebraska in the Sugar Bowl. In my senior year we beat our biggest rival, Auburn, in a rain storm in Birmingham. I look around the walls of my office at things I collected from those years, and they really bring back a lot of fond memories.

LEE ROY JORDAN, '62

It was an honor to play for an outstanding organization like the University of Alabama football program, and to play for a man such as Coach Bryant.

One of my most memorable games was the 1960 Georgia Tech game in Atlanta my sophomore year. We were behind 15–0 at the half, and everyone knew that Coach Bryant was going to get on us something awful. But he didn't; all Coach said was, "We got 'em right where we want 'em," and we came back and played one of the best halves of football we had played all year. Richard O'Dell, who had never attempted a field goal before in his life, came on to kick the game winner, and we beat Tech 16–15.

HARRY GILMER, '47

One of the most dramatic days for me was going to play Tennessee in Knoxville in 1946 because my 91-year-old grandfather came to watch the game. We lost, but it was one of the best games I ever played, and my uncle asked him after the game, "What did you think of the boy's play?" "Oh, it was alright," he said, "but what interested me was seeing all these people." There were about 50,000 people there, and he never dreamed of seeing so many people in one spot.

FRED SINGTON, '30

I had just lost my father in 1925, and we didn't have much money, so getting a scholarship to Alabama to get an education meant a great deal to me. I treasure my Phi Beta Kappa key just about as much as I do my All-America football.

Back when I was playing there were no lights, and one day at practice Coach Wade was not very happy with what we were doing, so he divided the team into squads and told us to run the single slot. After about ten minutes Coach Wade had a long distance phone call, so he took care of it and then went on home. We were still out there running plays in the pitch black dark. And we would still be out there if somebody hadn't gone in to call and ask Coach Wade if it was alright for us to quit. He was a tough coach.

HOYT "WU" WINSLETT, '26

In 1925 we were practicing at Rickwood in Birmingham prior to playing Georgia for a Rose Bowl bid. (Assistant) Coach Crisp called us all into a huddle and went over everybody until he got to right end Ben Hudson from Montgomery. He dropped his voice and said, "Hudson, the people of Montgomery think you're yellow." Then he switched over to me and said, "Winslett, we've been keeping you around here for three or four years, and you haven't done anything yet. We're gonna try you one more time." Then he turned to Pooley Hubert: "Hubert, your mother is depending on you over in Meridian. She's sick in bed and hoping you'll do her a good job." Well, Pooley started crying then and there, and Coach Crisp said, "Let's go to the ball field." We beat Georgia 27–0 that day."

INTRODUCTION

If the Crimson Tide of Alabama has become synonymous with gridiron glory from Spokane to Winter Haven, there's a reason for it—lots of reasons.

From that day in 1892 with Bill Little brought football home to Alabama from his eastern prep school, to this current 100th season, Alabama has recorded a football history without parallel.

After running through almost as many coaches as players during the pre-World War I era, the Crimson Tide established itself as a national football power with the arrival of Coach Wallace Wade in 1923. In 1925 Wade led 'Bama to its first National Championship by edging Washington 20–19 in the Rose Bowl, and the Tide has occupied that exalted throne ten times since then.

Wade also led the Tide to its first Southern Conference Championship, and another twenty-one Southern/Southeastern Conference Championships have followed—including an incredible eight during the 1970s.

The Rose Bowl that Alabama participated in in 1925 was the first of forty-two bowl appearances for the school. Starting in 1959, his second year as head coach of his alma mater, Bear Bryant took the Tide to a bowl game every year until his retirement, a total of twenty-four straight.

No less than seventy-four Alabama players have been named first-team All-Americans, beginning with "Bully" VandeGraaff in 1915, and dozens of those names still ring loud in the annals of college ball: Pooley Hubert, who quarterbacked the first National Championship team; Millard "Dixie" Howell and his great receiver Don Hutson; the amazing jump-passer Harry Gilmer; not to mention such huge stars of the modern era as Lee Roy Jordan, Joe Namath, Ray Perkins, Kenny Stabler, Johnny Musso, John Hannah, Ozzie Newsome, Bobby Humphrey, and three-time All-American Cornelius Bennett.

If Wallace Wade was Alabama's first coach of legend, he was certainly far from the last. Frank Thomas led the Tide for sixteen years, 1931-1946, garnering three SEC Championships and one National Championship during his tenure. Of course, only one man coached Alabama longer than Thomas, and that man was Bear Bryant. In addition to the twenty-four straight bowl games his teams played in, Bryant won thirteen SEC Championships and six National Championships. His grand total of 323 victories earns Bear Bryant the ultimate distinction of being the winningest coach in the history of college football.

Excitement, achievement, excellence, and the greatest names in the history of the sport—these are the hallmarks of Alabama football, a tradition celebrating its first hundred years and anticipating its second hundred.

Roll, Tide!

CRIMSON TIDE

1
IN THE BEGINNING

1892–1922

Ironically, football came to the University of Alabama through the misfortune of William G. Little, a Livingston, Alabama, youngster who had been sent to Phillips Exeter Academy in New Hampshire in the late 1880s to prepare for his entrance to Yale. Before he could graduate from prep school, however, his older brother died, and Bill left Phillips Exeter to return to his family in Livingston.

During his prep school days, though, Bill had fallen in love with football, the somewhat rugby-like game whose popularity had been steadily growing on eastern campuses for the past several decades. American football had repudiated its kicking-and-heading, soccer-like origins by 1871, when Harvard initiated the so-called "Boston Game," wherein players could pick up or catch the roundish ball and run with it if pursued, and in 1876 Harvard and Yale played the first football game with eleven men on each side.

Interestingly, this same Harvard-Yale game marked the appearance of Yale's Walter Camp, and thus began the career of one of the most illustrious figures in the history of American football. For the next fifty years, Camp would figure prominently as player, coach, organizer, legislator, chairman of the rules committee, and selector of the recognized All-America teams. Camp's guidance and influence would prove largely responsible for football's evolution away from rugby and into the uniquely American sport it has become.

So it was that when William Little enrolled at the University of Alabama, he wasted no time intriguing his schoolmates with his football outfit and his stories about the game he had played at the academy. He instructed them in the few simple rules of the game, and in short order Little and his friends had formed a University of Alabama team.

Since Bill was the only player with actual

experience, he was elected captain of the first Alabama football team in 1892. At six feet tall and 220 pounds, he was an imposing guard on that inaugural team. Other charter members of Alabama football included: E. L. Cope, guard; H. M. Pratt, center; F. M. Savage, tackle; Eli Abbott, left tackle; D. A. Grayson, right end; Burr Ferguson, left end; Bill Walker, quarterback; Hub Keyser, right halfback; Dan Smith, left halfback; and Bill Bankhead, fullback.

Eli Abbot, charter member of Alabama football.

The day after a practice game against "Prof. Taylor's team at the Ball Park" (according to the *Birmingham News*), University of Alabama football officially began with a game against the Birmingham Athletic Club on November 12, 1892. The Cadets, as the Alabama team was then called, lost a hard-fought contest to the heavier, more experienced Athletic Club by the score of 5–4, but a month later the Alabama squad ran roughshod over the Athletics and recorded their historic first victory, 14–0. (In those days a century ago,

a touchdown counted for four points, a goal after touchdown was worth two, and a field goal was good for five.)

On the afternoon of February 22, 1893, George Washington's Birthday, the city of Birmingham and the entire state of Alabama were caught up in a frenzy of excitement over the first-ever football battle between Auburn and Alabama. Special trains had arrived from Montgomery, Selma, Anniston, and other points around the state, and by game time, carriages, carts, and wagons had rolled into Lakeview Park, the site of the game.

Promptly at three-thirty the crowd of three thousand settled down as the two teams made their way onto the field: Alabama in white uniforms, red stockings, and a large "U of A" on the sweaters; Auburn in blue sweaters inscribed with a large orange "A," white pants, and blue stockings. The team captains, Auburn fullback Tom Daniels and Alabama's Bill Little, met at midfield for the toss of the coin.

Auburn had played its first football game a year earlier, whipping the University of Georgia 10–0, and had played Trinity (now Duke University), North Carolina, and Georgia Tech later in the year. Auburn's greater experience showed in the opening minutes of this inaugural state-championship game, as their backs repeatedly drove through the lighter Alabama line. Two touchdowns by Rufe Dorsey gave Auburn an early 8–0 lead.

But then Alabama's Frank Savage tore off runs of fifteen and twenty-two yards to bring the ball to Auburn's 10-yard line, and Savage again smashed through the Auburn defenders to give 'Bama its first score against Auburn. Bill Bankhead kicked the goal after touchdown and quickly cut the lead to 8–6.

The second half belonged to Auburn and Rufe Dorsey, however, and Alabama

Tough practice in the early days.

dropped the first game in what would become a vaunted series, 32–22. After the game, Captain Daniels and his teammates hoisted a trophy emblematic of the state championship, awarded by the City of Birmingham. The story on the front page of the *Birmingham News* ended on this note: "As the game ended, a series of cheers rent the air; then the sun went down, blotting out the day of the greatest football game that was ever played in the state of Alabama."

Unfortunately, the Auburn game set the tone for an 1893 season in which Alabama went without a victory. Indeed, the story of Alabama football for the next decade was few victories but many coaches. The first coaching change took place when Eli Abbott, who had coached for the first three seasons but had lost all four games on the 1895 schedule, was replaced by Otto Wagonhurst. Wagonhurst was to be paid $750 for the '96 season, but the senior class

could raise only $50. Some thirty years later, after Alabama had become a national power and had won a Rose Bowl Championship, the Athletic Association located Wagonhurst and paid him the balance of his salary. Coach Wagonhurst was no doubt shocked and delighted.

Wagonhurst served only one season before being replaced by A. G. McCants, but such turnover was not peculiar to Alabama. Football was still a relatively new game in the South, and finding qualified coaches was a difficult problem. Adding to the predicament were the poor salaries, the lack of proper and safe equipment for the players, and the dearth of adequate playing and practice facilities.

Hill Ferguson, a fine halfback on the 1895 and '96 teams, recalled his experiences for the school yearbook, the *Corolla*: "The teams I played on had very crude uniforms. We had pants that had some sort of tuft padding in the knees; occasionally we had jerseys with a big monogram "A" on the front, and sometimes there was some padding about the elbows. The backs did wear nose guards which seemed to give them a measure of protection, but there were plenty of broken noses. In lieu of head guards, the fellows let their hair grow in the spring in order to have some sort of protective mop for the following fall."

This absence of protective gear, in combination with the violence inherent in the game, led to an increasing number of severe injuries during the 1890's. Von Gammons, for example, a University of Georgia star, was knocked unconscious—and subsequently died—after hurling himself against a "wedge play" favored by many teams.

To address this growing problem, officials from Yale, Harvard, Princeton, and Penn convened at the University Athletic Club in New York. After consulting with leading coaches and other football officials throughout the nation, the committee proposed the following rules changes—changes that saved football and added to the color and excitement of the game:

- mass plays like the wedge and the flying wedge, which had caused so many of the injuries, were banned;
- the length of the game was reduced from ninety minutes to seventy, divided into thirty-five-minute halves;
- on the kickoff, the ball had to travel at least ten yards to be put into play;
- players were prohibited from laying hands on an opponent unless that opponent had the ball; and
- every game had to include the following officials: a referee, an umpire, and a linesman.

For Alabama football, the first years of the new century brought more coaches (Mike Harvey, Jim Heyworth, Eli Abbott again, and William Blount) and an increas-

ing number of games per season. The 1902 schedule included eight opponents, and Alabama played a full slate of ten games in 1904. The team's records during these years generally hovered at the break-even mark; however, the 1904 squad, despite tough losses to Clemson, Tennessee, and Auburn, followed their fine quarterback Billy Wyatt to seven victories, the most successful campaign in Crimson history thus far.

Despite the rule changes of 1901, the early 1900s brought no end to football's violence. In 1905, officials reported that nineteen deaths and 159 serious injuries had occurred during the 1904 season, and their report unleashed a storm of protest against the brutality of the game. President Theodore Roosevelt, an avid football enthusiast, called in representatives from some fifteen colleges and demanded that they clean up the game. Out of this meeting at the White House came a new rules committee, later called the Intercollegiate Athletic Association. The IAA's efforts on behalf of a cleaner, safer game produced the following changes in the rules of football: the legalization of the forward pass; the reduction of the halves to thirty minutes; increased first-down yardage from five to ten yards; and the establishment of a neutral zone separating the two teams by the length of the ball.

At Alabama, 1906 marked the arrival of yet another new coach, but in this case an extremely successful one. Over the next four seasons, Jack "Doc" Pollard, a Dartmouth all-around star, led the Crimson to twenty-one victories, five ties, and only four losses.

The 1906 Auburn game in Birmingham featured a couple of interesting twists. Just as the excited crowd of five thousand were settled in for the kickoff, Coach Mike

First Alabama Football Team.

Donohue of Auburn filed an official protest against Alabama player T. S. Sims, alleging that Sims was not a legitimate Alabama student. Pollard conceded that Sims had been off-campus for a time in order to tend to personal problems, but that he had met all academic requirements of the university. After lengthy discussion among the two coaches and the officials, the protest was denied and Sims was allowed to play.

Then, once the game was underway, Coach Pollard surprised the Auburn defense with a completely new formation, which he called the "Shift," or the "Military Formation." This new offensive wrinkle, which the team had practiced for a week behind closed doors, called for the linemen to step back from the ball just before the snap and shift to an unbalanced line. Each time the shift was employed, Auburn was caught off-

balance, and the Crimson Tide slashed through for long gains. Coach Pollard's new scheme has to be credited for Alabama's huge 10–0 victory over its bitter rivals.

A loss to a strong Vanderbilt team spoiled an otherwise perfect season for Alabama, but they nevertheless finished with what was for Coach Pollard a typically fine five win—one loss record.

For the Auburn game in 1907 Coach Pollard once again dug deep into his bag of tricks, but his new plays, and even the game itself (which ended in a 6–6 tie), proved secondary to what transpired between the two teams long after the game was over. The constant bickering between the two rivals ever since their first meeting in 1893 erupted into a serious disagreement over the game contract for the 1908 contest. Three points were in dispute: Auburn wanted to bring more players to the game than Alabama consented to; Auburn demanded an increase in expense monies; and the two schools could not agree on the officials for the game. By the time the three points of contention were settled, schedules had been finalized. Alabama offered to play between Thanksgiving and December 5, but Auburn was set on ending its season on Thanksgiving.

Thus, one of the fiercest and most colorful rivalries in Southern college football was suspended . . . and was not resumed until 1948!

Derrill Pratt, captain of Alabama's 1909 team, talked about his football memories with sportswriter Clyde Bolton of the *Birmingham News*:

"We played football because we loved the game. Those were good days then. I think I hold a lot of records for placekicks. I kicked one for about forty-seven yards against the Haskell Indians, and we beat them 9–8.

"Against Georgia, I kicked one ball that went twenty yards into the stands. I still have the ball I kicked against Georgia about sixty years ago. It's about the size and shape of a watermelon. It's so big you couldn't hold it, and if you wanted to pass it off, you had to lay it in the palm of your hand and spin it off.

"The equipment was terrible. The headgear was a piece of leather with some cotton under it. Big thing was the nose guard. That was about the only protection we had, and Coach Pollard made most of them. It was a leather pad that fitted over your nose, and it had a piece on it that you could bite to hold it in your mouth. If you wanted any pads for your shoulder or your pants, you had to make them for yourself.

"Doc Pollard designed one play for us where we grabbed our fullback by the seat of his pants and tumbled him over the center for a gain every time. . . . We were only allowed to dress eighteen men for a game in those days. I noticed that when Bear Bryant opened practice in 1979 he had ninety-six men suit up. But we only had 350 students at the university in 1907.

"Doc Pollard was the first real good coach we had at Alabama. Everybody liked him. After four years with us he was appointed head coach at Washington & Lee, and I went there as his assistant. I later joined the Alabama coaching staff."

Several interesting rule refinements were instituted for the 1910 season, among them the reduction of the value of the field goal from four to three points and the elimination of the fifteen-yard penalty for an incomplete pass. But for Alabama, after Coach Pollard's resignation, it was back to short-lived coaches and less than spectacular records. Guy Lowman, Alabama's twelfth coach in fourteen years, guided the Crimson Tide to a four win-four loss record in 1910. He was followed in 1911 by D. V. Graves, a Missouri graduate, who led the team to an improved record of five wins, two losses, and two ties.

However, 1912 proved a crucial year in the annals of Alabama football. On this year Dr. George Denny, an ardent booster of Alabama athletics, was named president of the university. At the time of his appointment, five hundred students were enrolled in the university. When he retired twenty-five years later, enrollment had grown to 4,800, and the Alabama Crimson Tide was a recognized national football power with four Rose Bowl victories to its credit. Early on, Dr. Denny realized that football could be a rallying point for students and alumni, and he did everything in his power to support the program.

Strange as it seems today, with Auburn off the schedule Sewanee emerged as Alabama's fiercest rival during the years

Bully VandeGraaff, Alabama's first All-American, led the Tide to a big win over Sewanee in 1915.

immediately before World War I. As Alabama star Bully VandeGraaff recalled for Clyde Bolton, "We had a terrible time beating Sewanee back then in the 1912–1914 period. ... They had great teams every year. We finally beat them [in 1915]. That was just about the greatest thing that happened while I played ... winning a game against Sewanee."

That 1915 Sewanee game was indeed memorable. Alabama clung to a 10–0 lead going into the final period, only to see Sewanee rally to tie the score. The huge crowd in Birmingham were now on their feet, roaring with every play. Threatening to take the lead, Sewanee quarterback Herring dropped back to pass, but VandeGraaff

charged in to force a hurried throw. Bully leapt into the air and deflected the ball — into his own hands — then sprinted sixty-five yards for the touchdown that nailed down Alabama's first win over Sewanee since 1894.

Alabama concluded the season with six wins and two losses, and Bully VandeGraaff was the first player in Alabama football history to be named to the All-American team.

Guiding the Crimson Tide during this wartime era was hard-driving Irishman Tom Kelly, selected by Dr. Denny in 1915 with the mission "to give Alabama the best football teams possible." And indeed, playing in the just-completed Denny Field, it appeared that Alabama was on a mission, as

Riggs Stephenson helped new coach Xen Scott inaugurate the post-war era.

IN THE BEGINNING

it opened Kelly's first season by routing its first three opponents (Howard, Birmingham Southern, and Mississippi College) by a total of 151–0. While that kind of success proved impossible to sustain, Coach Kelly, during his three-year tenure at the Alabama helm, produced a distinguished record of seventeen wins, seven losses, and one tie.

Because of the war, Alabama did not field a football team in 1918, but Dr. Denny wasted no time getting the post-war era off to a strong start. He hired a Cleveland sportswriter by the name of Xen Scott as his new head coach for the 1919 season, and Coach Scott brought instant success. Led by stars Riggs Stephenson and Luke Sewell, Scott's inaugural team streaked to five straight shut-outs, capped by a 40–0 thrashing of despised Sewanee. The next week, however, the Tide stumbled and fumbled its way to a tough 16–12 loss to Vanderbilt in Nashville, its only loss of the season. By the end of the 1919 season, Alabama had outscored its opponents 280–22 while compiling a record of eight wins and one loss, the finest in twenty-seven years of Alabama football.

In Coach Scott's second season, 1920, the Tide was riding a streak of *six* straight shutouts as they headed into the Vanderbilt game. Vandy had won all five previous encounters between the two teams, but this year Riggs Stephenson led 'Bama to a bitterly contested 14–7 victory, the team's seventh win in a row. After win number eight against LSU, it was time to face Georgia.

A record crowd of fifteen thousand sat enthralled as the two powers, tied at 14–14, entered the game's final minutes. Stephenson advanced the ball to Georgia's 30-yard line, but Georgia withstood three Alabama drives to force a fourth-down play. The veteran Talty O'Connor attempted the drop-

kick for the win, but Georgia smashed through the line to block the kick, and defender Cheeves snatched up the ball and streaked eighty yards for a touchdown. A crushing defeat, but the Tide bounced back for three more wins and a superlative 10–1 record for the season.

The graduation of such stars as Riggs Stephenson, Luke Sewell, Mully Lenoir, Talty O'Connor, and Walt Hovater resulted in a lackluster 1921 record of five wins, four losses, and two ties, but the schedule makers at the university were far from discouraged. They included on the 1922 slate two of the nation's powerhouses — Texas, with a winning streak of fifteen games in a row, and Pennsylvania, coached by football genius John Heisman.

After big wins over Marion and Oglethorpe, a tough loss to Georgia Tech, and a tie against Sewanee, Alabama traveled to Austin for its first-ever game against Texas. A stubborn Tide defense came to play, but seven fumbles by the offense gave the game away. Six days later, having traversed half the nation from Texas to Tuscaloosa, Alabama headed north to face Penn, winner of its last four out of five games. For years Alabama had heard stories of those football giants of the North — Yale, Harvard, Princeton, Penn — and Alabama was the first Southern team to ever venture into the den of any of these lions. Searching for a psychological boost, Coach Scott halted his team in Washington to watch Navy play Penn State. Here were two fine teams, but the point was made: Alabama could play in this league.

A crowd of 25,000 was gathered at Penn's Franklin Field, by far the largest house Alabama had ever played before. But the Tide was not intimidated. After an exchange of kicks in the opening minutes, Bill Baty took a great pass from quarterback Stumpy Bartlett on the 27-yard line. Bull Wesley

'Bama's 1922 squad, the first southern team to take on a northern power, defeated Penn, 9–7.

then kicked a perfect field goal for a 3–0 Alabama lead. However, that lead was erased in the second period when Penn's Ted Sullivan caught a pass on the Alabama 35-yard line and sprinted for a touchdown.

Perhaps the biggest play of the game came when Penn's huge All-American tackle Thurman was caught slugging Bill Baty, Alabama's smallest player, and was ejected from the game. Thurman had been the defensive anchor, and with his removal, Alabama's backs began to penetrate. In the third period, Bartlett battled his way from the Penn 27-yard line down to the four. On third down, Pooley Hubert smashed through the line for an apparent touchdown, but fumbled the ball. Luckily, the Tide's Clyde "Shorty" Propst was there to pounce on the loose ball and preserve the touchdown. Wesley's attempted point-after sailed wide, but Alabama clung to its 9–7 lead until time expired. The Crimson Tide

had won the biggest game in its history and struck a huge blow for Southern football.

The euphoria did not last long, though. Alabama won three of its last four games, but within weeks of the season's end, Xen Scott was dead from cancer. The entire campus went into mourning for its hugely popular and successful coach.

Scott's untimely passing brought to an end the early era of Alabama football, but it was an end that hailed a great new beginning. The smashing victory over powerhouse Penn brought national recognition to the strength and quality of Alabama football. In his syndicated column following that game, premier American sportswriter Grantland Rice had written, "Coach Xen Scott's Alabama Crimson Tide football team proved that Southern football is now on a par with the finest teams in the country."

2

THE
WALLACE WADE
ERA

1923–1930

Wallace Wade was one of five sons of a prosperous Tennessee farmer. After attending high school in Trenton, he went on to prep school in Chicago, then enrolled at Brown University and became a star guard. Wallace Wade was the only man to both play and coach in a Rose Bowl game.

Following his discharge from the Army in 1919, Wade was offered a coaching post at the Fitzgerald-Clarke prep school in Tullahoma, Tennessee. In two seasons there, Wade won fifteen games and lost but two. That record attracted the attention of Dan McGugin, who hired him at Vanderbilt, and the two of them did such a magnificent job that the Commodores did not lose a game in 1921 and '22. When McGugin recommended Wade to Alabama in 1923, Dr. Denny wasted little time signing him up.

Under Xen Scott, football practices were short and intense and fun. Under Wade, practices were grueling affairs that started early and ended late. He was a tough, strict disciplinarian, and he worked his young, inexperienced team into exhaustion.

Wade contended that "Nobody ever got back-slapped into winning anything." He stressed efficiency rather than theatrics, production rather than excuses. The best you can do, he claimed, is not good enough unless you beat the other team.

On September 29, 1923, Alabama opened the season with just two players with more than a year's varsity experience: end Al Clemens, the captain, and tackle Jack Langhorne. Graduation had taken such stars as Stumpy Bartlett, Bull Wesley, Shorty Cooper, Jack Hovater, and Tommy Newton.

All-Conference tackle Bill Buckler, one of Coach Wallace Wade's stalwarts.

Now Wade would have to rely on Johnny Mack Brown, Bill Baty, Jim Johnston, Andy Cohen, and Grant Gillis in the backfield; tackles Ben Compton, Bill Buckler, and Langhorne; guards Bruce Jones, Jim Camp, and Ben Enis; and center Clyde Propst.

After opening the season with wins over Union College and Ole Miss, the Crimson Tide travelled some 1,500 miles to battle a Syracuse University team rated as one of the powerhouses in the East. Alabama fought a courageous battle against the bigger, more experienced Orangemen and left the field at halftime on the short end of a 3–0 score. However, the Tide tired under the constant pounding of the big Syracuse backs and suffered a 23–0 defeat. In later years, Wade would maintain that he learned more about coaching in the game against Syracuse than in any other in his life.

On October 20, Alabama and arch-rival Sewanee fought each other ferociously for three quarters, with neither team scoring. But with just two minutes left in the game, Johnny Mack Brown intercepted a Sewanee pass and raced to midfield before he was brought down. Then Pooley Hubert took over. Carrying the ball on five successive plays, he cracked off-tackle for the touchdown. Ben Compton kicked the extra point, and Alabama had earned a hard-fought 7–0 victory.

After an easy win over Spring Hill, Alabama battled Georgia Tech to a scoreless tie before a crowd of 10,000 spectators. Tech racked up eighteen first downs to none for Alabama, yet failed to score. It was the marvelous kicking by Grant Gillis that saved the day for the Tide. Gillis kicked on at least five occasions from behind his own goal line, each kick measuring at least forty yards.

Before a big Homecoming Day crowd at Tuscaloosa, Grant Gillis starred on offense and defense as Alabama defeated a stubborn, challenging Kentucky Wildcat team, 16–8. After big victories over LSU and Georgia, Alabama squared off against Florida in a quagmire of mud and rain. It was the season finale for the Tide, and Florida slipped away, 16–6.

Thus, Coach Wade's first season included seven wins, two losses and a tie, with Alabama running up a total of 222 points while holding opponents to fifty. Captain Al Clemens and Grant Gillis were named to the All-Southern Conference team at season's end.

1924

When practice was called early in the fall of 1924, Coach Wade beamed at the veterans who were returning from the 1923 season: the great fullback and team captain

Coach Wallace Wade won three National Championships during his eight-year tenure at Alabama.

Pooley Hubert, who could run, pass, and kick the ball; Johnny Mack Brown, who would run wild in every game during the next two years; Grant Gillis, another triple-threat back; and Davey Rosenfeld, who could batter a brick wall. It was a talented, experienced team, and Wade was in great spirits as he directed each practice session as if it were a championship match-up.

Fulfilling Coach Wade's highest expectations, Alabama, led by Brown and Hubert, opened with shutout wins over Union, Furman, Mississippi College, and rival Sewanee. Georgia Tech, fresh from a smashing 15–13 victory over Penn State, was next, and Tech had not suffered a defeat to a Southern College since 1920. The Yellow Jackets figured themselves a heavy

favorite to defeat Alabama, but Tech reckoned without Johnny Mack Brown. What Johnny Mack did that October 25 will be remembered forever, for he gained 135 yards in ten plays, teaming with Dave Rosenfeld to defeat Tech 14–0 before a crowd that jammed every inch of the stadium in Atlanta.

Alabama rolled onward with a 61–0 thrashing of Ole Miss and then, on Homecoming Day at Tuscaloosa, crushed Kentucky 42–7. The feature of the afternoon was a sensational 99-yard jaunt by Johnny Mack Brown through the entire Wildcat team, a spectacular touchdown that brought the huge crowd up on its feet cheering for fully five minutes. The next week, however, a Centre College team that had lost but once all year long played an oustanding game to defeat Alabama by a 17–0 score. Alabama's fast and shifty backs, Brown, Rosenfeld, and Hubert, were helpless against the strong defense put up by Centre College. The Tide never penetrated beyond Centre's 50-yard line as it dropped its first game of the season.

Alabama had no trouble rallying for its final game of the season. In Birmingham on November 27, the Crimson Tide scored in every period to win easily over the Georgia Bulldogs by 33–0. Pooley Hubert was brilliant as he tossed touchdown passes to Caldwell and Ben Hudson. When he wasn't tossing passes, Hubert ran the ball in for a touchdown and intercepted two Georgia passes for good measure.

The marvelous eight win–one loss season was over. Alabama had won the Southern Conference Championship for the first time, and Pooley Hubert, Johnny Mack Brown, and guard Bill Buckler were named to the All-Southern Conference team.

1925

"Alabama will field the greatest collection of backs in the South," wrote Zipp Newman in his feature story describing Crimson Tide prospects for the 1925 season. "With Johnny Mack Brown, the finest back in the South; Pooley Hubert, the Tides' All-American quarterback; Grant Gillis, a great punter; Red Barnes, a fine all-around star; Jimmy Johnston, a marvelous linebacker; Red Pepper, a strong, sturdy, 200-pound fullback; Davey Rosenfeld, Herschel Caldwell, and Red Brown, Johnny Mack's flashy brother; Harry Holder, Bill Morrison, and Dick Hammer. Here is a collection of backs that can do everything. Coach Wade can shut his eyes and pick a great combination of backs from this group that cannot be equalled."

In its first two games of the 1925 season,

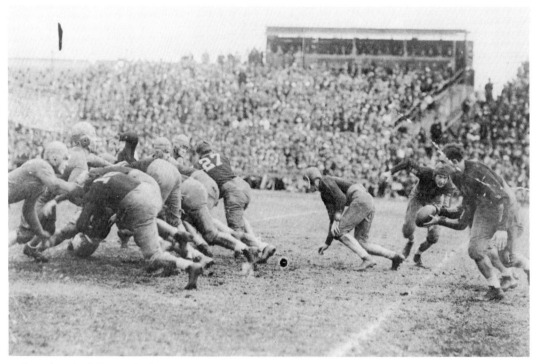

Pooley Hubert (no helmet) and Johnny Mack Brown (coming to ball) lead the Tide over Georgia in 1925.

Alabama crushed Birmingham-Southern, 50–7, and then manhandled Union 53–0. LSU was expected to provide stiff opposition, but the Tide smashed the Tigers, 42–0, with Hubert and Brown sweeping the ends and tackles for huge gains and six touchdowns. Sewanee, always one of the top Southern teams, went down to defeat, 27–0, as Emile Barnes, Hubert, Wu Winslett and Herschel Caldwell starred.

It was Johnny Mack Brown who provided the great thrill in the crucial game against undefeated Georgia Tech. Early in the game, Brown took a Tech punt on his 45-yard line and, behind the magnificent blocking of Hubert and Buckler, threaded his way fifty-five yards for the only score of the game. The following week provided another tough, savage, but thrilling contest as the Tide prevailed over a scrappy Mississippi A & M squad. Pooley Hubert passed to Winslett for thirty yards and the only score of the game, and 'Bama notched its sixth* win of the season. Johnny Mack Brown and Red Barnes ran over and through the Wildcats of Kentucky for a convincing 31–0 victory, and the Florida Gators went down 34–0 the following week, with Hubert tossing touchdown passes to Brown and Barnes. In the season finale Coach Wade employed a dizzying array of lateral passes and spinners, and the Tide flashed to an easy 27–0 win over Georgia.

After a spectacular season of nine wins and no losses, a season in which its defense had allowed a grand total of seven points, sportswriters voted the Alabama team Champions of the twenty-two-team Southern Conference. Quarterback Pooley Hubert was named the conference MVP and hailed as the finest quarterback the South had ever seen. At the annual banquet at the end of the season, the 1925 squad was voted "The Greatest Team in Crimson Tide History."

Triple-threat Pooley Hubert led the Tide to its first National Championship in 1925.

An even more important honor was yet to come, however — an invitation to represent the Southern Conference in the 1926 Rose Bowl. Coach Wade was excited, but left it up to his players to decide whether they wanted to take the trip to Pasadena to play Washington.

Wade called a team meeting and said to his squad, "Fellows, this is what a trip to the Rose Bowl means: There will be three weeks of tough, hard practice. I want you all to realize that to the full and think about it. But here's something else to remember. Southern collegiate football is not recognized as being anywhere near what it is in the East, West, and Midwest. So here's your chance to be part of history."

The players then voted unanimously to accept the challenge.

Commentators agreed that Washington had the better backfield and also a wide edge from tackle to tackle. What advantage Alabama might have, if it meant anything, was the expected balmy weather. Accordingly, the Huskies were installed as three-to-one favorites.

Meanwhile, at Pasadena, Coach Andy Smith of the University of California, whose team had lost to Washington by a 7–0 margin, called the Huskies "one of the greatest college football teams I've seen in my coaching career." Only a tie with Nebraska marred the perfect Washington record.

If the Crimson Tide players were eager to remove the cloak of inferiority that had clouded Southern football in the minds of many of the nation's sportswriters and fans, the Washington Huskies were equally determined to demonstrate the superiority of Western football.

Immediately a series of wire stories appeared on the sports pages extolling the fearsome prowess of George Wilson, the Huskies' All-American halfback, who two years before as a sophomore had run wild in the Rose Bowl against the Navy. Another story reported that Wilson had turned down the then tremendous sum of $3,000 to play professional football in order to test his crushing drives against the greatest team in the South."

Once the battle was joined, however, it quickly appeared to the Huskies that the Tide eleven was faster and tougher than they had expected. Alabama drove up the field with several short passes, the last of which brought the ball to the Washington 15-yard line. But on the next play Winslett's pass to Brown was high, and as Johnny Mack leapt for the ball, Wilson appeared out of nowhere, snatched the ball, and carried it back to the 47-yard line.

On successive line smashes, Wilson and halfback Patton cracked down to the Alabama 3-yard stripe, and on third down Patton hit the left side of the line for a touchdown. Washington took a 6–0 lead as the all-important try for the extra point was missed. Wilson and Patton combined for another score in the second period. With the ball at the Alabama 25-yard line, Wilson faked a run, faded back, and tossed a beautiful pass to Patton in the end zone. After another missed extra point, it was Washington 12, Alabama 0.

During the half-time, Coach Wade talked with quarterback Hubert: "Go ahead Pooley; give 'em everything you've got. Run the ball yourself all you want. It's rough and tough out there but you can do it."

Coach Wade was right. But he was fortified by the certainty that George Wilson had been knocked unconscious shortly after Washington's second score and would not be in the Huskies' line-up for the third period. The circumstances of the injury were revealed after the game. Wilson had been routinely charging through the Tide's line and breaking up plays that ordinarily gained a good deal of ground. So Captain Jones, Hubert, and guard Bill Buckler allowed Wilson to break through the line one more time, then mousetrapped him and knocked him out.

Taking advantage of Wilson's absence, and with the ball on the Huskies' 41-yard line, Pooley Hubert carried on five successive plays and drove all the way in for the touchdown. Buckler kicked the extra point to make the score Washington 12, Alabama 7.

On its next possession Alabama drove seventy yards for its second touchdown. Gillis, the Tides' fine halfback, took the pass from center, faded back to his 41-yard line, and shot a great pass to Johnny Mack Brown, who caught the ball on the 25-yard line and sprinted over the goal line for the touchdown. Buckler's conversion was good and Alabama had a 14–12 edge. Moments later Ben Enis recovered a Washington fumble at mid-field to set up the Tide's

Johnny Mack Brown scored two touchdowns in Alabama's first Rose Bowl game in 1926.

third touchdown. Pooley Hubert tossed a perfect strike to Johnny Mack Brown on the 20-yard line, and Brown dashed home for a 20–12 lead.

With the Tide close to another score in the final period, George Wilson returned to the game, and the embattled Huskies dug in and took over the ball on downs. Then Wilson sped off-tackle for seventeen yards, and subsequent smashes through the line brought the Huskies to the Alabama thirty.

Wilson then passed to his quarterback, Gottormsen, who raced fifteen yards for the Huskies' touchdown. Gene Cook's extra point made it Alabama 20, Washington 19, and that's how it ended. The Washington Huskies, one of the finest teams in West Coast history and the three–one favorite over Alabama, went down to defeat in one of the most stunning and exciting games in the history of college football.

Coach Wallace Wade, cool, crafty, and

1925 National Champions: *Front row:* Rosenfeld, Winslet, Gillis, Jones, Barnes, Enis, T. Brown. *Second row:* McDonald, Morrison, Perry, Pickhard, Buckler, Hudson, Bowdoin. *Third row:* Hubert, Vines, M. Brown, Payne, Pepper, Holmes, Camp, Caldwell, Dismukes.

quiet-spoken, had enjoyed considerable success in his three years at Tuscaloosa but this was a crowning achievement. The 1925 season ended with the Crimson Tide winning its second consecutive Southern Conference Championship. Alabama had one of the nation's three unbeaten, untied elevens and had been scored on only once during the regular season. When the Crimson Tide was declared National Champions, the South marched into big-time football.

When the game was finally over, Coach Wade scanned more than 300 congratulatory wires from elated Dixie supporters and then paid a solemn tribute to Hubert and Brown: "I'll never forget my touchdown twins: Hubert, one of the greatest quarterbacks I've ever seen, and Brown, the kid with the hands of a magician."

Following the 1926 contest there developed a bond between the West and South which contributed much to the glamor and popularity of the Rose Bowl game and to the subsequent bowl craze throughout the nation. And in the heart of Coach Wallace Wade, Alabama's first Rose Bowl appearance retained a place of special honor. Twenty-five years later, he observed, "I still regard the 1926 Alabama-Washington game as the most spectacular, exciting, and dramatic college football game that I ever saw and the most important football game in Alabama history."

The more than 45,000 spectators who saw the game agreed with Coach Wade. And so did the nation's sportswriters, who voted the 1926 Rose Bowl game "one of the ten great college football battles of all time."

1926

The Helms Athletic Foundation of Los Angeles presented the Alabama Football team its "Team of the Year" trophy, emblematic of the 1925 National Championship, but few of Alabama's most supportive fans gave the Tide a chance to repeat their 1925 triumphs.

Graduation had taken some of the finest players in Alabama history, and even Coach Wade was at his gloomiest. He pointed out that Alabama would have no players as experienced and as skillful as the ones we lost, that the '26 squad would be lighter, both in the line and in the backfield, and that teamwork would not be as good and the passing would not be as good as last year." "But," he concluded, "the prospects are that Alabama will have a good team, almost as good as any in the South."

As it happened, the Crimson Tide of 1926 streaked to a second straight perfect season of nine wins and no losses. If the offense supplied fewer fireworks than the '25 squad, the defense was no less imposing, giving up a total of three touchdowns all year. For example, in its 21–0 triumph over a highly rated Georgia Tech team, Alabama's great line held the fast Tech backs to just two first downs in the game. Alabama had its only real scare in the fifth week of the season, as Sewanee fought the Tide tooth and nail for the better part of four periods. But then, with only two and a half minutes to play, Fred Pickhard blocked a Sewanee punt that rolled out of the end zone for a safety and a hair-raising 2–0 win.

The Tide defense was dominant in consecutive shutouts over LSU and Kentucky. In fact, against the Wildcats, the Alabama line allowed a total of thirty-five yards.

With impressive victories over Florida (49–0) and Georgia (33–6) to close out the season, Alabama had once again captured the Southern Conference Championship. This was the third in three years, and the Helms Athletic Foundation unanimously voted Alabama the National Champions. The Tide agreed to meet Stanford on January 1 in the Rose Bowl at Pasadena, California.

Wu Winslett helped lead the Tide to a 7–7 tie in the 1927 Rose Bowl versus Stanford.

Despite the remarkable showing of Alabama's great team a year earlier, the West Coast sportswriters were still having difficulty accepting the credibility of Southern football. Ernie Nevers, the former great Stanford star, said the Indians would beat Alabama by at least two touchdowns. Coach Pop Warner rated his Indians "a remarkable team led by All-American Ted Shipkey, a great end, the incredible running of 'Tricky Dick' Hyland, and the passing of fullback Bill Hoffman."

The Pacific Coast smugness appeared justified during the opening moments of the game as Stanford's Bill Hoffman passed to Dick Hyland for thirty-five yards. Three

1926 National Champions: *Front row:* Douglas, Holder, Ellis, Rosenfield, Barnes, Hamner, Brown, Caldwell, Dismukes. *Second row:* Enis, Morrison, Smith, Skidmore, Vines, McDonald, Black, Winslett, Hagler, *Third row:* Johnson, Bowdoin, Pepper, Holmes, Pickhard, Pearce, Hurt, Payne, Perry, Taylor.

plays later George Bogue tried a field goal from the sixteen, but the kick was wide. After an exchange of possession, Hyland made a fair catch on the Indians' 37-yard line, and Stanford steadily advanced down the field. With the ball on Alabama's 18-yard line, Bogue faded back and tossed to Ed Walker for the score.

The score remained 7–0 until there were just two minutes to play. The fans were streaming from the Stadium when Alabama's great center Babe Pearce cracked through the Stanford line and blocked Frank Wilton's fourth-down punt on the Sanford 47-yard line. But the ball bounced crazily in favor of Alabama, and the Crimson Tide pounced on the ball on the 14-yard line. Here Coach Wade sent in Jimmy Johnston, who had been one of Alabama's great backs during the season but had injured his shoulder. Now it was Alabama's last chance, and Johnston alternated in carrying the ball with All-American Wu Winslett over the next five plays, and Alabama smashed across the Stanford goal line for its first score. Alabama's Herschel Caldwell calmly brushed the dirt from his

shoe and kicked the extra point for a 7–7 tie.

Tackle Fred Pickhard, who had been oustanding all season long and had been a defensive bulwark in holding Stanford to one touchdown, was named the outstanding player of the 1927 Rose Bowl.

1927

The University of Alabama began the 1927 season with an incredible record of twenty-two consecutive victories. Heading into his fourth year at the Tide's helm, Wallace Wade stood tall as one of the nation's leading football coaches. He had lost but three games in four seasons, his record an astounding 34–3 with two ties. But Wade knew that 1927 would be a year in which he had to completely rebuild the team. Graduation had taken its toll on his Rose Bowl Champs, and there were few players on the roster with any varsity experience.

Indeed, 1927 proved to be the year of Alabama's return to mortality. After wins over Millsaps and Southwest Presbyterian and a 0–0 tie against LSU at Birmingham, a smooth, revenge-seeking Georgia Tech team defeated Alabama, 13–0. It was Alabama's first loss in twenty-five games. The team shook it off, though, and rolled over Sewanee 24–0. Then, in a last-minute thriller, Alabama defeated Mississippi State by a score of 13–7, and the following week came from behind to beat a strong Kentucky eleven, 21–6.

At this point, however, with the season record standing at a highly respectable 5–1–1, the proverbial wheels came off. For the first time in recent memory, Alabama lost three straight games. Clyde Crabtree, with a thrilling 95-yard touchdown run, led Florida to a hard-fought 13–6 win. Ten days later, a superior Georgia eleven defeated Alabama 20–6 in the first game for the two teams at Birmingham's Legion Field. And in the season's final game, Vanderbilt's All-American triple-threat star Bill Spears passed and ran the Commodores to an upset victory over Alabama by 14–7.

So the Tide closed out the season with a disappointing 5–4–1 record. Fred Pickhard, the outstanding team captain, was named to the All-Southern Conference team.

1928

The 1928 season saw some improvement over the previous campaign, but not enough. Alabama opened the season by defeating Ole Miss by a score of 27–0 and Mississippi State by 46–0, but the following week they lost a heart-breaking, bitter battle to underdog Tennessee, 15–13.

The frustrating pattern was repeated over the next four weeks. Alabama romped to a lopsided 42–12 win over ancient rival Sewanee, but the next week they traveled to Madison, Wisconsin, to meet a Badger squad that had won five games in a row. In a tough battle that had a crowd of 35,000 fans on edge throughout, the Badgers made the Tide their sixth victim with a 15–0 victory. The Crampton Bowl in Montgomery provided a much-needed 14–0 victory over Kentucky. Just one week later, however, a powerful, aggressive Georgia Tech eleven roughed up the Crimson Tide, 33–13.

The Tide ended the season with wins over Georgia and LSU for a 6–3 season, but now the howls of anguish from the alumni rent the air in Tuscaloosa. Wallace Wade, a most sensitive coach, heard the unhappy wails and began to look for an out.

1929

The voices of dissent became louder and longer in 1929 as Alabama once again came up with a season record of six and three. The bright spots included wins over Mississippi College, Mississippi, and Chattanooga, along with a huge 35–7 demolition of Sewanee. But with a loss to Vanderbilt and another to Georgia in the final game of the season, the lamentations of the Alabama alumni began in earnest.

On April 1, 1930, the *Birmingham News* featured a screaming headline that shocked every football fan in the state. The story reported that Coach Wade had resigned to take a similar post at Duke University. Wade still had one more year to fulfill his Alabama contract and began to plan for that final year as soon as the hysteria had calmed down.

Fred Sington, All-American tackle in 1929, 1930.

1930

With Wallace Wade feeling the pressure that only football in Tuscaloosa can generate, Alabama opened the 1930 season with an easy 43–0 win over Howard University. The Tide featured a wide-open running attack sparked by sophomore quarterback John "Hurri" Cain and John Henry "Flash" Suther. The two Alabama tackles, Fred Sington and Captain Foots Clement, stopped Howard's ball-carriers on just about every play.

The following week, Alabama defeated Ole Miss on Denny Field in Tuscaloosa by scoring sixty-four points, and the Tide chalked up its third victory of the season by easily beating the Sewanee Tigers, 25–0. After the win over Sewanee, an Atlanta sportswriter picked a new nickname for the Alabama team. He wrote: "'The Crimson Tide' is a thing of the past. From now on they are to be called 'The Red Elephants.' Their every move reminds me of the king of the jungle . . . the elephants. When the Tide team moves the earth thunders . . . like the rumble of the elephants."

In the first really big game of the season, Alabama defeated the Tennessee Volunteers, 18–6, with Cain, Suther, and John Campbell scoring, and Vanderbilt was beaten 12–7 the following week. Then, after Alabama shutouts of Kentucky and Florida, the Rose Bowl Committee had announced that the winner of the Alabama-Georgia game would be invited to the Rose Bowl. Hurri Cain, the sophmore quarterback for Alabama, used his tremendous punting to handcuff the Georgia backs and keep the Georgia offense pinned in their own territory for most of the game. Campbell scored in the third period, then sped fifty-five yards in the final period to set up a touchdown by Cain. Alabama scored its biggest win of the year, 13–0, and secured the trip to the Rose Bowl.

The 1930 team outscored its opponents 247–13, while compiling its 9–0 undefeated mark. Fred Sington and "Flash" Suther were named to the All-American team, and crooner Rudy Vallee, one of the most popular singers of the era, composed a song called "Football Freddy" that was played on radio stations throughout the nation for years to come. The 1930 squad was hailed as the "Champions of the Universe" by the *Corolla*.

Few teams have ever achieved mastery over another on Pasadena's historic gridiron with the thorough workmanship displayed by Alabama in the Rose Bowl against Washington State in 1931.

Alabama did not win on sheer power. With Wade directing the strategy from the bench like a field general, shifting his line-up around to get the very most out of every changing situation, and with Johnny Cain calling a perfect sequence of plays, Alabama stunned the Cougars in a second period tornado of three successive touchdowns as a roaring crowd thundered their applause.

The surprise of the afternoon came as the teams trotted onto the field: Alabama's reserves were facing the Cougars! This daring bit of strategy was just enough to keep the Washington players off balance. The Tide's second stringers played the Washington varsity on even terms throughout the first quarter, and when Coach Wade inserted his regulars into the game, the

John "Hurri" Cain ran, passed, and kicked the Tide to the 1930 National Championship.

J. B. "Ears" Whitworth's field goal was the final tally in the Tide's 1931 Rose Bowl victory.

result was overwhelming. Alabama racked up those three touchdowns within a six-minute span.

First, Jimmy Moore faded back from the Bama 39-yard line and tossed a beautiful pass to "Flash" Suther, who took the ball over his shoulder and sped over the goal line. Then, after an interception on the Washington forty-seven, Ben Smith made a magnificent one-handed catch of a pass by Moore and spun over the goal line. The huge throng had just resettled into their seats when Campbell slashed right guard for nine yards, then on the next play broke through his left guard, cut for the sidelines, and raced forty-three yards for the third touchdown. The final tally came in the third period when "Ears" Whitworth, with

quarterback Tucker holding the ball, booted the field goal to give Alabama a 24–0 margin.

In his nationally syndicated column sportswriter Grantland Rice said: "Great praise should be given to Hurri Cain . . . his judgment of plays was the closest thing to Notre Dame's Frank Carideo we have seen all this year . . . and that great All-American tackle, Fred Sington, why he was all over the field bringing down the Cougar backs whenever they threatened to gain ground. Frankly, I've never seen a better exhibition of tackle play than Sington. He has to be one of the greatest in football."

Alabama and Wallace Wade had now made three trips to the Rose Bowl and had yet to meet defeat.

1930 National Champions: *Front row:* Houston, Holley, Taylor, Miller, Bellini, Causey, Elmore. *Second row:* Moore, Frey, Brown, Suther, Campbell, Dotherow, Laslie, Cain, Long. *Third row:* Sington, Sims, Howard, Whitworth, Clement, Sharp, Smith, Jackson, Tucker, Boykin, Erdreich (mgr.). *Back row:* Sanford, Hanson, Miller, Dobbs, Hood, Barker, Eberdt, McRight, Godfrey.

THE WALLACE WADE ERA

3

FRANK THOMAS COMES TO ALABAMA

1931–1946

"There's a young backfield coach at Georgia who should become one of the greatest coaches in the nation," Wallace Wade had told Dr. Denny when he resigned. "He played football under Knute Rockne at Notre Dame, and Rockne called him one of the smartest players he ever coached. His name is Frank Thomas, and I don't believe you could pick a better man."

Frank William Thomas, the youngest of six children, was born to James Thomas, an ironworker, and Elizabeth Thomas on November 15, 1898, in Muncie, Indiana. It was only sixteen years after the Thomases had come to America from Cardiff, Wales. The Thomases moved to East Chicago when Frank was ten. He played his first football there at Washington High school, and when Western State Normal College in

Kalamazoo found that Frank was Washington's first four-sport letter man, they offered him a job for his room and board and a chance to complete his education at Kalamazoo.

Tommy Thomas checked into Kalamazoo with a bank-roll of $7.50 and two pairs of pants. The first Saturday there he played against the University of Michigan. He weighed only 135 pounds, but he played fifty-five minutes and ran eighty-seven yards for a touchdown. In 1918, Tommy Thomas, all 135 pounds, was captain of the Western State team. When the season was over, the old Notre Dame star Clipper Smith arranged for Thomas to go to Notre Dame and Knute Rockne.

In 1920 and '21, Tommy was Notre Dame's number one quarterback, and in

1923 Georgia coach Kid Woodruff offered Thomas $2,500 to coach his backfield. Tommy joined the Woodruff staff, and in 1923 Georgia defeated everybody except Yale and Alabama. After three years as head coach at Chattanooga, Harry Mehre, Georgia's new head Coach, brought Tommy back as his chief aide. In 1930 Thomas was named head coach at Alabama . . . and a new era was to begin.

1931

The ink was hardly dry on Frank Thomas's new Alabama contract when President Denny jolted Thomas with a meaty bit of his philosophy.

"Mr. Thomas," Denny said deliberately, "material is ninety percent of football, and coaching is ten percent. We will furnish you with the ninety percent and you will be held strictly accountable for delivering the remaining ten percent."

Thomas promptly went to work with a vengeance. He hired as assistants Red Drew and Dick Donaghue, then shelved Wallace Wade's successful single-wingback with an unbalanced line and introduced his own Notre Dame box. The immediate problem was that halfback John Cain, the only varsity player left from the 1930 season, was too modest to call his own signal. So Thomas promptly turned the signal-calling over to Hillman Holley and began to prepare his squad for the opening game of the season, September 26.

In the first ever game under Coach Thomas, before more than 20,000 fans in Tuscaloosa, a hard-running, fast-moving Crimson Tide demolished Howard University 42–0. Halfback Leon Long scored three

touchdowns, Hillman Holley scored twice, and Larry Hughes added another score. The following week Johnny Cain scored three touchdowns as Alabama racked up a 55–6 win over hapless Ole Miss. The grueling two-a-days their new coach had put them through in September were paying off; once again the Tide was rolling.

After trouncing Mississippi State, 53–0, the Tide hit its first snag of the new era. The Tennessee Vols, led by Gene McEver's three touchdowns, broke the string of thirteen successive Alabama wins by ripping Alabama's defense for a 25–0 victory in a game played at Knoxville.

The Tide quickly recovered from the Tennessee defeat and came back strong to defeat Sewanne, 33–0. The following week featured brilliant individual performances by Johnny Cain and Kentucky's great back, Ralph Kercheval, whose booming punts kept the ball in Alabama territory most of the first three periods. But in the final period, with the score tied 7–7, a long punt by Cain put the ball on the Wildcats' 8-yard line, and when Kercheval attempted to kick out of danger, Tom Hupke, Alabama's scrappy guard, blocked the kick. Alabama recovered behind the goal line for a safety and a 9–7 win.

With four more wins in a row, including a heart-stopping 14–6 victory over Vanderbilt in Nashville, Alabama closed out its first season under Frank Thomas with a marvelous 9–1 record.

1932

The 1932 season picked up where the '31 campaign left off. The Tide rolled over Southwestern of Memphis, 45–6; thrashed

Mississippi State 53–0 as Captain Johnny Cain scored three touchdowns; and then traveled to Washington D.C., to defeat a spirited squad from George Washington University, 28–6. Two newcomers — a long, lanky, pass-catching end named Don Hutson and a shifty triple-threat halfback, Millard Howell — were improving with each game, and Thomas had high hopes for these would-be-stars.

Once again it was Tennessee that brought the Tide to a standstill. Played in a torrential downpour, the game featured a spectacular punting duel between Johnny Cain and Beattie Feathers of Tennessee. Alabama led 3–0 in the third period when Feathers punted high into the air and the ball settled down on the Alabama 1-yard line. On the next play, Johnny Cain dropped back to kick out of danger, but the center pass was low, and John's hurried kick traveled just twelve yards. Tennessee took over, and in four plays Feathers went off tackle for the score. Wynn kicked the extra point, and the game ended with Alabama on the short end of a 7–3 score.

The Tide came back the next week to defeat Ole Miss by a 24–13 margin, then

(L-R) Assistants Red Drew, Happy Campbell, and Hank Crisp with new coach Frank "Tommy" Thomas.

Millard "Dixie" Howell, Alabama passing star in '32, '33, and '34.

FRANK THOMAS COMES TO ALABAMA

barely squeaked by Kentucky (12–7) and V.P.I. (9–6) before their luck ran out in a loss to Georgia Tech, 6–0.

Alabama then shut out Vandy, 20–0, and in the final game of his illustrious career Johnny Cain scored the game's only touchdown as the Tide defeated St. Mary's, 6–0. Alabama ended the season with an 8–2 record, and John Cain and guard Tom Hupke were named to the All-Southern Conference team.

1933

Coach Frank Thomas had won seventeen and lost but three games in the two years he had coached at Alabama. But the big game of the year was against Tennessee and Tommy had lost twice to the Vols. As a matter of fact Tennessee had defeated Alabama in four of the last five games between the two schools and the wolves were beginning to howl.

Having noticed the fine passing and kicking skills of young Millard "Dixie" Howell, Thomas promptly shifted the kid into the backfield, and by the second game of the 1933 season the skinny youngster proved that he would be a capable replacement for Johnny Cain, who had graduated. Thomas installed a new set of plays built around Howell, and by mid-season the forward passing combination of Howell to Don Hutson was creating all kinds of defensive problems for every Alabama opponent.

Alabama's record stood at 2–0–1 (including a 0–0 tie against Ole Miss) when, on October 21, more than 25,000 fans turned out for the big game of the year against a powerful Tennessee team coached by wily Bob Neyland. Tennessee had run up a string of thirteen consecutive wins, then

had dropped a squeaker to Duke University, 10–2, a week before the Alabama contest. Now they were ready to start a new streak by defeating Alabama.

Beattie Feathers, Tennessee's All-American and Alabama's nemesis, scored the first Tennessee touchdown in the second period on a 23-yard dash off-tackle. But in the third period, Howell received the center snap, spun completely around and deftly handed the ball off to Erskine Walker. Dixie continued his run as if he still had the ball, and Walker cracked off-tackle and dashed forty-five yards to tie the score 6–6. Then, with the game's last seconds ticking away, Howell slashed over the goal line from the 5-yard line, giving Alabama a 12–6 victory in one of the most thrilling games of the year.

The following week, October 28, the Crimson Tide traveled to New York City's famed Polo Grounds to take on Fordham University, one of the nation's top teams. A jam-packed crowd of more than 60,000 fans were on hand to cheer as Alabama lost a heart-breaker to the Fordham Rams, 2–0.

The only score came in the first period when Alabama gained possession of the ball on the 2-yard line. Dixie Howell attempted to punt, but Ram tackle Tony Sarna blocked the kick, and it bounded across the end zone for a safety.

Alabama finished the season in a blaze of glory. It shut out Kentucky and V.P.I.; then Dixie Howell, by intercepting a pass and running three straight times, eased them past Georgia Tech, 12–9. In the final game of the season Howell sparkled again to give Alabama a close 7–0 win over Vanderbilt.

By winning its last four games and finishing with a 7–1–1 record, Alabama clinched the first-ever Southeastern Conference Championship. Dixie Howell and guard Tom Hupke were named to the first All-SEC team ever selected.

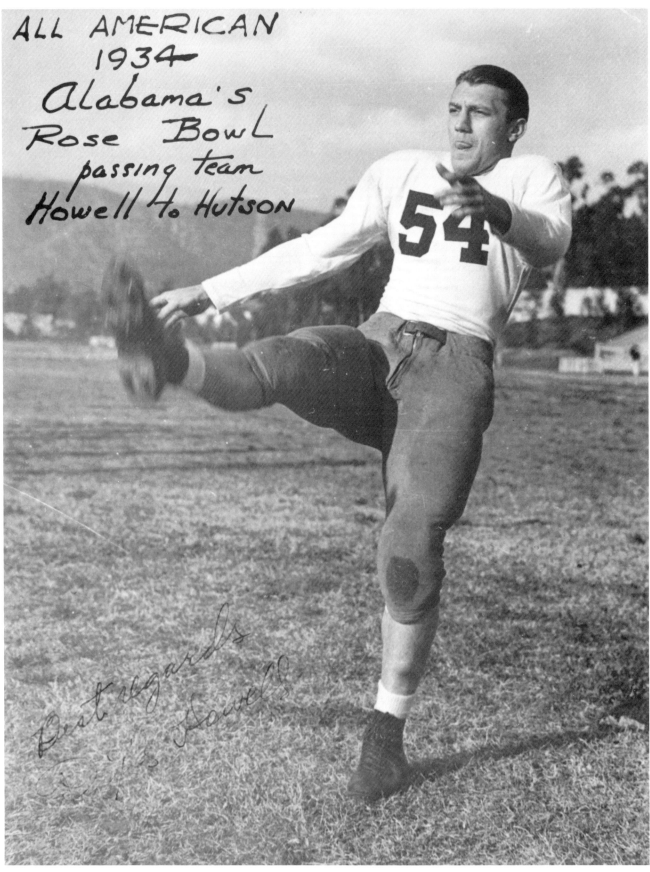

ALL AMERICAN
1934
Alabama's
Rose Bowl
passing team
Howell to Hutson

Best regards
Dixie Howell

Howell to . . .

FRANK THOMAS COMES TO ALABAMA

ALL TIME
ALL AMERICAN END
ALABAMA
1934—

Hutson, Alabama's All-American combination.

What was more, as Tommy Thomas savored the fruits of the 1933 campaign, he looked forward to a season with several of the brightest young stars that he had ever seen together on one team. He couldn't wait for the 1934 season with Dixie Howell, Don Hutson, Paul "Bear" Bryant, Riley Smith, Joe Demyanovich, Charley Marr, and Bill Lee. Tommy knew he had a strong team and with a bit of Irish luck could go all the way.

1934

Don Hutson was born January 31, 1913, in Pine Bluff Arkansas, a railroad town in the southeastern corner of the state. He showed little interest in high school football, but Bob Seawall, a boyhood chum and the star of the team, urged him to try out. After graduation, the heavily recruited Seawall said he would go to Alabama, but only if the college would take his buddy Don Hutson, too. Grudgingly, Alabama agreed. Ironically, Seawall dropped out of school after two years, while Hutson became one of Alabama's greatest stars.

"The best story about Hutson," said Bear Bryant, "the one they still talk about on the campus at Tuscaloosa is the one about his love for other sports. Once during an Alabama baseball game, Hutson wore his track suit under his baseball flannels because a dual track meet was scheduled simultaneously on the track adjacent to the diamond. Between innings, Don stripped of his baseball togs, got into the starting block, and ran the 100-yard dash in 9.8 to win the race.

"That was the big thing some people forget about Hutson," added Bryant, "the speed that propelled him beyond the

defenders and enabled him to catch all those passes for us and for the Green Bay Packers, when he played for them."

Coach Thomas built his 1934 offense around the deft ball-handling and passing of Dixie Howell and the great receiving of Don Hutson. The other end was well taken care of by the six-foot-three, 225-pound Bear Bryant, who knocked down any player in the path of an Alabama ball carrier. Then there were Bill Lee and Jim Whatley, two fine tackles; Charlie Marr and "Tarzan" White at the guard positions; centers Kavanaugh Francis and Joe Dildy; and an all-star backfield that consisted of Howell, Riley Smith, Joe Riley, Joe Demyanovich, Young Boozer, Charley Stapp, and Tilden Campbell.

The Tide opened the '34 season with

Arthur "Tarzan" White was an All-SEC guard on the 1934 National Championship team.

lopsided wins over Howard, Sewanee, and Mississippi State, then came the big game against Tennessee at Birmingham. The match was a toss-up until Hutson took over in the third period. First he took a pass from Riley for fifteen yards. Then on an end-around play he picked up another 10 yards, and on another end-around play he cut back over his own left tackle and scored the winning touchdown.

The Tide surged over its next four opponents, whipping Georgia, 26–6; holding off stubborn Kentucky, 34–14; and whitewashing both Clemson and Georgia Tech, 40–0. Then, in the locker room, prior to the final game of the season against Vanderbilt, Coach Thomas talked to his squad:

"Men, there is much talk about the Rose Bowl game. The Committee is considering Alabama or Minnesota to play Stanford, and I believe we have a great chance of getting that bid . . . if we have a great win over Vanderbilt. I know you fellows want the game. So do I. Let's go out there and get into the Rose Bowl. Now, I want you to go out there and play the best game of your life."

In the "big game" of the year, played in Birmingham on November 20, Dixie Howell played the greatest game of his career. He passed and kicked and ran the ball until Vanderbilt's defense didn't know where the next play was coming from, and Alabama whipped Vandy, 34–0. A number of sportswriters covering the game declared that this Alabama team was the most versatile in the history of Southern football.

The Minnesota Gophers had also won their crucial game over Wisconsin by 34–0, so the Rose Bowl bid for the moment was still undecided. When Coach Thomas and the players returned to their Birmingham hotel, the hotel clerk said, "Coach, Los Angeles has called several times. They want you to call back."

Tackle Bill Lee was the captain of the '34 Championship squad.

Tommy made the call, and when he returned to the lobby, he informed his team that the Rose Bowl wanted Alabama. The roar of the players as they got the news could be heard back in Tuscaloosa.

"The Alabama squad left for the Rose Bowl on December 21," said Bear Bryant. "I remember how the cold chills ran up my back, and I think what won the game for us was the way Coach Thomas prepared us. I surely remember that. We were going to Pasadena by train, and the day before departure we worked out in the stadium at Tuscaloosa just as we had worked twice daily for the past two weeks. Evidently, we weren't pleasing Tommy because he blew the whistle and ordered head-on tackling for the last half of the practice.

"I clearly remember that train ride," said Bryant. "How long it was. And all that free food. I remember them having to take one of our players, Bill Young, off the train at Del Rio, Texas, when he suffered an appendicitis attack. And then we stopped at Tucson where we ran wind sprints for an hour and almost collapsed in the thin air.

"I remember falling in love with everything about California," said Bryant. "We stayed at the Huntington Hotel where all the movie stars hung out. A lot of name sportswriters were there: Grantland Rice, Henry McLemore, Paul Gallico, and there was a cub reporter named Ronald Reagan working sports for a local station. Reagan covered our practice sessions at Occidental everyday. Years later, I reminded him of those early days.

"There were movie stars all over the place—Dick Powell, Mickey Rooney, Jack Oakie, Tom Mix. Mix, the cowboy star, brought a couple of big linemen to watch us practice, two of the University of Southern California tackles, Marion Morrison and Floyd Herman. Morrison later became Duke Wayne, and Babe Herman was one of the great Brooklyn Dodger Baseball stars. I'll never forget that trip and all those great people we met," said Bryant.

Tommy Thomas was ashen-faced and trembling with the excitement just before the game began. "I didn't have a single hot line to deliver to my team," he later told Zipp Newman. "I wanted to say, 'this is like one of those great mythical battles and from yonder pyramids, forty centuries of warriors are watching you.' But instead I was thinking that beyond the Rockies lies a lot of railroad track. And if Stanford beats us it will be a long, sad ride back to Tuscaloosa."

As the game began, it appeared that Stanford would turn back Alabama as they struck quickly in the first few minutes of play. Stanford's right end, Keith Topping, recovered an Alabama fumble on the Tide's 29-yard line, and several line smashes later Bobby Grayson plunged across for the Stanford score. The kick was good and Stanford had a 7–0 lead.

But in the second period, Howell and Hutson took over.

A punt exchange gave 'Bama the ball on the Indians' 45-yard line. Howell took the ball in deep punt formation, started as if to go between end and tackle, then swung outside and downfield. Aided by magnificent downfield blocking, Howell streaked along the sideline, cut back towards the middle of the field, faked out the safety man, and crossed the goal line for Alabama's first score. Riley Smith missed the extra point and it was 7–6 Stanford.

Then the Crimson Tide unleashed an offensive barrage that has never been matched in all the years of Rose Bowl football. In the last ten minutes of the second period, Alabama scored sixteen unanswered points, including a 30-yard field goal by Riley Smith, a 67-yard touchdown sprint by Howell, and then a long, beautiful touchdown pass from Smith to Don Hutson.

By the end of the third period, Stanford had narrowed the gap to 22–13, but in the final quarter Howell lofted another tremendous pass to Hutson on the Stanford 20-yard line. Once again Don leaped high into

Frank Thomas congratulated by USC Coach Howard Jones, as Don Hutson (1) and Dixie Howell look on.

the air, took the ball over and out of the hands of a big Stanford defender, and galloped over for a touchdown. The game ended as Alabama intercepted a Stanford pass to give the Tide a tremendous 29–13 victory and the Championship.

Grantland Rice in his marvelous story of the game wrote: "Dixie Howell today gave you the impression of a Dizzy Dean throwing strikes all day long; he was an antelope along the ground and one of the greatest kickers the Rose Bowl has ever seen." But a

West Coast writer put it more poetically:
Nae man can tether "Time or Tide"
When Millard Howell and Hutson ride
The Rose Bowl airways down the field
And Stanford's choice is but to yield
Before the surge of Dixie's pride.

One of the greatest ever, the 1934 Alabama team had won the Rose Bowl, the Southeastern Conference, and had three players selected for the All-American team: Dixie Howell, Don Hutson, and tackle Bill Lee.

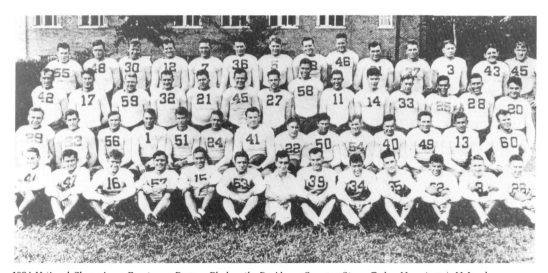

1934 National Champions: *Front row:* Rogers, Bludworth, Davidson, Granger, Stapp, Taylor, Marx (mgr.), McLeod, Williamson, Goldberg, Thompson, Riley, Shepherd. *Second row:* Ryba, Gandy, McDaniel, Howell, Boozer, Cochrane, Lee, Campbell, Angelich, H. Walker, Danelutti, A. White, Peters, Griffin. *Third row:* Dildy, Smith, Lyon, Morrow, Baswell, Ellis, Dobbins, Sneed, R. White, Tipton, Rhordanz, Nisbet, Scott, Stacy. *Back row:* Young, Radford, Coffman, Bryant, Moye, J. Walker, McGahey, Whatley, Keller, Marr, Hutson, Francis, Freeman, Demyanovich.

Paul Bryant was born in 1913, the eleventh of twelve children, the youngest of Wilson Monroe Bryant, of Georgia, and Ida Kilgore, from a family of Texas farmers. There were no paved roads in Moro Bottom, a few miles from the little Arkansas town of Fordyce, just timberland and wild hogs for hunting and cotton farms.

As the last boy still at home Paul had to do all the hard chores around the farm. He plowed and chopped wood, drew water for the cows, and was up every day at four on the days his mother made her selling trips, getting the wagon ready. Some people turn their childhoods into a fantasy and grow nostalgic over the Depression. Not Paul Bryant. He hated making those rounds in the wagon, and never let go of the pain he felt. Before he started school, the rounds would take mother and son past the schoolyard as the other kids were getting out for lunch. Even as late as the 1960s he remembered the names of the ones who laughed at him and made fun of the elderly mules hitched to the wagon.

Among the people who knew him in Fordyce, there were no glowing predictions of future success, not in coaching or anything else. A high school teammate named Ike Murray, a lawyer who later became the attorney general of Arkansas, once said, "If I had been writing the class prophecy for our senior class, I'd have written this about Paul: 'He'll be lucky to stay out of jail.' "

Paul played in the first football game he ever saw, in the eighth grade. At Fordyce High, he became an all-state end for the team. He had the size and he was mean. He was working one summer in a meat market when assistant coach Hank Crisp recruited him for Alabama. Later that summer, Crisp piled Bryant into his car and drove him to Tuscaloosa, where he became known as Alabama's "other end." *The* end, of course, was Don Hutson.

Paul "Bear" Bryant at Fordyce High in Arkansas and at the University of Alabama.

FRANK THOMAS COMES TO ALABAMA

1935

Young Boozer, Jr., was an outstanding halfback on the '35 and '36 squads.

In 1935 Coach Frank Thomas received a new five year contract to coach the Alabama team, but without such stars as Dixie Howell, Don Hutson, Bill Lee, and several other stalwarts of the 1934 eleven, the Tide started poorly. In the first three games, Alabama tied perennial opening-day patsy Howard, trounced George Washington, and lost to underdog Mississippi State, 20–7. Adding to the misery of the loss was that Bear Bryant was injured and taken from the game. On the sidelines, the team's trainer thought that Bryant had fractured his leg and quickly got Paul into the hospital.

Tennessee was next on the Tide's schedule, and Bryant made the trip to Knoxville on crutches and with his right leg in a cast. Just before the kickoff, the Alabama team doctor removed the cast and told Paul he could suit up for Tennessee, even if he didn't play. Coach Thomas turned to Bryant and asked him if he thought he could play. Bryant nodded, started the game, and in the first couple of minutes caught a pass that led to a touchdown. Several plays later Paul caught another pass, lateraled the ball to Riley Smith, and Smith dashed in for a touchdown. Alabama stunned Tennessee, 25–0, and the team's historians called it the finest game of Paul Bryant's college career.

Despite being riddled with injuries, the Tide rolled to victories over Georgia, Kentucky, Clemson, and Georgia Tech before being upset 14–6 by Vanderbilt in the season finale. The Tide finished 1935 with a record of six victories, two losses, and one tie, a merely ordinary record for a team accustomed to winning every game.

ALL AMERICAN
1935

U of ALA.
BACK

Riley Smith, All-American in 1935, had been one of the heroes of the Rose Bowl at the beginning of the year.

1936

Alabama opened the 1936 season with several new additions to the coaching staff, including Paul Bryant. Bryant had taken several assignments for Coach Thomas during the summer and had performed so well that Thomas asked Paul if he would be interested in coming back to Alabama.

"We were watching the Alabama baseball team," said Paul, "and I was sitting with coach Tommy. He asked me if I thought I could like to coach with him."

"Do you mean full-time" asked Bryant, who had just married his college sweetheart, Mary Harmon Black, and needed a job.

"Yes, I mean full-time," said Thomas. "Do you think you could handle coaching the varsity guards?"

"Yessir," said Paul, "I think I can."

"OK," said Thomas. "I'll give you $1,250 a year."

"I'll take it," said Paul Bryant. "I'm a married man now and need the job."

Alabama opened the season by avenging the 7–7 tie of 1935 and defeating Howard University, 34–0. The Tide then manhandled Clemson, 32–0, and, in the big Homecoming Game, struggled to a 7–0 win over a determined Mississippi State eleven. A tough, no-nonsense Tennessee team held Alabama to a scoreless tie in the fourth game of the season. Alabama put on a strong offensive drive in the second period, but Joe Riley was tackled on the 1-yard line as the half ended. Neither team threatened in the second half of the game.

From that point on, Alabama marched through Loyola, 13–6; defeated a favored Kentucky, 14–0; blasted a rugged Tulane squad 34–7; and defeated Georgia Tech,

20–16. This heart-stopper ended with Tech filling the air with passes in a vain attempt to pull the game out of the fire, but 'Bama's stubborn defense, led by guard "Tarzan" White, stopped Tech whenever they approached within scoring distance.

Alabama ended the successful season with a great win over a strong, determined Vanderbilt team. Vandy surprised Alabama by jumping off to a 6–0 lead in the first two minutes of the game, but in the third period Joe Riley passed to Ben McLeod for a touchdown, and Joe Kilgrow kicked the extra point to make it a 7–6 game in Alabama's favor. With but two minutes left to play, Riley tossed a perfect pass to Joe Kilgrow for Alabama's second touchdown and a hard-fought 14–6 victory.

After defeating Vanderbilt for an impressive 8–0–1 season record, Coach Tommy sat back and waited for a bid to the Rose Bowl, but no such bid was forthcoming. Instead the Rose Bowl Committee selected the Mustangs of Southern Methodist University. And Coach Thomas and his squad packed away their equipment and waited . . . for the next time?

Alabama's great guard "Tarzan" White and quarterback Riley Smith were named to the All-American and the first-team All-Southeastern Conference squads.

1937

The 1937 season owed at least some of its success to a young kicking specialist, one of Paul Bryant's first recruits.

"Recruiting was something new to me," recalled Bryant, "and when Coach Thomas asked to me check out a boy named Sandy Sanford, out of Russelville, Arkansas, I

2ND.
ALL AMERICAN
1937
U. of ALA.

"TACKLE"

[signature: Sincerely yours, Jim Ryba]

Tackle Jim Ryba, All-American in 1937.

set plans to get him for our team.

"Sandy was at a junior college in Russellville, and I went there with Coach Drew to try to change his mind about going to the University of Arkansas. We talked to Sandy and talked and talked. It got to be late at night, and Coach Drew said he was going back to his hotel. I wasn't satisfied. I went back to Sandy's dorm. He wasn't in and so I waited for him.

"About 2:00 a.m. he finally came in, and by 3:30 I was working out some math problems so he could turn in a paper he needed to graduate. I had finally talked him into coming to Alabama, but I still had to get him away from the Arkansas people before they showed up to claim him. Then I had to take him to his mamma and daddy in Adona, Arkansas. And I never told Sandy I didn't know the first thing about the math problems he had to finish."

Back on the campus in Russellville, recounted Bryant, "Coach Drew and another recruit, Al Davis, were walking out of the dining room. They didn't know I had Sanford. Then Drew walked out to the car and almost swallowed his cigar when he saw I had Sanford all set for Alabama."

'Bama started the 1937 season with six big wins in a row: 34–0 over Howard, 65–0 over Sewanee, 20–0 over South Carolina, 14–7 over Tennessee, 19–0 over George Washington, and 41–0 over Kentucky. Then came a terrific battle against Tulane. Playing in Tulane's Stadium before a crowd of 35,000 fans, the teams were tied 6–6. Then in the last two minutes of the game Alabama got the ball to the Tulane 41-yard line, and Sandy Sanford calmly walked in and kicked a magnificent field goal to win the game by three points.

After beating Georgia Tech in the closing moments of another tense battle, 7–0, the Tide faced yet one more titanic struggle, this time against Vanderbilt. The Crimson Tide trailed an aggressive Commodore team, 7–6, with only six minutes left to play when Coach Thomas once again called upon Sanford. This time Sandy booted one from a difficult angle on the 27-yard line, and Alabama had come for behind to win the final game of the season by the narrow margin of Sanford's kick, 9–7.

The victory over Vanderbilt gave Coach Thomas an incredible perfect season . . . nine wins and no losses. The very same afternoon there was a call from the Rose Bowl Committee with the invitation to play

a great University of California team in the New Year's Day game.

Coach Frank Thomas brought a solid, well-balanced team to Pasadena in 1938. The line was bulwarked by Captain Leroy Monsky, the All-American guard, while the tricky and fast Tide backfield featured Hal Hughes at quarterback, Joe Kilgrow and George Zivich at the halfback spots, and Charley Holm at fullback. The Tide also had one of the best placekickers in the nation in Sandy Sanford.

Coach Stub Allison's Golden Bears were probably the closest-knit group ever to play in the Rose Bowl. Allison's molding job was all the more remarkable since every one of the six seniors on the first team—end Perry Schwartz, quarterback John Meek, halfback Sam Chapman, center Bob Herwig, guard Claude Evans, and right guard Vard Stockton—had the distinction of making one or more All-American teams.

In the second period, California found a weak spot in the Alabama defense after Bob Herwig intercepted an Alabama pass on the California 6-yard line. Chapman punted out to Herky Mosley, the Alabama safety, but Perry Schwartz hit Mosley so hard the ball squirted out of his hands, and Schwartz pounced on it on the Bears' 39-yard line. Thirteen straight running plays produced the game's first touchdown. Chapman kicked the extra point, and it was California ahead 7–0.

Toward the end of the third period, Chapman and Bottari began pounding through the line again, and Bottari finally smashed over from the 'Bama 5-yard line.

Alabama fumbled away both of its best scoring opportunities, once on the two and again on the seven, and the clock ran out with California still up 13–0. After the game was over, Coach Thomas said that California had the hardest-hitting team he had ever encountered and the most powerful since the Stanford eleven of the 1935 game.

1938

For the first time since 1917, Alabama opened the football season away from home. The 1938 Crimson Tide began the year with a trip to Los Angeles to tackle the University of Southern California in one of the biggest intersectional battles of the season.

USC, coached by the great Howard Jones, had won seven conference titles, had beaten three Rose Bowl opponents, and in 1938 fielded one of the leading teams on the Coast. Key Trojan players included the triple-threat Grenny Lansdell, fullback Bob Peoples, and burly Ray George, one of the nation's top guards. Southern California had been pointing toward the Alabama challenge ever since the Tide had lost to California in the Rose Bowl.

USC was favored to defeat the Crimson Tide, but Coach Tommy Thomas, starting his eighth season at Tuscaloosa, had other plans.

"I've been meeting with my coaches and some of my players, and I think we might have a bag of surprises for Southern California," said Thomas.

On September 24, with a crowd of some 65,000 spectators looking on, the Crimson Tide and USC exchanged punts and straight running plays in an effort to feel out the other team's weakness. But in the second period, after Alabama took the ball over on the USC 31-yard line, Herschel Mosley streaked for seventeen yards. Two plays later Mosley passed to Bill Slemons for Alabama's first score. Vic Bradford kicked the extra point, and it was 7–0, Alabama.

USC looked to counter immediately. Lansdell returned the kickoff to his 34-yard line, then passed to Peoples, who sped to the Tide 24-yard line. But here Alabama's great defense stiffened, and in four tries USC failed to gain a first down. Then the Tide began to dominate. Zivich, Mosley, and Charley Holm ripped through the USC line and advanced to the Trojan 35-yard line. Mosley then completed two passes to Gene Blackwell, the second of which was good for the touchdown.

Alabama scored on an intercepted pass in the third period to take a commanding 19–0 lead. USC's only score came when the Tide's Charley Boswell was hit hard by two USC players and fumbled a punt on the 1-yard line. USC scored on the next play, but it was Alabama in a big win, 19–7.

The Tide rolled over Howard and North Carolina State in the next two weeks, then came up against Tennessee. The Volunteers fielded one of the finest teams in their long history in 1938, and, with triple-threat George Cafego running wild, defeated Alabama 13–0 in Birmingham.

A week later the Tide rebounded for a 32–0 trouncing of Sewanee, then held off Kentucky, 26–6. Next, Tulane and Alabama were locked in a scoreless battle until the final moments of the game, when Halfback Vic Bradford kicked the ball squarely through the crossbars to give Alabama a narrow 3–0 victory. A 14–14 tie against Georgia Tech and a 7–0 win over Vanderbilt gave the Crimson Tide another successful season with seven wins, one loss, and one tie.

1939

In 1939 Alabama opened its ninth season under coach Tommy Thomas with an unimpressive 21–0 victory over Howard. But the entire nation was impressed when, just one week later, Alabama faced a powerful Fordham University squad in New York City's famed Polo Grounds. A crowd estimated at more than 65,000 jammed every inch of the old baseball park to witness the battle between two of football's great coaches: Jimmy Crowley, one of Notre Dame's Four Horsemen, against Frank Thomas, ex-roommate of the immortal George Gipp.

Alabama slowly established field position in the early going, finally taking possession on the Rams' 35-yard line. A series of running plays advanced the ball to the 13-yard line, and then Charley Boswell took the pass from center, faked a hand-off to John Hanson, spun around and slipped the ball to Jim Nelson, who slashed his way off-tackle for the touchdown. Sandy Sanford, who looked as if he didn't have a care in the world, calmly kicked the ball through the uprights for the extra point, and Alabama had a 7–0 margin.

In the fourth period, Herschel Mosley attempted a quick-kick, but a charging Fordham line broke through and blocked it.

End Holt Rast would be named to the 1941 All-American team.

Dom Principe, Fordham's great fullback, then ripped the Alabama line twice and scored from the 17-yard line. Then, as the huge crowd stood and screamed, Fordham missed the extra point, and Alabama had a hard-fought but well-earned 7–6 victory.

But the huge win may have taken some of the color out of the Crimson. After defeating Mercer, Alabama was handled with relative ease by Tennessee. The '39 Vols were one of the nation's finest teams, with a consecutive winning streak that covered the better part of two seasons, and with All-Americans George Cafego, Bob Suffridge, and Bowden Wyatt, they measured the Tide, 21–0.

During the following weeks, the Crimson Tide continued to play inconsistently. A 7–0 win over Mississippi State was followed by a 7–7 tie with Kentucky. Then came two tough losses—13–0 to Tulane and 6–0 to Georgia Tech.

However, on November 30, nine Alabama seniors played the best game of their lives as Alabama defeated a strong Vanderbilt team by a 39–0 score. Halfback Paul Spencer starred in this last game of the year as he ran, passed, and kicked his way to account for three touchdowns.

The easy victory meant a less than spectacular 5–3–1 season for the Tide. Captain Carey Cox was named to the All-American team.

1940

Coach Tommy Thomas, beginning his tenth season at Alabama, could not have been very happy as he sized up the prospects for the 1940 season at the team's first workout early in August. Thomas had lost nine of his best players to graduation, including the All-American center Carey Cox, and with the lackluster record in 1939, the poorest in ten years, there were the unmistakable grumblings from the alumni.

But worst of all for Tommy was the realization that he was losing his favorite former player and assistant coach, Bear Bryant. Bryant had been one of Tommy's pets as a player, and as a coach during the past four years had developed into a most valuable aide. But Red Sanders had been quietly putting a top-notch coaching staff together at Vanderbilt, and when he offered Bryant a post as his number-one assistant, Bryant reluctantly said his goodbyes.

As the 1940 season got underway, star halfback Paul Spencer led the tide to three straight convincing wins. However, on October 19, an undefeated Tennessee eleven, led by Johnny Butler and All-American Bob Suffridge, once again defeated an inexperienced but determined Crimson Tide by a 27–12 margin. Tennessee went on to an undefeated season and lost to Boston College in the Sugar Bowl.

The next four weeks produced a 25–0 upset over a strong Kentucky team, a close 13–6 win over Tulane, a nail-biting, come-from-behind win over Georgia Tech, 14–13, and an equally thrilling 25–21 victory over Vanderbilt in Birmingham. Halfback Jim Nelson started the game with a damaged knee, but threw two marvelous touchdown passes, then returned an intercepted pass for still another score. The winning margin came with but three minutes to play when Nelson received the snap from center Joe Domnanovich, faded back, evaded two would-be tacklers, and tossed a flat pass to Russ Craft. The left halfback snatched the ball with one hand on the 25-yard line, dodged two enemy tacklers, and dashed into the end zone.

A loss in the final game of the season to

Joe Domnanovich
All-AMERICAN-1942
University, Alabama
Center

Good luck to you Jimmy
Your friend
Joe Domnanovich

Joe Domnanovich emerged as a great center in 1940; by 1942 he would captain the team and become All-American.

undefeated Mississippi State gave Alabama a record of seven victories and two defeats. Tackle Fred Davis, end Holt Rast and halfback Jim Nelson were named to the All-Southeastern Conference team.

1941

As the first week of practice ended in 1941, Coach Thomas turned to his chief aide, Red Drew and said, "Red, I've never seen as many outstanding backs on one team." They did seem innumerable—Jim Nelson, Bill Harrell, Julius Papias, Paul Spencer, Dave Brown, George Gammon, Russ Mosley, Al Sabo, Carl Mims, Lou Scales, Howard Hughes, and Don Salls.

"I think we'll be all right this year," added Tommy, "that is, if we can stay healthy."

The Tide opened the season with a hearty drubbing of Southwestern Louisiana, but the very next week the Mississippi State Maroons defeated Alabama for the second straight year. Alabama fumbled the ball six times, threw several pass interceptions, and lost to an alert, fast-moving Mississippi State squad, 14–0.

Alabama quickly rebounded to defeat a hapless Howard eleven 61–0, and in the annual battle against Tennessee at Knoxville, Alabama's star halfback Jim Nelson, passed and kicked and led the Tide to a close, hard-fought, 9–2 victory over the Vols.

A week later, when Alabama's All-American candidate Jim Nelson faced Georgia ace Frank Sinkwich, it proved to be a stirring individual battle between these two stars as well as a great team battle. The highlight of the game came in the third period, when Nelson intercepted a Sinkwich pass and scampered, dodged, and fought his way seventy-four yards for the touchdown that lifted Alabama to a huge 27–14 win.

Kentucky was no match for the geared up Crimson Tide on Homecoming Day, November 1, but it was a different story against Tulane in New Orleans the following week. The Green Wave led Alabama 14–6 at the half and assistant coach Red Drew was so angry at the calibre of the Alabama line that he chewed up the entire squad in the locker room. Coach Thomas followed Drew's fire-in-hell talk with a calm summation: "All we need is a touchdown and a field goal and we've got the ball game."

The Tide went out in the third period and promptly drove seventy-five yards in eleven plays, with Nelson passing to Rast for a touchdown, and it was Tulane 14, Alabama 13. Then, with four minutes to play, Salls smashed through the line for a touchdown, and Alabama had a 19–14 lead. Tulane filled the air with passes in the waning moments, but Alabama's defense held the Wave at bay. It was a great Tide comeback and one of the great games of the entire season.

Alabama won two of its last three—a 20–0 drubbing of Georgia Tech, a tough 7–0 loss to Vanderbilt, and a 21–7 victory in its first-ever game against Miami. The season record of eight wins and two losses was impressive enough for an invitation to the Cotton Bowl to play Texas A & M.

The A & M squad, coached by Birmingham native Homer Smith, had the better day in yards from scrimmage, but fumbles and interceptions gave Alabama a win in one of the most unusual games in the history of the Cotton Bowl.

A minute after a first-period A&M touchdown, Don Whitmire recovered a fumble, and then Nelson on a reverse circled his left end and dashed in for a touchdown that tied the game at 7–7. In the third

1941 National Champions: *Front row:* Baker (mgr.), Blackmon, Strange, Moseley, Harrell, Martin, Cox, Killian, Craft, Sessions. *Second row:* Johnson, Jones, Gresham, McWhorter, Papias, Brown, Spencer, Avery, Lane, Salls. *Third row:* Hecht, Sharp, Weeks, Kimball, Pope, McKosky, Baughman, Hargrove, Nelson, Huges. *Fourth row:* Scales, Lockridge, Wyhonic, Leon, Chorba, Mims, McCoy, Bailey, Beard, Sabo, Roberts. *Fifth row:* Tollett, Stewart, Jergensen, Cook, Wise, Wesley, Bires, Aland, Rast. *Back row:* Gammon, Leeth, McKewen, Domnanovich, Richeson, Whitmire, McAllister, Fichman, Olenski, Langdale.

period Jimmy Nelson gathered in a punt by Moser and sped seventy-five yards for Alabama's second score. A few plays later, Daniels fumbled a Tide punt and Jim Sharpe recovered. On the first play Nelson flashed twenty-one yards for Alabama's third touchdown and it was Alabama 20, Texas A&M 7.

At this point Coach Thomas sent in his second and third string players, and they increased the margin to 29–7 before A & M rallied for two final-quarter touchdowns. The final score, 29–21, made the game sound closer than it was. Indeed, the victory was so decisive that Football Thesaurus named Alabama the 1941 National Champions.

1942

With the United States still reeling from the treacherous attack on Pearl Harbor and U.S. forces retreating throughout the South Pacific, it was with a heavy heart that college football officials decided to play the 1942 schedule rather than abandon the game for the duration. The White House supported this decision, and most colleges played out the year.

Alabama inaugurated war-time football with a host of veteran stars held over from the 1941 squad: Captain Joe Domnanovich, the All-American center, superb tackle Don Whitmire and halfbacks Russ Craft and Dave Brown.

After opening with a lopsided win over Southwestern Louisiana, the Tide came looking for revenge in the second game against Mississippi State. Halfback Russ Craft found it for them. He returned the opening kickoff to the State 25-yard line before he was tackled. In the third period, he broke off-tackle and raced thirty-eight yards for a touchdown, and in the fourth period he caught a pass on State's 4-yard line, then bucked over for another score. Alabama won, 21–7.

Two weeks later, in one of the toughest games ever played between Alabama and Tennessee, the Crimson Tide scored a touchdown with just three minutes to play to wrap up a nail-biting 8–0 win over the Vols. Then, in a big Homecoming Game the following week, 'Bama out-fought a stubborn Kentucky team for its fifth straight win of the '42 campaign.

The unblemished record was spoiled, however, when Frank Sinkwich and George Poschner assumed control of the big game between Georgia and Alabama. The Bulldogs scored two touchdowns on passes from Sinkwich to Poschner and toppled the Tide from the ranks of the undefeated with a smashing 21–10 win. Sinkwich was brilliant as he passed thirty-seven times and completed eighteen to give Georgia 231 yards in the air.

The Tide bounced back over South Carolina, 29–0, but then were shut out 7–0 by a rugged Georgia Tech team in Atlanta. Just one week later, Alabama, led by Russ Craft and Jim August, defeated Vanderbilt, 27–6,

but then the Crimson Tide lost again to the Georgia Pre-Flight Skycrackers, a team composed of a galaxy of stars from American and Southern college football.

Despite the three losses, the Orange Bowl Committee selected Alabama to meet Boston College on New Year's Day in Miami. "Alabama's brilliant past bowl record weighed heavily in the decision of the Orange Bowl Officials to invite a three-time defeated team here," the Associated Press reported when the 1942 Crimson Tide received its invitation.

"Every sportswriter of note in the nation said we didn't have a ghost of a chance," recalled Joe Domnanovich, Alabama's All-American center, who starred in the Orange Bowl Game. "They outweighed us 20–30 pounds per man and they were so big and so fast, five of their players later on played in the National Football League.

"The Eagles came out fast," said Domnanovich, "using the new-style offense that the Chicago Bears used so well. It was the T-Formation, and they quickly scored two touchdowns for a 14–0 lead. Halfback Mike Holovack shot through our line for sixty-five yards and their first score, then he went off-tackle for thirty-five yards and another touchdown before we quite knew how to handle that very tricky formation. Then I called time-out and changed our defense. Our end went inside and I charged outside and that stopped them for a while."

The defensive change worked, and an inspired Alabama line didn't give up another score until late in the game. Russ Craft, Dave Brown, Johnny August, and Russ Mosley tore off big chunks of turf, and as the Eagle defense slowly began to give ground, Bobby Jenkins raced across the Eagles' goal line for a touchdown. Boston came right before the half to go ahead 21–19, but George Hecht kicked a 25-yard field goal to give 'Bama a 22–21 half-time edge.

FRANK THOMAS COMES TO ALABAMA

In the second half Alabama added 15 points as Leeth scored on a 14-yard pass from Mosley; Ted Cook scored on another pass from Jim August; and Domnanovich added a safety to give Alabama a 37–21 victory.

Such a great comeback win over the heavily favored Boston team added another brilliant page to the history of Alabama football.

1944

Alabama, along with most of the major teams, abandoned its football schedule in 1943, as most of the young men of college age were called into the various services. However, Coach Thomas told the university's athletic committee that he felt he could field a team in 1944, and the Committee agreed to allow him to go ahead.

There was one player that Coach Thomas had been carefully scouting in 1943. He was a slight tailback playing at Woodlawn High School in Birmingham, and his name was Harry Gilmer. A smallish youngster with thin shoulders and a thin chest, Gilmer had developed a jump-pass that was almost impossible to defense. In high school and on the playgrounds, Harry had been too small to identify his receivers, so he would jump high into the air and fire off passes with amazing accuracy. He could also kick and run with the ball and was one of the best defensive players in high school football.

Coach Thomas, in order to induce Gilmer to attend Alabama, hired Woodlawn's coach Malcolm Laney and Gilmer quickly followed his coach to Tuscaloosa.

In the opening game of the 1944 season, Alabama met LSU for the first time since

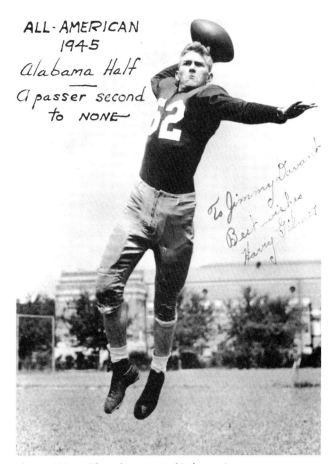

ALL-AMERICAN
1945
Alabama Half
—
a passer second
to NONE

To Jimmy Durant
Best wishes
Harry Gilmer

The great Harry Gilmer demonstrates his famous jump-pass.

1930 and in a game that was packed with excitement from start to finish the two teams battled to a 27–27 tie game. Gilmer made his college debut a memorable one with a 95-yard kickoff return for a touchdown.

Alabama ran up huge scores in the next two games against Howard University and Millsaps; then on October 21, Alabama and Tennessee fought to a 0–0 scoreless tie. Kentucky was next on the schedule, and the Tide played the best game of the year in completely dominating the Wildcats, 41–0. Gilmer scored two touchdowns and passed for two more scores, while the Wildcats were never able to advance the ball beyond the Alabama 26-yard stripe.

On November 4, however, Alabama's unbeaten record came to an end as Georgia prevailed in a 14–7 squeaker. The Tide bounced back for wins over Mississippi, 34–6,

Gilmer makes his college debut with a 95-yard kickoff return for a touchdown.

and Mississippi State, 19–0, to end the season with a record of five wins, two losses, and two tie games.

Surprisingly, the Sugar Bowl Committee invited Alabama to meet Duke University in the annual New Year's Day game at New Orleans, and Coach Thomas asked his "War Babies" to vote on whether they wanted to participate. The players elected unanimously to accept the invitation, and it turned out to be one of the most exciting Sugar Bowls ever.

The crowd of more than 72,000 people had just about settled in their seats when the Tide's kickoff was returned to the 33-yard line. Two plays later it was 7–0, Duke, and the game was just a minute old. But Alabama was just getting started. After

Ralph Jones recovered a Duke fumble, a series of running plays by Norwood Hodges and Lowell Tew were good for a first down on the Duke 8-yard line. The pass from Gilmer to Hal Self got the ball to the 1-foot line, and then Hodges smashed in for the score. Hugh Morrow missed the extra point, but Alabama wasn't through. On its next possession, Gilmer went off-tackle for twenty-five yards, then faded back, leaped into the air, and passed to Jones who was downed on the 2-yard line. Hodges again scored the touchdown, and Alabama now led 12–7. Late in the second period Gilmer passed fifty-one yards to Jones, who sped ten more for another 'Bama touchdown and a 19–7 lead. Duke rallied for a touchdown, and at the half it was 19–13, Alabama.

Hard-running fullback Norwood Hodges starred in the Tide's Sugar Bowl win capping the 1944 season.

Fred Digby of the *New Orleans States Item* described the contest as "the greatest game I ever saw in more than thirty years of sportswriting."

1945

Coach Thomas knew that he would have an outstanding team in 1945, his fourteenth season. After all, his "war babies" were back, and they were just a little bigger, tougher, and more experienced. But he never thought his team would be quite that good. . . .

Thomas's returning veterans included: Alabama's great triple-threat star Harry Gilmer and such backfield stalwarts as Lowell Tew, Henry Self, Fred Grant, Hugh Morrow, Jim Robertson, and Norwood Hodges; back also were the All-American center Vaughn Mancha; tackles Tom Whitley and Francis Cassidy, Jack Green, and Dick Flowers; guards John Wozniak and Jim Bush; and ends Rebel Steiner, Jim Cain, and Dick Gibson. Tommy drove his "War Babies" and his newcomers from morning till late afternoons in a relentless effort to shape the squad into the form he thought they should reach for one of the most formidable schedules in history.

After shutting out the Kessler Field Flyers, 21–0, to open the '45 campaign, the Tide traveled to Baton Rouge for a night game against LSU. In this battle of forward passes, Harry Gilmer battled the great Y. A. Tittle in a thrilling match-up, but Gilmer prevailed as he completed eight of sixteen passes for 188 yards and three touchdowns.

After two more solid wins against South Carolina and ancient rival Tennessee, Alabama faced its most severe test yet—the

In the third period, the heavier Duke team pounded away, marching sixty-three yards for another touchdown and a 20–19 advantage. But in the fourth quarter, Morrow intercepted a Duke pass and re-returned it for eighty yards and an Alabama score. Now it was 26–20, Alabama in front.

Late in the game, with 'Bama taking possession on its own 2-yard line, Coach Thomas decided to give Duke a safety rather than have his inexperienced players handling the ball so close to the Duke goal line. The strategy backfired. Duke returned the kick to the 'Bama 40-yard line, and with two minutes to play, Clark sped twenty yards to put Duke in front for good, 29–26.

One of Coach Thomas's "war babies," Lowell Tew scored three TDs against the Kessler Field Flyers in 1945.

powerful Georgia eleven—on October 27. Georgia's attack was built around its sensational triple-threat star, Charley Trippi, but once again Gilmer outplayed his rival, passing for three touchdowns as Alabama defeated Georgia 28–14.

With five successive victories, Alabama, a team of destiny this year, rolled on to four more, all by hugely lopsided scores: 60–19 over Kentucky, an incredible 71–0 over Vanderbilt, 55–6 over the Pensacola Fliers, and 55–13 over Mississippi State.

Alabama had ended the season with an incredible 9–0 record, and only Army's powerhouse team of Blanchard and Davis stood in the way of a National Championship. Army was indeed declared National Champions by the Associated Press, but Alabama was invited to its sixth Rose Bowl Game. The stage was set for the battle of the year between Alabama and the mighty University of Southern California.

"We were supposed to get knocked off that day against Southern California," said Gilmer, "and they were all set to defense

our passing attack. So Coach Thomas told us to stick to the running game and we had them completely baffled."

The game opened with both teams sparring, feeling out each other's defense carefully, anxiously. Then Trojan halfback Bobby Morris fumbled an Alabama punt on his own 17-yard line, and Alabama recovered the ball. Gilmer carried three times, then Self scored the game's first touchdown on a quarterback sneak.

Four minutes later a 38-yard burst by Gordon Pettus set up another score, with Lowell Tew, whose broken jaw had been wired shut for the game, cracking the center of the line for the touchdown.

Alabama scored again in the first half and twice more in the second half to take an astonishing 34–0 lead over the mighty Trojans. With the victory secured, Coach Thomas inserted every player making the trip. He even called upon third-string quarterback Clem Gryska, a seventeen-year-old freshman, to try a punt in the final quarter . . . even though the young quarterback had

All-Americans Gilmer and center Vaughn Mancha led the Tide to a brilliant 10-0 season in 1945.

no fingers on his right hand. The final score was Alabama 34, Southern Cal 14.

The final statistics underscored the wisdom of Coach Thomas's game plan. Alabama wound up with 351 yards gained, 292 running. USC had only forty-one yards. In one of its truly remarkable performances, the Crimson Tide scored more points than all eight of the Trojans' previous Pasadena foes combined.

1946

The 1946 season was a terrible one for Coach Thomas. He had developed a heart condition, and then high blood pressure complicated his life. His doctors placed him on a strict diet and ordered him to stop smoking and to cease all outside activities. He coached the 1946 team from an elevated platform and used a bullhorn to make himself heard because his voice became so weak. When not coaching he was in bed. His doctor, Joe Hirsh, would not let him stand.

Nevertheless, behind the marvelous leadership of Harry Gilmer and Vaughn Mancha, Alabama easily defeated Furman in the opening game of the schedule and a week later nosed out Tulane by virtue of an extra point, 7–6. At Columbia, South Carolina, the Gamecocks pressed Alabama to the last whistle, just losing to the Tide, 14–6. Then Southwest Louisiana went down under a barrage of eight touchdowns and a 54–0 defeat.

By this time Thomas's condition had so deteriorated that University President Ray Paty asked Thomas to step down, "for his own sake." But Thomas refused, saying he could not quit on his players in the middle

of the season. In later years he would regret his decision.

His illness, however, took its toll on Tommy and his players. They lost four of their last seven games: 12–0 to Tennessee, 14–0 to Georgia, 31–21 to LSU, and 13–7 to Boston.

Thus, a year that started out as a most promising one produced a disappointing 7–4 record and bore witness to a coach who refused to quit under the most heartbreaking circumstances.

Thomas resigned his coaching position after the season, but his condition steadily worsened. Relegated to the athletic directorship through 1951—when he gave that up too—Tommy never lost interest in "his" team; he would analyze each game on his Birmingham radio show. His immortality was secured when he was named one of the twenty-one charter coaches in the National Football Hall of Fame. Thomas died in the Druid City Hospital in Tuscaloosa, May 10, 1954, and all of Alabama mourned this great coach.

4

YEARS OF TRANSITION

1947–1957

Harold "Red" Drew, an assistant coach under Frank Thomas since 1931, was hand-picked by Thomas to succeed him, and while Red's record from 1947 to 1954 was a successful one, he never quite reached the pinnacle that Alabama teams of the Thomas era approached. Still, Red Drew knew and loved the great winning tradition at Alabama and was determined to continue it. In his pursuit of that end, he became one of the most popular and beloved figures on the Alabama campus.

In 1947 Drew welcomed back most of the seniors who had won eleven straight games, including the Tide's sixth Rose Bowl Game. Harry Gilmer, everybody's All-American, was back for another year. So was one of the nation's top centers, Vaughn Mancha, along with halfbacks Lowell Tew, who had been a sensation in 1946, Norwood Hodges, and a youngster who was a year away from greatness, quarterback Ed Salem. In addition to Mancha on the line, Drew had Jim

Cain, Rebel Steiner, Tom Whitley, and Captain John Wozniak to give Alabama a veteran aggregation, able to compete with any defensive unit in the nation.

In the opening game of the season, a night game at Birmingham, Alabama easily defeated Mississippi Southern by a 34–7 win. But suddenly the tide turned against Alabama, and they lost a heart-breaker to Tulane, 21–20, followed by a bruising 14–7 loss to Vanderbilt.

Alabama had not lost two of three early season games since 1895, and suddenly Coach Drew realized he had been too lenient with his players. He had been treating his stars more like his pals than his players. Now, he took his gloves off and drove his seniors through their practice sessions like a military unit. They responded by completely dominating a powerful Duquesne University squad, 26–0. This was a contest that saw the former "War Babies" at their level best. Harry

Gilmer was unstoppable with his great jump-passing, sizzling off-tackle jaunts, and pin-point punting that kept Duquesne from mounting any kind of offensive threat. Lowell Tew, Mancha and Jim Cain also performed like the All-Stars they were.

After that performance against the Dukes, the Tide played every game as if the national championship were at stake. In

All-SEC end Rebel Steiner.

turn they defeated Tennessee, 10–0, won out over a strong Georgia eleven, 17–7, and took a tough 13–0 win from Coach Bear Bryant's Kentucky Wildcats.

After a narrow victory over Georgia Tech the following week, Harry Gilmer's great

passing, coupled with the outstanding defensive play of the entire line, sparked Alabama to a 41–12 win over Louisiana State. Miami became the eighth victim, losing to Alabama 21–6.

In its lopsided win over LSU, the Crimson Tide had been so impressive that Cotton Bowl officials at the game hunted down Coach Drew and got him to sign a contract for a Sugar Bowl game on New Year's Day.

The match-up in the 1948 Sugar Bowl on New Year's Day in New Orleans showcased two of the most spectacular individual performers in college football: Harry Gilmer, Alabama's great triple-threat star, and Bobby Layne, Texas's sensational halfback.

But unfortunately for the Tide, Gilmer failed to live up to his billing as one of college football's spectacular backs. He completed but three of eleven passes, though one of them resulted in a touchdown that tied the score 7–7 at the end of the half. In the third period, however, Bobby Layne and his Texans went to work with a vengeance. When Alabama's Norm Mosley attempted to punt from his 25-yard line, the entire Texas line charged through, blocked the kick, and guard Vic Vasicek of Texas recovered in the end zone for a 14–7 Texas lead.

The Tide remained only one touchdown behind until the closing minutes, when Gilmer tossed a desperation pass that was partially deflected right into the hands of Texas end Lew Holder, and Holder raced into the end zone for another Texas score. Then, a few plays later, Gilmer was hit hard on the 5-yard line, fumbled the ball, and again it was Holder who recovered. On the next play Layne darted over for Texas's fourth touchdown and a 27–7 margin.

It was a tough loss for Alabama in a game that was much more closely contested than the final score indicated.

1948

The highlight of the 1948 season was the resumption of the natural intra-state rivalry between Alabama and Auburn University. The last game between these bitter rivals was played in 1907 and resulted in a 6–6 tie. There had been periodic efforts on the part of both schools to revive the series, but it was not until 1947 that the Alabama House of Representatives approved a joint resolution for the two schools to resolve their differences and resume full athletic competition.

On April 20, 1948, Dr. John Gallalee, president of Alabama, phoned Dr. Ralph Draughon and suggested a meeting to discuss the resumption of the series. Several meetings later, on May 2, they reached an agreement to renew the state rivalry on December 4, 1948, at Legion Field, Birmingham.

Auburn, under a first year coach Earl Brown, had opened the season with a 20–14 win over Mississippi Southern, followed with a 13–13 tie against Louisiana Tech, and then lost the next seven games on the schedule. But it hadn't been the best of times for Alabama either. The Tide had wins over Duquesne, 48–0, Mississippi State, 10–7, Mississippi Southern, 27–0, Georgia Tech, 14–12, and Florida, 34–28. But it also had four losses: to Georgia, 35–0 (the Tide's worst defeat since 1910), to Tulane in the opening game, and to Tennessee and LSU. The record also included a 14–14 tie against Vanderbilt.

But the schools' records didn't dampen the excitement of the Alabama–Auburn game. Though no championship was involved, the National Broadcasting Company had its top broadcaster, Bill Stern, on

hand to bring the play-by-play to more than 250 stations from coast to coast, and every major newspaper in the State proclaimed the banner event in glaring, blank-ink headlines.

Coach Red Drew had a number of surprises for Auburn this day, the biggest of which was a cocky, young quarterback, Ed Salem. All that Salem accomplished this day was to pass for 159 yards, including three touchdowns, to score one himself, and to kick seven conversions as Alabama resumed the rivalry with a 55–0 rout of the Tigers.

The onslaught began when Auburn fumbled the ball and Herb Hannah, a guard, recovered on the 23-yard line. Three plays later Gordon Pettus passed to Butch Avinger, and Butch went in for the first score.

In the second period, Alabama had the ball on its 11-yard line when Clem Welsh dashed for a 23-yard gain. From there, Salem completed three passes, the third of which was a 20-yard scoring strike to Welsh. Just before the half ended, Welsh blasted ten yards for the third Alabama score. The half ended with the Tide in front, 21–0.

Auburn fumbled the kickoff to start the second half, and Steiner recovered for Alabama on the 19-yard line. Two plays later Salem sped off-tackle for the touchdown, and the lead had swollen to 28–0. Auburn's next possession ended in a punt, and Alabama took the ball over on its 47-yard line. On the first play from scrimmage, a Salem to Steiner pass was good for a 53-yard gain and yet another touchdown.

Auburn's humiliation continued with three more Tide touchdowns, and with Coach Drew utilizing every player who made the trip to Birmingham.

"But wait till next year," said Coach Earl Brown of Auburn. "We'll get you all."

Herb Hannah, star guard in the late '40's, along with the next generation—John, David, and Charley.

1949

In 1949 Alabama opened its 55th football season, third under Coach Red Drew, by dropping a hard-fought contest to Tulane University, 28–14. This was the third straight loss to Tulane in three seasons and caused mutterings among alumni who were still disappointed over the four losses in 1948. When the Tide lost a squeaker to Vanderbilt the next week, the alumni grumbling turned into growling.

Coach Drew's practice sessions became longer and tougher as the team prepared to face a very strong Duquesne University team in a game at Tuscaloosa, October 7. The veterans on the squad responded: Ed Salem, Butch Avinger, Jim Franko, Floyd Miller, Rebel Steiner, Ed White, Herb Hannah, Bill Cadenhead, Ed Holdnak, Red

Noonan, and Larry Lauer played their hearts out and swamped Duquesne 48–6.

Tennessee, one of the nation's top teams, came into Birmingham a week later and in a tough, hard-fought contest tied Alabama 7–7, but from that point on, the Tide rolled over its next five opponents—bashing Mississippi State, 35–6; slipping by Georgia, 14–7, and Georgia Tech, 20–7; taking a thriller from Mississippi Southern, 34–26; and pasting Florida 35–13. A victory over Auburn would conclude a most successful season for Coach Drew and for Alabama.

Coach Earl Brown of Auburn had been humiliated in 1948, and from the very first day of practice in 1948, he never let his Auburn squad forget that day of ignominy. He had signs with 55–0 posted all over the campus, and in practice he drove his players as if he were preparing to play a championship game.

A rip-roaring crowd of more than 45,000 frantic football fans were packed into

Legion Field as Eddie Salem returned the kickoff to the 'Bama 13. On a second down, Salem faded back to pass but got the ball off too high, and it was intercepted by Johnny Wallis, who promptly dashed nineteen yards into the end zone. The kick was good, and Auburn had a 7–0 lead with but two minutes gone.

The two defenses held until the final minutes of the half. Salem returned an Auburn punt thirteen yards, and in just two plays Alabama drove to the Auburn thirty-three. Ed White picked up thirteen more yards, and then Salem, in a brilliant display of running, streaked across the goal line for an Alabama score. The kick was good, and it was 7–7 at the half.

Auburn's fine All-American quarterback, Travis Tidwell led the Auburn charge in the third period, as the Tigers drove relentlessly down the field. A Tidwell fumble had Tide fans screaming — briefly — until Max Autrey of Auburn recovered the ball on Alabama's 11-yard line. Then on the first play Biff Davis blasted through Alabama for Auburn's second score, and the Tigers led 14–7.

With three minutes to play, the Tide was desperate but not done. A long Auburn punt went out on the 47-yard line, and Alabama began a fearsome last-minute drive. Jim Melton, Salem, and then Melton again pounded at the Tigers' line. Yard by yard the fighting Tigers stubbornly gave ground. Salem was sacked for a 10-yard loss, but on the very next play he uncorked the best pass of the day, a 40-yard toss to Melton that went to the Auburn 3-yard line. Eddie Salem cracked over the goal line with just 1:13 remaining in the game.

Then Alabama's halfback Jack Brown took the center pass and placed it down on the turf. Salem put his toe into the ball, and it shot off wide to the right. No good!

Auburn had upset Alabama 14–13 for the biggest win in Tiger history.

1950

Surveying his veteran 1950 squad, Coach Red Drew had reason to smile. Ed Salem, Alabama's triple-threat star was back for his senior year, as were Bobby Marlow, a sensational halfback; Pat O'Sullivan, an All-SEC linebacker; Mike Mizerany, a rough and tough guard; Herb Hannah, another outstanding guard; halfbacks Bobby Luna and Jim Melton; and outstanding end Al Lary.

However, after opening with big wins over Chattanooga, 27–0, and tough Tulane, 26–14, the team went into a funk. The Tide lost to Vanderbilt, turned around to trounce Furman, 34–6, and then lost to a superior Tennessee eleven, 14–6.

All-SEC end Al Lary helped lead the Tide to revenge over the Auburn Tigers in 1950.

All-SEC guard Mike Mizerany captained 'Bama in 1950.

53–0, in a torrent of touchdowns by Salem, Marlow and Milton; walloping Georgia Tech, 54–19; and trouncing Florida, 41–13. Then it was time for Auburn on December 2.

Auburn was suffering in 1950, for the Tigers had not won a football game since their surprise upset win over Alabama the year before. However, previous game records went out the window when such bitter rivals met on the gridiron, and Alabama was wary.

But the Tide set the tone for the game on its first possession. Al Lary, Ed Salem, and Bobby Marlow took turns gouging the Tiger line, and then, from Auburn's 26-yard line, Salem took the center pass and lofted a beautiful touchdown throw to Bobby Marlow.

Auburn responded with a drive to the Alabama 16-yard line. But when quarterback Bill Tucker threw a pass just off the fingertips of Biff Davis, Auburn's only scoring threat of the day was over. Alabama proceeded to score once more in the first half and then thrice more in the second half to paste the Tigers 34–0 and gain sweet revenge for the bitter loss of a year ago.

Alabama finished the season with an outstanding 9–2 record and waited and waited for a Bowl bid. When none came, Coach Drew and his team were downcast. But on the positive side, for his all-around play during 1950, Ed Salem was named to the All-American team and the All-SEC squad. Center Pat O'Sullivan, guard Mike Mizerany, and end Al Lary were also named to the All-SEC team.

1951

For Coach Drew, 1951 looked like a good year to start over. He had few veterans

But just as it seemed that the season's bright prospects had dimmed, Alabama ran up a string of five consecutive victories over the strongest teams in the Southeastern Conference — winning over Mississippi State, 14–7; beating Georgia 14–7 in a tense struggle; swamping Mississippi Southern,

returning from the 1950 squad, and with the departure of his great triple-threat star Eddie Salem and such fine backs as Butch Avinger and Tommy Calvin, he was faced with a total rebuilding job. All through the torrid heat of August, Drew drove his team through twice-a-day practice sessions, hoping that by opening day the Crimson Tide would be ready.

On September 21, Alabama opened the season in a night game in Montgomery against Delta State, and its starting backfield of quarterback Clell Hobson, Bobby Marlow, Jim Melton, and Tommy Lewis ripped and tore apart a hapless Delta State defense for an 89–0 victory. But just when it looked as if Coach Drew had finally put together a solid winning combination, a suddenly helpless Tide lost four games in a row: to LSU, 13–7; to Vanderbilt in a 22–20 heartbreaker; to Villanova, 41–18; and finally to Tennessee, 27–12.

Attempting to turn the season around, Coach Drew and his staff burned the midnight oil, tried every offensive combination, switched his defense around, and turned the daily practice sessions into tough, grueling hours on the gridiron. It looked like the hard work paid off when the Tide defeated a tough, aggressive Mississippi State, 7–0, and then outplayed a strong Georgia Bulldog, 16–14. Hope was brightening when Mississippi Southern was routed 40–7 by a sizzling Alabama offense led by Marlow and Lewis.

But in the next two weeks Georgia Tech defeated Alabama, 27–7, and Florida tagged on another defeat, 30–21. So it was that the Tide took a 4–6 record into the Auburn game, hoping against hope for a victory.

In the opening period both teams missed out on scoring opportunities. Auburn fumbled on the Alabama 27-yard line, and Joe Davis missed a field goal from the Auburn three. But then Bobby Marlow and

Sensational halfback Bobby Marlow led the Tide's ground attack in the early '50s.

Tommy Lewis took over for the Tide. Marlow slashed off-tackle for twenty-seven yards, Lewis rambled for seventeen more, and suddenly Alabama was at Auburn's 35-yard line. Melton and Bobby Wilson advanced the ball to the twenty-two; then Wilson faked a field goal attempt and flipped a short pass to Brown that brought the ball to the Tigers' six. On fourth down on the 6-yard line, Bob Marlow followed great blocking into the end zone, and Alabama had a 7–0 lead.

In the second period, Auburn's fine quarterback Vince Dooley was intercepted by Jesse Richardson at the 36-yard line. Three plays later Melton bucked over for Alabama's second touchdown. The kick was no good, and Alabama had a 13–0 lead.

Auburn scored once in the second half behind Dooley's fine passing, but the Tide scored twice more to seal the victory. The Crimson and White had a 25–7 win over Auburn to celebrate, but the jubilation for many Alabama fans had a slightly hollow quality. With a five win–six loss record, Alabama had suffered its first losing season since 1903.

Bart Starr led the Tide through some rough years, then became one of pro football's Hall of Famers.

BART STARR REMEMBERS –

Every kid growing up in or near Alabama admired the Tide's legendary players—Don Hutson, Fred Sington, halfback Dixie Howell, quarterback Harry Gilmer, and all the rest of the great All-Americans. And I was thrilled to death when Joe Kilgrow, an All-American halfback in the 1930s, and Bubba Nisbet, another great halfback from the same era, invited me to visit the Tuscaloosa campus during the fall of my senior year in high school. They brought me over to the Football Office, introduced me to the great former Notre Dame star, now athletic director at Alabama, Frank Thomas. Thomas, incidentially, roomed at Notre Dame with George Gipp. It was Thomas who helped establish Alabama as a perennial football power, leading the Tide to five Rose Bowl wins, four SEC Championships, and three National Championships during his fifteen-year tenure.

What I remember most about Coach Thomas, however, was his emphasis on academics.

"Son," he said, "you'll enjoy playing football here. And from what these two players have told me about you, you're gonna be a darn good one. But you'll get a good education here. That'll be something to stay with you for the rest of your life."

I accepted Alabama's four-year scholarship a couple of weeks later.

I spent my spring semester at Sidney Lanier High playing varsity baseball and earning some money for Alabama. Coach Moseley helped by giving me a job repairing his football field. My responsibility was to rescue the stands and to re-sod the middle of the football field where the ground was bare. After completing one patch, I yelled across the field, "Coach, I need some more horse manure."

When I looked up, I noticed my English teacher standing on the sidelines with Coach Moseley. In a loud stage whisper, she said, "Bill, can't you get Bart to say 'fertilizer'?"

He responded, "Miss Persons, do you have any idea how long it took us to get him to say 'manure'?"

That fall I joined a Crimson Tide football team that was touted as one of the strongest in the nation. My transition from high school to college was made a great deal easier by the presence of Nick Germanos and Bobby Barnes, high school buddies who also accepted scholarships to play at Alabama. We were excited because the collegiate rules had recently been changed, making freshmen eligible to play varsity football.

Red Drew, who had succeeded Thomas in 1947, all but abandoned the Notre Dame box offense and relied primarily on the split-T formation, which required the quarterback to be equally adept at running and passing. I was not an accomplished runner at the time. However, I presented no immediate threat to Clell Hobson and Bobby Wilson, our first two quarterbacks. Coach Drew decided that he would carry three quarterbacks on the squad, which meant that I had to battle Hobson, Wilson, and Albert Elmore. Elmore was a strong, talented athlete, but I just managed to edge him out. My goal from that point was to get enough playing time to earn a Varsity letter."

Coach Drew expected to have an outstanding team in 1952 and had good reason for such great expectations, for his record-breaking backfield star, Bobby Marlow, who had posted 728 yards rushing in 1951, the fifth highest total in Alabama history, was back. In addition, such outstanding veteran backs as Cecil "Hootie" Ingram, Clell Hob-

Cecil "Hootie" Ingram intercepted ten passes in 1952, still an Alabama record.

son, Bobby Luna, Bob Conway, Tommy Lewis and Bobby Wilson were on hand for another season. And there was a freshman quarterback who could pass as well as any back on the squad and punt better than any man on the squad. His name was Bart Starr, and he would be heard from over the next four seasons.

Alabama opened the season with four straight wins, including a heart-stopper, 21–20 against LSU. But then old nemesis Tennessee, on the way to a national ranking, defeated a sluggish Alabama, 20–0. It was the Vols fourth win in five games against the Tide.

In the next three games, however, Alabama's vaunted backfield swung into high gear and rolled over Mississippi State, 42–19; swept by Georgia, 34–19; and battered Chattanooga 42–28 in a wild scoring fest. Then, on national television, Georgia Tech eked out a hard-fought battle over the Tide, 7–3, but a week later Alabama beat a tough Maryland team 27–7. Now the Crimson Tide, floating on an impressive 8–2 record, sped home to Tuscaloosa for the always bitter battle against ancient rival Auburn.

November 29 was wet, cold, and windy at Birmingham as Alabama kicked off to Auburn in front of more than 40,000 screaming fans. But Alabama wasted little time heating up its offense. On its first possession, two fine running plays by Lewis gained twenty-two yards, and then Bobby Marlow smashed inside guard all the way down to the 16-yard line. Two plays later, Tommy Lewis sped over from the 13-yard line. Bob Luna converted for the extra point, and it was 7–0, Alabama.

A dodging, twisting 43-yard gain by Auburn's Fob James brought the Tigers within striking distance, but Hootie Ingram intercepted a pass at the 16-yard line and Alabama took over. The Tide used a series of bruising running plays to advance relentlessly down the field, until Tommy Lewis hit paydirt for his second touchdown of the day. Luna's kick gave Alabama a 14–0 lead.

In the third period, Alabama mounted yet another grueling ground attack starting from its own 40-yard line. Marlow carried the ball four out of seven times for forty-three yards, then Bobby Luna cracked the final four yards for the Tides' third touchdown of the day. Luna again kicked the extra point and it was Alabama 21, Auburn 0.

For Alabama it was one of the most successful grid seasons in years: nine victories, two defeats, and the first post-season invitation since 1947. The Tide would play in the Orange Bowl against one of the best Syracuse teams in history on New Year's Day, 1953.

BART STARR –

At the 1953 Orange Bowl, our team was led by the tremendous running of All-American Bobby Marlow and Bobby Luna, who scored two touchdowns and kicked a record seven points after touchdowns for a total of twenty-one points. Then there was a marvelous 80-yard punt return through the entire Syracuse team by "Hootie" Ingram. Corky Tharp scored on a tremendous 50-yard pass play from Clell Hobson. I threw a pretty good pass for about twenty-five yards to Joe Cummings for another touchdown, and we beat a pretty good Syracuse team, 61–6. It was the most one-sided victory in major bowl history, and I'm happy that I had a small part in the establishment of another record that day.

I entered the game in the fourth quarter with strict instructions to throw to receiver Joe Curtis. He was within one catch of setting an Orange Bowl record for receptions. After dropping the first three passes,

Curtis was subjected to some badgering from our other receiver, Joe Cummings, who kept yelling, "Hang onto the ball, you dummy."

My touchdown pass to Curtis ended the scoring and silenced Cummings.

In my sophomore year, 1953, I became Alabama's starting quarterback and shared the punting duties with halfback Bobby Luna. My average of 41.4 yards per kick was second in the nation behind Zeke Bratkowski of Georgia. I had additional motivation to kick them long and high – a recent rule change prohibited unlimited substitution, and I was starting at defensive back.

The 1953 season was a strange one. We opened with a 25–19 loss to Mississippi Southern, but then went on to win the SEC Championship despite winning only four of seven conference games.

After winning three conference games, the Crimson Tide tied LSU, 7–7, Tennessee, 0–0, and Mississippi State, 7–7. They desperately needed a win over Auburn.

A huge crowd of more than 43,000 fans jammed into Birmingham's Legion Field for the annual battle, and Auburn boosters rent the sky with war whoops as Charles Hataway and Vince Dooley ripped off large chunks of Alabama territory to put Auburn in front, 7–0. But Alabama's Bill Stone and Hootie Ingram teamed up for huge gains, and then Stone rammed the ball over for an Alabama touchdowns. Bobby Luna's kick was good, and at halftime it was a 7–7 game.

The score remained tied, with both teams playing a tough defensive game, until midway in the final period when Auburn fumbled on the Alabama 37-yard line. Defensive back Bart Starr pounced on

Halfback Corky Tharp was one of Bart Starr's favorite receivers during the 1953 season.

the ball, and the complexion of the game changed then and there.

Two beautiful Bart Starr passes to Bill Oliver for thirteen and then for forty-four yards brought the Crimson Tide to the Auburn 11-yard line. But on fourth down an Alabama field goal attempt sailed wide. The Tide was undaunted, though, and the defense quickly forced a punt to the Tide's 40-yard line. Then the offense took over and advanced the ball to the Auburn twenty-four. Coach Drew then sent in Bobby Luna for a field goal attempt. Al Elmore knelt at the 28-yard line, took the center-snap and placed the ball on the turf, and then Luna booted a perfect three-pointer for a 10–7 lead.

Bobby Luna's kick won not only the Auburn game, but the Southeastern Conference championship and an invitation to the Cotton Bowl on January 1.

BART STARR –

Our great record of 6–2–3 led to a Cotton Bowl invitation to play Rice, who featured the All-American running back Dickey Moegle. And my two interceptions in the game did little to stop the Owls, as they manhandled us 28–6.

The game's most memorable play, however, was made by one of our running backs. Unfortunately, it occurred when our defense was on the field. With Rice in the hole at their own 5-yard line, Moegle swept right. I quickly moved up to make the tackle, but one of their blockers wiped me out. As I scrambled to my feet, I saw Moegle sprinting down the sidelines on a 95-yard jaunt. Suddenly, as he crossed midfield, he was slammed to the turf by an Alabama player who had run onto the field from our bench. It was Tommy Lewis, our fullback. It had been a frustrating day for us offensively, and Tommy just lost his head. Rice was awarded the touchdown. Tommy received great notoriety and an appearance on the Ed Sullivan TV Show.

Years later, Tommy, who had become an insurance executive, volunteered as an assistant coach at Huntsville High School. During a game against Sidney Lanier, a Lanier running back began streaking down the sideline toward an uncontested touchdown. As he passed the 50-yard line, a kid from the Huntsville bench ran out and tackled him. Coincidentially, he was wearing number 42, the same one Tommy had worn at Alabama.

When Tommy and I talked about the incident, he said, "Bart, for the first time in my life, I knew exactly how to console someone.' "

"Tommy," I replied. "You coached the boy well."

The Cotton Bowl defeat was disappointing, but I looked forward to two more seasons as Alabama's starting quarterback.

However, while punting in a workout during the summer of 1954, before my junior year, I noticed a sharp pain in my lower back. Instead of stopping, I continued to kick. The next morning I couldn't raise my leg above my waist. Like a fool, I kept on trying to raise the ball when I should have been resting an injury. As it turned out, I suffered a severe back strain that would threaten to end my career and flare up intermittently for years to come.

When Alabama reported for fall practice, I was in traction and remained there for several days. As I lay in the hospital bed, unable to even sit up, I wondered whether I could ever take another snap. Fortunately, I did recover, but saw only brief action during the last month. The Tide's lone bright spot all that year was the play of Al Elmore at quarterback. The team's 4–5–2 season was a great disappointment; mine was a washout.

1955-1957

After a 28–0 loss to Auburn to conclude the 1954 season, Coach Red Drew resigned and was replaced by J. B. Whitworth.

J. B. "Ears" Whitworth had been a fine tackle on the great Alabama teams of 1930 and 1931. He had kicked a field goal in the 1931 Rose Bowl game as Alabama defeated Washington State 24–0. After graduation, Whitworth had remained at Alabama as an assistant coach, then became an assistant at LSU and Georgia, and then was named head coach at Okalahoma State. He still had a year remaining on his contract with the Oklahoma Aggies, but they were willing to release him.

"Whitworth arrived at Tuscaloosa," said Bart Starr, "with a commitment to clean house. With the exception of two seniors, he elected to field an entirely new starting lineup. He also installed the offensive system perfected at Oklahoma, college football's dominant power at the time.

"He prefaced nearly every statement with, 'This is what they're doing at Oklahoma.' What they were doing at Oklahoma," said Starr, "was utilizing a split-T offense that emphasized a quarterback's running rather than his throwing ability. I quickly realized I would not be starting that fall."

Starr injured his leg in the opening game of the season against Rice, and the Tide went down to a 20–0 defeat. In the second game against Vanderbilt, Coach Whitworth shook up his starting backfield and started Al Elmore at quarterback, halfbacks Obie Linvelle and Bill Hollis, and fullback Jim Bowdoin. The change-over did not help as Alabama lost not only that game but every game on the schedule. The only time during the all-losing season that Whitworth sent in his seniors was when a game was hopelessly lost.

"When I'd get out there on the field," said Bart, "I just wasn't the quarterback I should have been, the kind of leader I'd been as a sophomore and junior."

The 1955 season saw Alabama with a record of ten losses and no wins, easily the poorest season in Alabama's football history.

In 1956 Coach Whitworth's Alabama eleven struggled through the first four games against Rice, Vanderbilt, TCU and Tennessee before striking pay dirt. On October 20, the Tide managed to win its first game under Whitworth by squeaking through to a one-point, 13–12 victory over Mississippi State in a big Homecoming battle at Tuscaloosa. As the game ended, a jubilant group of Alabama players rushed to Coach Whitworth, hoisted him onto their shoulders, and happily danced into the locker room to celebrate the victory.

After a loss to Georgia the next week Alabama regained some semblance of its old glory and upset Tulane in New Orleans, 13–7. However, the jubilation was short-lived. Georgia Tech, ranked fourth in the nation, blasted over for three touchdowns in the final period to win 27–0. Then Mississippi Southern tied Alabama, 13–13, and in the final game of the year, Alabama was hammered by arch-rival Auburn, 34–7.

Meanwhile, Bear Bryant's Texas A&M Aggies had just come through a 9–0–1 season, and the fans and alumni began to pressure Alabama officials to bring Bryant back to Alabama.

The 1957 season wasn't much of an improvement for Coach Whitworth, and

the howls from the alumni were heard throughout the state. The Crimson Tide opened against a strong, hard-running LSU and the Tigers, led by Billy Cannon, dominated an Alabama squad that had little purpose. The next week, October 6, in a game at Nashville, Vanderbilt scored a touchdown to tie Alabama, 6–6, and then followed three more Tide losses—to TCU, Tennessee, and Mississippi.

Coach Whitworth drove his squad through the most grueling workouts of the year preparing for the upcoming game against Georgia. The team took the field in a fighting mood and played the best game of the season to eke out a 14–13 win over the Bulldogs. But the Tide who promptly dropped the next two games to Tulane, 7–0, and to Georgia Tech, 10–7. Another tough week of practice and tongue-lashing and Alabama easily defeated Mississippi Southern, 29–2, on November 23.

In the final game of the season, Auburn, on its way to a National Championship, romped over Alabama, 40–0, and the Tide closed out the season with a discouraging two wins, seven losses, and one tie.

During Coach Whitworth's three years as Alabama's head Coach, his teams had won but four games, lost twenty-four and tied two games for the most dismal three years in Alabama football. Whitworth had been informed in October that his contract would not be renewed, and on November 30, after the Auburn game, his tenure at Alabama ended. Three days later, December 2, President Frank Ross of the University of Alabama announced that Coach Bear Bryant of Texas A & M had agreed to return to Alabama and had signed a ten-year contract.

The era of Bear Bryant had begun at Alabama.

5

BEAR BRYANT COMES HOME

1958–1970

"This is the most difficult thing I've ever had to do," Coach Paul Bryant said to a group of sportswriters gathered in the Shamrock Hotel, in Houston, on December 3, 1957.

"You don't stay at Texas A & M as long as we did without learning to love it, the traditions, the boys, everything about the school. The only reason I'm going back home to Alabama is because my school called me."

With that pronouncement, Bear Bryant and his wife Mary Harmon returned to Tuscaloosa to take up his duties as Alabama's new football coach. As they drove into town in a shiny new air-conditioned Cadillac, they were greeted by a billboard which had huge pictures of Bryant and Mary Harmon and the simple message: "Welcome Home Bear and Mary Harmon."

After four years as an aide to Coach Frank Thomas, Bear joined the staff of Red Sanders at Vanderbilt in 1940 and worked

with Sanders for two years before enlisting in the Navy at the start of World War II. Upon his discharge, Bryant was named head coach at Maryland, and in his only year there the Terrapins had a 6–2–1 record.

Bryant then moved his winning touch to Kentucky, where the Wildcats won sixty games, lost twenty-three and tied five in eight seasons. Bryant had nine years left on his unprecedented twelve-year Kentucky contract when he departed in 1954 for a downtrodden Texas A & M, doormat of the Southwest Conference at that time. The predominance of basketball at Kentucky, plus an attractive salary and the prospect of another rebuilding job, lured him to Texas.

The Aggies won only one game in 1954, then lost but one in 1955. They went undefeated in 1956, and his 1957 team won eight and lost two.

Now he was back at Alabama and at the crest of a career that had been filled with storm and thunder and continuing success.

Paul "Bear" Bryant settles in to coach his alma mater.

BEAR BRYANT COMES HOME

He could well afford to let the chips fall as they may. He new he would not have to move again. He knew he could rally an entire state behind him, even the press, and he would never again have to turn his head or wink at a rich alumnus to recruit the best of the schoolboy talent.

BEAR BRYANT REMEMBERS –

I had no doubt that we would win at Alabama. I just didn't know how long it would take.

The team that I inherited was a raggedy bunch. The best players quit us, and recruiting was actually over, so we weren't going to get much for the following year except the boys Coach Hank Crisp and Jerry Claiborne signed while I was still in Texas.

I wasn't able to talk with each one of the players, so Jerry and I and Coach Hank lined it up so I could visit some of them by phone. I remember I talked with Pat Trammell, the quarterback, who turned out to be the very best leader I ever had, from New York, where I was at a banquet.

I came back from the Coaches All-American Banquet in New York and ordered the entire squad to assemble at Friedman Hall for a meeting. I didn't even mention football. I talked to the players about their lives and what they had to do to be successful. I told them how I wanted them to conduct themselves, how to look and act. Little things like writing home and smiling and recognizing the contributions of others on the campus. Fred Sington, who was an All-American tackle in the 1930s, had two boys on that team, Fred Junior and David. He came to me later and told me how much the boys were impressed that day.

After I talked along those lines for a few minutes, I said, "What are you doing here?" And I waited. It was so quiet you could hear the boys breathe. Then I yelled, "If you're not here to win the National Championship you're in the wrong place."

And they believed all through the four years – Pat Trammell, Lee Roy Jordan, Jim Sharpe, Billy Rice, Richard Williamson, Bill Oliver, Charlie Pell, Bill Battle. Just special boys. Trammell, Gary Phillips, and Tim Davis became doctors after they graduated. Billy Neighbors was a fine professional player. Every one of the boys on that first team was a winner.

We built our offense in that first year around quarterback Bob Jackson. He was a senior. He could pass and run, and so we ran an option most of the times. We lined up in a number of offensive sets and then let Jackson keep the ball. Or we'd quick-kick. We did that a lot, and that gave us a big advantage 'cause lots of teams had all but forgotten the quick-kick.

On September 27, 1958, Bear Bryant's Crimson Tide took the field in a night game at Mobile against one of the strongest LSU teams in history. Coached by Paul Dietzel, led by one of the great triple-threat halfbacks in Billy Cannon, the Tigers were a cinch to beat any team in the nation, and Dietzel's "Chinese Bandits," his second-team defensive specialists, were tougher than most teams' first string.

But LSU got the surprise of their lives when Duff Morrison snatched a Billy Cannon fumble in midair and dashed to the LSU 4-yard line before he was brought down. Three Alabama line smashes did not gain, and Fred Sington, Jr., kicked a field goal to give Alabama a 3–0 lead at half time. The Crimson Tide line held the great Cannon scoreless for three periods, and just when it seemed that Bear Bryant had an incredible upset in the making in his first game, the LSU Tigers struck for two quick scores for a final score of 13–3.

"We won one of our first four games," recalled Bryant. "We got a scoreless tie with Vanderbilt, beat Furman, 29–6, beat Chattanooga, 13–0, lost to Tennessee, 14–7, beat Mississippi State, 9–7, beat Georgia, 12–0, lost to Tulane, 13–7, beat Georgia Tech, 17–8, then beat Memphis State, 14–0, and lost to 4th-ranked Auburn 14–8."

In his first season Coach Bryant finished with a 5–4–1 record, including Alabama's first win over Georgia Tech since 1953. In this first year Bear Bryant had won more games than Alabama had won in the previous three. He had performed a coaching miracle in one year.

1959

"In 1959 we began to play a real tough defense that characterized the early Alabama teams of the Frank Thomas era," said Bear. "I had a sophomore, Pat Trammell, one of the finest boys to ever play for me and without doubt the best leader on the field I ever had." Billy Neighbors, Lee Roy Jordan, Bill Battle, Charley Pell, Jimmy Sharpe, Fred Sington, Jr., Stan Bell, Wayne Sims, Don Cochrane, Leon Fuller, Marlin Dyess, and Duff Morrison would make up the heart of Alabama's 1959 team."

The opening game of the season saw a strong Georgia Bulldog, headed by quarterback Fran Tarkenton, take an early lead in the first quarter, 3–0, then turn on the offensive heat to score two touchdowns to defeat Alabama 17–3 in a fast-moving, exciting game played at Athens.

Fred Sington's 25-yard field goal late in the third period enabled Alabama to eke out a 3–0 win over Houston in a game at Houston, September 26. A week later Ala-

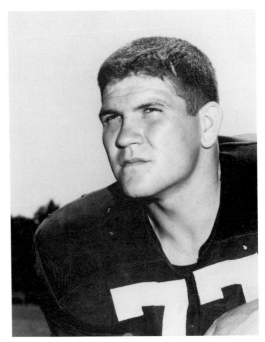

Emerging lineman Billy Neighbors would become an All-American in 1961.

bama and Vanderbilt struggled to a 7–7 tie. The rest of the way, the Tide won seven, tied Tennessee, 7–7, and finished the regular season with an amazing upset win over Auburn, 10–0, the Tides' first win over Auburn since 1953. For that vital game, Coach Bryant shifted Marlin Dyess, a 150-pound halfback, to split end, and Dyess caught a pass from Bobby Skelton at the 35-yard line and raced across the goal line for the only touchdown of the game.

That win, among so many others, illustrated perfectly Bryant's theory that all games are decided by five or six plays. The key is to have the right people on the field, in the right place, when those plays occur.

The Liberty Bowl Committee extended an invitation for Alabama to meet Penn State's Nittany Lions, and on December 19, on a bitterly frozen day in Philadelphia, the Crimson Tide battled Penn State on even terms until just before time ran out in the first half. Tommy White, attempting to punt, got off a kick that traveled against a blustery wind for a distance of three yards.

With the ball on the Alabama 18-yard line, Penn state went into field goal formation without a huddle. Quarterback Galen Hall knelt on the 25-yard line as Sam Stellatella stood ready for the kick. Hall took a high snap, stood upright, and rolled to his right. He tossed a high, arching pass to end Roger Kochman, who charged in for the only score of the game.

1960

The Crimson Tide of 1960 was a team on the verge of greatness as they took field against the highly-rated Georgia Bulldogs in a nationally televised game in Birmingham on September 17. The Bulldogs had one of their most aggressive teams, quarterbacked by future All-Pro Fran Tarkenton, who could run, pass, and kick the hell out of the ball. The Bulldogs were odds-on favorites to win.

But from the opening gun, an impressive Crimson Tide offense ran at full throttle. Alabama's speedy halfback, Tommy White, capped an 89-yard drive to score Alabama's first touchdown, as he bucked over from the 3-yard line. Just a few plays later, quarterback Bobby Skelton took a hand-off and skipped over for Alabama's second touchdown to climax a 52-yard march. Still in the first half, Skelton dashed nine yards for Alabama's third touchdown. Georgia failed to score until the final two minutes, as Alabama took the upset win, 21–6.

After a surprise 6–6 tie with Tulane, 'Bama's offense came to life in the second half to score three times to beat Vanderbilt, 21–0. Three Alabama fumbles resulted in a tough loss to Tennessee in Knoxville, but the Tide rebounded for big wins over Houston, Mississippi State, and Furman.

Pat Trammell, Bob Skelton, Bobby Wilson, and Cotton Clark all played well for the Tide as they prepped for the upcoming game against Georgia Tech, the biggest game of the year.

Coach Bryant.

BEAR BRYANT –

It's a game that I'll never ever forget. If it wasn't the greatest comeback I have ever seen, it certainly was the greatest one I've been involved in.

We were behind 15–0 at the half. We hadn't even made a first down until the last play of the second quarter. When we came into the locker room, I didn't know what to do or say. I was going to really get at the players, make them look me in the eye and tell me what the hell they were doing. A coach has to have a plan, but I had none. I had to stall and try to come up with a plan.

So I went the other way. First thing I said was, "Where are the Cokes?" And I walked around, patted the guys on their backs. I said, "Damn, this is great. Now they'll see what kind of mammas and pappas we got. They'll all see what we're made of." The players didn't know what to expect. My coaches nearly passed out. Bebes Stallings talked about this for years afterwards.

Well, you've never seen anybody play the way that Bobby Skelton did the last six minutes of the game. He had fourth down plays four times on that first drive, and then scored a touchdown.

Then Georgia Tech had the ball and they couldn't gain and punted to us, and we got possession on the 45-yard line. Then Skelton called for a sideline pass to Butch Wilson, and he took the ball to the 12-yard line.

We called our last time out. We had a kid, Richard O'Dell, a big end, who had been on the squad for two years but never had tried a field goal.

I patted him on the back and said, "Get out there, Digger and kick one." O'Dell looked at me kind of surprised, then gamely walked out and kicked a field goal, and we had won the biggest game of the year, 16–15.

The Crimson Tide rolled over Tampa 34–6, then, in a bitter defensive battle in the final regular-season game, Alabama kicked a field goal in the first period to defeat nationally ranked Auburn 3–0. The big win concluded a great 8–1–2 season and earned Alabama a bid to play Texas in the Bluebonnet Bowl in Houston on December 17.

The Bluebonnet Bowl paired good friends, Coach Bryant and Darryl Royal of Texas. Both teams were surprisingly alike: the players were not very big, but emphasized hard-hitting defense, and that's exactly the type of game that some 68,000 fans witnessed—a hard-nosed, knock-down-drag-out affair that produced a 3–3 stand off.

Alabama's end, Tom Booker, kicked a 30-yard field goal to give Alabama a 3–0 lead in the third period. Then, with three minutes left to play, Texas began a drive from its 48-yard line. As the final minute ticked away, Dan Petty, a third-team sub, kicked the tying field goal from the 10-yard line.

1961

By his senior year, 1961, quarterback Pat Trammell was being described by Coach Bryant as the best leader he had ever coached. At six-two and 200 pounds, Pat was an average passer, average runner, but exceptional at doing whatever it took to win. Pat was bigger than most of the linemen in '61. It was not a big Tide team, but it proved to be an awesome winning machine.

Teammate Bill Oliver tells how Pat intimidated some of his rivals as a freshman. He charged into a room where the players were sitting around a table, flipped a big switchblade knife into the tabletop, and as it quivered he asked if any players there were quarterbacks. No one answered. "Right then," said Oliver, "they all became halfbacks."

The 1961 team had an offense directed by Pat Trammell, with a tough ground attack led by fullback Mike Fracchia. It had great defense led by All-American Lee Roy Jordan, Darwin Holt, Billy Neighbors, Bill Battle, Jimmy Sharpe, Charley Pell, Butch Wilson, Bill Richardson, and John O'Linger.

Quarterback Pat Trammell, called by Bryant the best leader he ever coached, blocks for Gary Martin.

In the season's opener in Athens on September 23, with Pat Trammell handling the team like a field marshal, the Tide easily defeated a strong Georgia Bulldog eleven, 32–6. Fullback Mike Fracchia, who gained seventy yards in sixteen carries, scored the first touchdown of the season in the second period, then came back to score another touchdown in the third period. Pat Trammell tossed a line-drive aerial to Butch Wilson in the third period for thirty-six yards and a touchdown. Fracchia, Trammell, and Wilson starred for the Crimson Tide, and the defense held the Dogs scoreless until the last play of the game.

A sluggish Tide offense generated just enough spark to defeat a tough Tulane, 9–0, in the second game of the season, then shifted gears to roll past Vanderbilt in Nashville, 35–6. Pat Trammell tossed passes to his halfbacks and ends for three touchdowns, and Fracchia scored on a flashy 68-yard sprint in the first period.

The next week, the great forward passing star Roman Gabriel led North Carolina State to a 7–0 half-time lead over Alabama. But in the second half it was sharpshooting Pat Trammell who out-dueled Gabriel. Pat connected for ten of fourteen passes to lead the Tide to a second-half comeback that gave Alabama its fourth straight win, 26–7. Then old nemesis Tennessee, who had not lost to Alabama since 1954, was soundly thrashed by a fast-paced Tide attack, 34–3. And a week later at Houston, Alabama ground out win number six, 17–0, with fullback Mike Fracchia picking up eighty-six yards on sixteen carries.

In the big Homecoming battle against Mississippi State, Fracchia blasted through the rain and sleet to rush for 116 yards on twenty carries to lead the Crimson Tide to its seventh straight, 24–0. Billy Richardson, Dink Wall, and Pat Trammell scored touchdowns for the Tide before a crowd of more than 40,000. Win number eight came

Pat Trammell, Tommy Brooker, Lee Roy Jordan, Mike Fracchia, and Billy Neighbors of the 1961 National Championship team.

easily the next week, as the Tide buried Richmond under an avalanche of nine touchdowns.

Georgia Tech loomed as 'Bama's next obstacle, and the game was predictably hard-fought. Alabama's offense was limited to a hard-nosed ground game, with Mike Fracchia scoring the Tide's lone touchdown. Tim Davis added a field goal from the 32-yard line in the third period to give 'Bama a 10–0 victory.

In the final game of the regular season, against Auburn, Alabama received the opening kickoff and marched down the field in an uninterrupted series of line plays, with Billy Richardson blasting in from the 11-yard line for the Tide's first score. Alabama then added seventeen more points on a touchdown by Trammell, a Tim Davis field goal, and a 20-yard pass play from Trammell to Richard Williamson. Williamson scored again on a 6-yard jaunt in the third period, and then Davis booted his ninth field goal of the year for Alabama's 34–0 victory.

The win over Auburn was the fifth

BEAR BRYANT COMES HOME

straight shutout for Alabama and gave the Crimson Tide its first undefeated season since 1945. Alabama's ten straight wins got them an invitation to the Sugar Bowl against Arkansas at New Orleans.

On January 1, 1962, before a jam-packed crowd of 85,000 spectators, Pat Trammell put the Tide out in front with a 12-yard dash off-tackle in the first quarter. In the second period, Tim Davis booted a 32-yard field goal to give the Crimson Tide a 10–0 lead. Late in the third period, Mickey Cissell of Arkansas kicked a 23-yard field goal—the first points registered against Alabama since October 21. But that was all the scoring in the game, and Alabama went on to capture its eleventh straight win, 10–3.

In four short years Bear Bryant had taken the Crimson Tide from its darkest days—a season without a single victory—to the head of the collegiate football world, the National Championship.

1961 National Champions: *Front row:* Richardson, Fracchia, Trammell, Clark, Moore, Wilson, Bible, Mooneyham, McGill, Davis, O'Linger, Hurlbut. *Second row:* Jordan, Brooker, Wright, Abruzzese, Wilson, Patton, Allen, Hopper, Martin, Sharpe, Pell, Morrison, Wall, Holt, Pette, Rutledge, Layton, Oliver. *Back row:* Wilkins, Battle, Weiseman, Henry, Tucker, Sanford, Versprille, Rice, Stephens, Burnham, Williamson, Nelson, Rankin, Cook, Lewis, Crenshaw, Neighbors, Boler.

Joe Willie Namath arrives in Tuscaloosa in the fall of 1961.

BEAR BRYANT COMES HOME

JOE NAMATH REMEMBERS –

Joe Willie Namath lifted himself up out of Beaver Falls Pennsylvania, a picturesque but poor town in the hills about thirty miles outside of Pittsburgh. He was the youngest of five children, and his parents were divorced when he was in the sixth grade. He lived with his mother, and there was not too much money around, so Joe was always hustling. He shot pool, shined shoes, ran messages for bookies; he got by.

"Where I came from," he said, "ain't nobody gonna out-hustle me." His brothers, Bobby and Frank, taught Joe how to throw a ball, and by the time he was ten years old he could hit a stump forty yards away. Joe liked football, but also starred on the high school baseball and basketball teams, and when he graduated, the Baltimore Orioles wanted to sign him. But a score of colleges wanted him to play football. His first choice was Notre Dame, but he did not get a happy welcome in South Bend.

"I then wanted to go to Maryland," said Joe, "because I thought it was down South. I didn't know much from outside Pittsburgh. All I knew was that I wanted to go down South."

Namath took the college Boards at Maryland and came up short. "I scored 745, but I had to do 750. They wanted me to take the test again, but I said the hell with it."

Howard Schnellenberger, who now coaches the fine Louisville football team, said, "I coached one of Joe Namath's brothers at Kentucky, and when I heard that Namath was not going to Maryland, Bear Bryant suggested that I go on up to Beaver Falls and get Joe to Alabama." Schnellenberger hauled Namath to Tuscaloosa in the fall of 1961.

When I left Beaver Falls and went off to college in 1961, I met Paul Bryant, the great Alabama Coach, on my first day in Tuscaloosa. Somebody took me out to the football practice, and Coach Bryant was up on the observation tower, watching and yelling and frowning on nearly every play. He waved his arms at me, so I climbed up the tower to him. He introduced himself, I introduced myself, and we started talking. And honest, I didn't know what the hell he was talking about. We must've talked for at least twenty minutes, and out of the whole conversation I only understood one word: he kept saying "stud," talking about the players on the field.

Pretty soon after that, I started practicing with the freshman team and I got to understand Coach Bryant. He made sure I understood him. The freshmen were scrimmaging the varsity third team one Monday night, and I ran out to my left on an option play, and as I started to pitch out, some big lineman hit me and the ball fell loose. I didn't scramble for the ball. Hell, the guy who had made the tackle was still holding on to me for dear life. It seemed he didn't want to get up either. Coach Bryant came out on the field and said, "Goldarn it, Namath, it's not your job to pitch the ball out and lay down there on the ground and not do anything. You don't just lay there." He kept on grumbling, and I started to walk away toward the huddle, half-listening to him, not looking at him, and suddenly he grabbed hold of my face mask and yanked it around, nearly lifting me off my feet. I was startled. The other players looked up at me.

"Namath," he shouted, "when I'm talking to you, boy, you say, 'Yes sir' and look me in the eye. I don't like no sideways looks." I said, "yes sir, yes sir." He scared me half to death. And from that day on, if Coach Bryant just said, "Joe," even if I was *fifty or sixty yards away, I'd run like hell to him, stop a yard away, come to attention and say, "Yes sir, Coach."*

We had a damn good freshman team in 1961 and beat a couple of very good teams. I made some nice plays, passed the ball pretty good, and got the coaches to really look at me with a sort of new-found respect.

My sophomore year, when I was the starting quarterback, we were playing a good Vanderbilt team, and I was having a lousy day. Coach Bryant pulled me out of the game, and I was really mad as hell. I threw my helmet down on the ground as I came off the field. Then I came over to the bench and sat down, and Coach Bryant came over, sat down next to me and put his arms around me. To the crowd, it probably looked like he was cheering me up. Cheering me up like hell; he was damn near squeezing my head off.

"Boy," he said, "don't let me ever see you come out of a game throwing your helmet around and acting like a showoff. Don't you ever do that again. You come on out, sit your ass down and look smart. Never mind what else is going on."

"Dammit, Coach," I said. "I'm not pissed off at you for taking me out or anything. I'm just pissed off at myself for playing so goddamn bad. I sure as hell deserve to be taken out of the game."

"Well, all right," said Coach Bryant. He understood me that time.

1962

Namath came close to dropping out after his freshman year and accepting a $50,000 bonus to sign a baseball contract with the Baltimore Orioles. Bryant sent Bubba Church, a former big league pitcher, to talk with Joe. "Look, Joe, "they'll give you fifty thousand and you'll blow that in two years. You know you will. Then suppose your arm goes bad. Then what have you got? No college. No degree. You've got nothing." Joe Willie stayed on for the 1962 season and began to fit in. By design or not, his voice developed a soft Southern edge that over the years confused his friends and fellow Easterners.

Coach Bryant did not adjust his offense to accommodate Namath's arm, not in 1962. Joe ran the split-T and he ran it well. In the season opener against Georgia, Joe Willie Namath threw for three touchdowns as Alabama shutout Georgia 35–0. The following week Joe passed for two more scores in a 44–6 win over Tulane. Not since World War II and the heyday of the great Harry Gilmer had a quarterback so excited the fans of Alabama.

Seven games later, the Crimson Tide was still unbeaten and ranked number one in the nation. Then 'Bama traveled to Atlanta to take on always-tough Georgia Tech. Unfortunately, the Tide offense never cranked up. Tech intercepted a Namath pass for a touchdown and still led 7–0 in the fourth period. Alabama finally scored in the waning moments, attempted a two-point conversion but failed, and lost for the first and only time that season.

The chance to repeat as national champions was gone. But in the final game of the season, the Tide clobbered Auburn, 38–0, in a game that saw Namath pass for two touchdowns and run for another on a 10-yard sprint.

The nine win–one loss season was good for an Orange Bowl invitation, and on January 1, Joe Namath quickly led his team sixty-one yards in ten plays for a touchdown. Cotton Clark took a pitch-out in the second period and bulled his way in for another score. Finally, Namath led the Tide

Lee Roy Jordan's amazing thirty-one tackles earned him MVP honors in the Orange Bowl after the '62 season.

to the Oklahoma 2-yard line, where Tim Davis booted a field goal to give Alabama a workmanlike 17–0 win. The shutout was largely attributable to Lee Roy Jordan, whose amazing thirty-one tackles earned him the honor of MVP.

1963

There was talk of a dynasty at Alabama in 1963; one could see it coming over the horizon like the rising sun. The Bear switched to a pro-style offense to take better advantage of Namath's gifts, and the Tide was ready to roll. Then, on March 23, 1963, the *Saturday Evening Post*, one of the nation's foremost magazines, featured an article called "The Story of a College Fix" by Frank Graham, Jr. The story charged that Coach Bryant and Georgia's athletic director Wally Butts had conspired to "fix" the outcome of the Alabama-Georgia game for betting purposes. Bryant got proofs of the story before the magazine reached the newsstands and went on television to completely refute the allegations. Then he met with his players to read the story and to deny its each and every statement.

The story created national attention and, in and around Alabama, provoked indignation and a storm of protest. In the end, Bryant and Butts were awarded damages. Butts received a settlement of $460,000, and Bryant and Curtis Publishing settled out of court, with Bryant receiving $300,000.

"For the next ten years," said Bryant, "I suffered night and day. I actually think that story took ten years out of my life. I used to wake up nights worrying about the way the story was harming my family. It was unbelievable."

Whether because of this unfortunate incident or not, 'Bama misfired twice during the '63 season, the first loss coming in the fourth game of the season. After wins over Georgia, Tulane, and Vanderbilt, the Tide fell to Florida, 10–6. No other team would defeat Alabama in Tuscaloosa until Bryant's very last game there.

The next week, against Georgia Tech, Joe tossed just three times, but he crossed them up by running thirteen times for fifty-three yards and a touchdown. The Tide earned a big 27–11 win that avenged the loss of the previous year. But Auburn immediately brought Alabama back down to earth. The Tigers ended a four-game losing streak with a 10–8 upset over the Tide, despite an 80-yard sprint for a touchdown by Alabama's Benny Nelson.

There were two more games to be played in the 1963 season, Miami on November 14 and the Sugar Bowl game against Mississippi. Both games were to be televised nationally. But Bryant had heard that Joe Willie had been out on the town and had broken some hard rules laid down by himself and the staff, and after talking to Namath, Bryant suspended him for the rest of the year.

Years later, as a pro, Joe Willie would tell a writer: "I deserved that suspension. Coach was 100% right."

Jack Hurlbut, a tireless worker who looked like an All-American but seldom prospered in a game, inherited Joe's post. Steve Sloan, a sophomore, was ready to back up Hurlbut. But the Alabama star proved to be Gary Martin, who took the opening kickoff and sped downfield for 102 yards and a touchdown. Thanks to that initial spark, Alabama out-lasted Miami to win a thriller, 17–12. George Mira, the Miami quarterback, passed for nearly 400 yards in a losing effort.

A freak snow storm hit the South just a few days prior to the Sugar Bowl, and when Alabama and Ole Miss players took the field January 1, the snow was piled all around. But the crowd of more than 85,000 ignored the weather and hollered for the start of the game.

It was Tim Davis's turn to carry the team. His four field goals gave the Tide a hard-fought 12–7 triumph and an impressive 9–2 season.

1964

In time for spring practice in 1964, Coach Bryant was satisfied that Joe Namath had repented sufficiently to earn his way back as the team's number-one quarterback. Joe would have a number of key players at the opening game: Ray Perkins, an end who could block and catch anything thrown in his direction; Paul Crane, who began the season at guard and was shifted

Ray Perkins was Joe Namath's favorite receiver during the great '64 season.

Ray Ogden's great kick return against Auburn in 1964.

to fullback; guard Wayne Freeman; tackle Dan Kearley; and end David Ray.

In the opening game against old Georgia in Tuscaloosa, Joe was at his very best, scoring three touchdowns in a 31–3 rout of the Bulldogs. Namath then followed that show by scoring two touchdowns and passing for two more to easily handle Tulane. The following week, Vanderbilt battled the Tide to a 0–0 tie at half time, that is until Joe struck for three touchdown passes, to go with a 28-yard field goal by David Ray.

In the fourth game of the season, undefeated North Carolina State provided a few anxious moments as the two teams battled on almost even terms. On a rollout in the second period, Namath cut to his right and sustained the knee injury that would plague him for the rest of his career. He was carried from the field. Steve Sloan replaced him and promptly passed and ran for two touchdowns, as Alabama defeated NC State, 21–0. After holding on for a tough 19–8 win over Tennessee, the Tide turned back the Florida Gators in a real thriller. Florida led 14–7 going into the final period, but the Tide scored ten points for the great comeback win.

The Tide rolled on to a spectacular undefeated regular season with wins over

Mississippi State, LSU, Georgia Tech, and a heartstopper over Auburn, 21–14. 'Bama agreed to another Orange Bowl contest, this time against fifth-ranked Texas. But its 10–0 regular-season record had already clinched another National Championship.

At game-time on January 1, both Alabama quarterbacks, Steve Sloan and Namath, were hobbling around on injured knees. Sloan started but gave way to Joe in the second period, and as Namath came off the bench the crowd went wild. But the tough Longhorns continued to prevail, and the score was still 21–17 late in the fourth period, even after Joe had thrown passes to Ray Perkins and Wayne Trimble.

Then Joe moved the Tide to a first down at the Texas 6-yard line. The winning touchdown was at hand, and the crowd was in a frenzy. Three straight line smashes by

1964 National Champions: *Front row:* Durby, Namath, Wall, Hopper, Simmons, Andrews, Mitchell, Harris. *Second row:* Ogden, McClendon, French, Stephens, Freeman, Kearley, McCollough, Bird. *Third row:* Bates, Crane, Cook, Calvert, Ray, Sloan, Dowdy. *Fourth row:* Bowman, Cole, Carroll, Thompson, Strickland, Williams, Fuller, Newbill, Perkins. *Fifth row:* Mosley, Duncan, McLeod, Tolleson. *Back row:* Gilmer, Tugwell, Kelley, Sullivan, Trimble, Moore, Rumsey, Bean, Kerr. *Not Pictured:* Canterbury, Elmore, Sherrill.

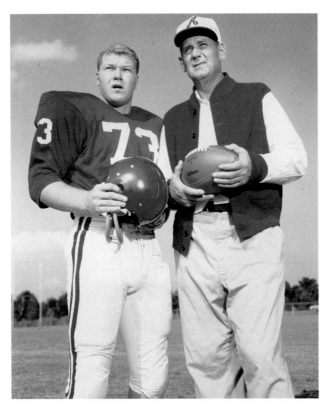

Tackle Jimmy Fuller, one of Bryant's favorite players in the mid-sixties—currently an assistant coach.

fullback Steve Bowman gained five, and on fourth down Alabama needed one yard to score and win the game. Namath tried a quarterback sneak. He was hit and hit hard right on the goal line. One official indicated Joe had scored, but the referee signalled otherwise. The ball went over to Texas as time ran out. The Longhorns won, 21–17.

"I don't think I scored," said Steve Bowman, "but I'll always believe that Namath scored."

And Namath agreed: "I'll go to my grave knowing I scored a touchdown on the play."

In August 1986, Joe Willie Namath, who shook from his white shoes the coal dust of Beaver Falls, who made headlines as a rebel, a playboy, and a quarterback, was inducted into the Pro Football Hall of Fame at Canton, Ohio.

In the middle of his talk at the induction ceremonies, a television audience across the nation heard Joe's voice crack when he said, "Coach Bryant, Mrs. Bryant, wherever you are, we miss you."

1965

BEAR BRYANT –

I just don't know how we ever got Steve Sloan to come to Alabama. Sloan had been an all-state in everything in Tennessee, and everybody tried to recruit him. I thought Georgia Tech had a lock on him.

But Bebes Stallings said, "Let me take a run at him."

If you were a football player in high school and you didn't want to play at Alabama, Stallings thought you were crazy. So Gene went to Cleveland, Tennessee, to Sloan's home, and found that both Tech and Tennessee had told him it was futile to go to Alabama.

When it came to a final decision, Steve asked to be excused. He wanted to go out and pray about this. If you know Steve you know that's the way he did things. He came back into the house within thirty minutes and said, "Gentlemen, I want to thank you all. But I'm going to Alabama."

I just couldn't believe it when Stallings called me and reported the decision.

As it turned out, I couldn't have been closer to Steve in his years at Alabama if he had been my own son. Steve became one of the most popular players in 'Bama history. A deeply religious boy, Steve was a regular speaker at schools and churches throughout the state.

That 1965 group of players was amazing. We were favored to win all of the games on our schedule. But right out of the box, in the first game of the season and on national television, Georgia beat us 18–17 in an amazing game.

Steve Sloan, Orange Bowl MVP culminating the 1965 championship season.

It was a spectacular pass-and-lateral play in the final two minutes of play that defeated Alabama (though films later showed that Georgia's player lateraled the ball with one knee on the ground). Two touchdown passes by Sloan and two field goals by David Ray beat Tulane 27–0, but the following week Ole Miss had a 9–0 lead at half time and still led 16–10 with six minutes to play. Then Steve Sloan showed his greatness. He produced a touchdown on three passes to Ray Perkins and Tommy Tolleson, and Alabama made the extra point as time ran out. Final score: Alabama 17, Ole Miss 16. Three costly fumbles prevented a victory over Tennessee the next week, but once again Sloan scored a touchdown. Ray kicked the conversion, and Alabama pulled out an exciting 7–7 tie.

Steve Sloan, Orange Bowl MVP.

BEAR BRYANT –

We won our next five games against Florida State, Mississippi State, LSU, South Carolina, and we trounced Auburn 30–3 to finish the regular season with an 8–1–1 record.

That night after the game, I told Steve Sloan, "Steve we're not going to win the National Championship by lucking out 7–6 or something like that. We have to win and win big. I don't care where you are on the field or what the score is, I want you to play like you're behind."

That's all the push Steve Sloan needed. He went out against a bigger, stronger Nebraska team, fired pass after pass to Ray Perkins, Tolleson, and even to tackle Jerry Duncan to run up a 39–28 margin over Nebraska. Perkins scored two touchdowns on passes from Sloan, Les Kelly scored on a 4-yard buck into the line, Steve Bowman scored twice, and David Ray kicked a field goal and four points after touchdowns.

Steve Sloan broke every Orange Bowl passing record in winning the MVP award. He hit for twenty of twenty-nine passes for 296 yards in a brilliant performance.

Before dawn on January 4, most of Alabama was sound asleep. One man, however, was up and around. It was just three-thirty in the morning when he tacked a slip of paper on the door of the football dormitory. The note said, "Congrats: National Champions. Let's start today make it three in a row." It was signed, "Paul Bryant."

Bryant carried off the field after 1967 Sugar Bowl win.

All-American quarterback Ken Stabler confers with his coach.

KENNY STABLER REMEMBERS –

From as far back as I can remember, the only thing I wanted to do with my life was to become a pro athlete. Somehow I just knew that eventually I was going to make a living playing ball. And I chose football over baseball because I felt I'd make more money in the long run pitching the pigskin instead of a baseball.

I was an All-State quarterback in high school and got offers to go to about fifty-two schools, but when I met Coach Bryant that was it. With his big body and a face that looked like it should be carved in Mt. Rushmore, Coach Bryant was the most imposing figure I had ever seen, next to my father. The amazing thing was how closely my father resembled Coach Bryant, who could have been his older brother.

When Coach Bryant came down to Foley and had dinner with my family, he didn't make any sales pitch to me. He just talked about hunting and fishing in that great voice that just about hypnotized you. So, I signed a letter of intent to go to Alabama, and with five dollars in my jeans and a few clothes I arrived in Tuscaloosa. One of the coaches had arranged a job for me to cut grass. It wasn't much, but it gave me spending money.

I did quarterback the freshman team in the four-game schedule in 1964. I played fairly well, and in the fall of 1965 after a couple of days practice, I was given the jersey with number 12, the same number Pat Trammell and Joe Namath had worn. But I did not win the starting job then; the quarterback for the '65 season was Steve Sloan, a senior, who led us to a 9–1–1 record followed by a sensational 39–28 win over Nebraska in the Orange Bowl, and we won the National Championship."

In 1966 we had a hell of a team, and I

was confident that we were going to have a big season. Coach Bryant was tough and demanding. The drills were long on conditioniong with lots of wind sprints from sideline to sideline, plenty of stamina work. In those days, all Alabama players were lean and mean. Quickness was the key, and the linemen averaged only 195 pounds. So we ran, ran, and ran.

In our season opener against Louisiana Tech, I tossed a pass to our flanker Dennis Homan for thirty-two yards and a score. Then in the fourth period I hit Denny with a long one – the play measured seventy-nine yards – for another score. I scored a touchdown on a 7-yard jaunt and we won going away, 34–0.

We beat Mississippi, 17–7, Clemson, 26–0, and then in a knock-down battle, we just squeezed out an 11–10 win over Tennessee. The Vols scored ten points in the first quarter, and nothing much happened in the second and third period; we just slopped around in the mud and rain. But in the final quarter, I got to the Tennessee 5-yard line and drove in for a touchdown, and it was 10–6, Tennessee. Then I passed to Wayne Cook for the two-point conversion and it was 10–8, Tennessee.

Then on an exchange of kicks we had the ball on the 25-yard line, and after a series of passes and runs we got to their 1-yard line. With three minutes to go, Steve Davis kicked a perfect three-pointer and we were out in front, 11–10. The game ended, finally, with Tennessee knocking at our doors from the 3-yard line.

Then in rapid succession we beat Vanderbilt, Mississippi State, LSU, South Carolina, Southern Miss, and Auburn, 31–0. We had ten straight and looked like a cinch for an undefeated season.

In January we went to the Sugar Bowl to play Nebraska and really trounced them. That gave us an 11–0 record, which seemed

Bryant with his outstanding '66 squad, featuring Stabler (12), Dennis Homan (88), and David Chatwood (31).

to us hard to beat. But the Associated Press and other pollsters voted the Championship to Notre Dame. Michigan State was second and we were number three. But in the minds of all of us at Alabama, we were the national champions.

"This is the greatest offensive team I've ever been around," Coach Bryant told us. "This team came a long way with less ability than any team I've ever had."

As if I didn't have enough problems at home with my Dad not working and messing around, I tore a cartilage in my knee early in spring practice in 1967. After the knee was drained, and it was drained, I could walk but not run.

Coach Bryant said, "Don't do anything, Kenny; just let that knee heal up."

But watching practice all the time wasn't much fun, so I started to run around with my girlfriend, and then I began to cut classes, never doing any homework.

Naturally, word got around, and one day while I was visiting my parents, a telegram arrived: "You have been Indefinitely Suspended. Coach Paul Bryant."

A few hours later I received another wire, this one from Joe Namath. His read: "He means it."

My father saved the whole ball of wax for me. He had a lawyer friend write a letter that appeared to be from the Draft Board, saying if I did not return to college I would be subject to induction.

I returned to school, but had to move out of the football dorm as part of my punishment. Finally practice began and I was

BEAR BRYANT COMES HOME

Stabler and Bryant celebrate trouncing Nebraska in the 1966 Sugar Bowl.

allowed to practice with the fifth team, even given brown T-shirts to indicate I was a member of the fifth squad. Here I was a senior, coming off the MVP Sugar Bowl award, and I had to wear a brown shirt. I had to work my way up through five different jerseys during the next couple of weeks.

In the opening game of the 1967 season, we were two touchdown favorites against Florida State, but the oddsmakers were way off. We had lost a great pass-catching end in Ray Perkins and five starting linemen, and we weren't the same team we had been the year before. That was some game. I passed for a few touchdowns, but Florida State pounded our line, and we were lucky to come off with a 37–37 tie. We had a huge crowd screaming on every play.

In the following weeks, Alabama easily defeated Mississippi, Southern Mississippi, and Vanderbilt, then lost to an inspired Tennessee eleven, 24–13. The loss to the Vols snapped the longest non-losing streak in college football, twenty-five games. The Tide then began another win streak as they defeated Clemson, 13–10, South Carolina, 17–0, and in the final game of the season

defeated the Tigers of Auburn in a close battle, 7–3.

My proudest moment of the year came after the Auburn game. The game was played in the mud and rain, and the footing was so insecure nobody could move the ball. That was why, with us trailing in the fourth period, no one was going to stop me when I got off a 47-yard run to win the game.

After the game, Coach Bryant came over and said, "Son, I am as proud of you as I am of anybody who's ever been here. You've done a great job for me on and off the field."

On January 1, 1968, teacher (Bryant) and pupil (Bebes Stallings of Texas A & M) met head-on in a cold, wet Cotton Bowl matchup that was one of the most dramatic games of any year.

The game opened with Kenny Stabler driving eighty yards and diving over the goal line to score from the 3-yard line. Then, still in the first period, an inspired Texas A&M team intercepted a Stabler pass, and Ed Hargett of A&M passed to Larry Stegent to tie the score at 7–7.

On the first play of the second period, Steve Davis kicked a long, low, but perfect 36-yard field goal to give the Crimson Tide a 10–7 margin. Then with but sixteen seconds to go in the half, Hargett lobbed a short 7-yard pass to Tom Maxwell for a Texas A&M score and a 13–10 half-time lead.

At the start of the second half, the Aggies quickly jumped further into the lead, driving some fifty-two yards in six running plays with Wendell Housley smashing the 'Bama line for a touchdown. But Kenny Stabler quickly drove eighty-three yards and bucked over from the 7-yard line. 'Bama tried for a two-point play, but it failed.

Stabler's 47-yard run to beat Auburn in 1967.

BEAR BRYANT COMES HOME

Stabler's 47-yard run to beat Auburn in 1967.

With seconds left in the game, Stabler just missed a touchdown on a pass that was intercepted by Curley Hallman, and as a delighted Stallings rushed over to embrace his former head coach, Bear Bryant picked up the big Stallings and carried him triumphantly off the field.

A&M had done the impossible, defeated Alabama 20–16.

BEAR BRYANT –

In 1968, after we won the first two games over Virginia Tech and Southern Mississippi, we lost a close one to Mississippi, 10–8, beat Vanderbilt, and lost to Tennessee by a point, 10–9. We then went on a tear and beat Clemson, Mississippi State, LSU and Miami, and then we had a two-week break before tangling with our ancient rivals, Auburn, for the final game of the regular season.

One evening just before the game, I received a phone call from Pat Trammell. Pat had graduated, then had gone on to medical school and had become a fine doctor.

Pat said, "Coach, I want to tell you something before somebody else tells you. I've got a tumor." He kept talking about it in big medical words. I didn't understand a thing.

I said, "Pat, what the hell are you talking about?"

He said, "Dammit, Coach, I got cancer."

My stomach turned over and I had to close my eyes for a minute.

He said, "There's a hospital in New York that's the best in the country for this. But I'm not going to let a goddamn Yankee work on me."

I said, "I'll go up there with you."

"Will you, Coach?"

"Sure."

Pat's doctor and his wife, Baye, took him

to New York, and I came up right after. Joe Namath and Ray Abruzzese picked me up at the airport, and we spent hours with Pat.

We talked for hours and when I finally left, Pat felt much better. And I certainly felt better. Felt he was going to be OK.

The operation went well. Pat went back to practicing medicine, and the following fall he brought his son down to practice. They stayed there in the dorm, and I wondered about it.

Just before he left, he got me aside and said, "Coach I got that damn tumor again."

The season wore on and, again the week of the Auburn game, I called Pat and invited him and little Pat to sit on the bench. They came to the hotel, sat on the bus with the team and sat on the bench, and after we beat Auburn, the players gave Pat the game ball.

A couple of days later, I got word that Pat was in the hospital and could be gone any minute.

Pat Trammell died a day later. He was just twenty-eight years old when he died. I still miss him. Everybody loved him.

All-American Dennis Homan caught a record fifty-four passes for 820 yards and nine TDs in 1967.

The big thing that I was concerned with in the 1969-'70 period was that I thought I was losing my touch. For the first time since coming back to Alabama in 1958 I felt like my program was missing. Some coaches might not think those years were so bad, because we went to different Bowl Games every year. But we also lost five games each of those years, and it was my fault.

Our selection of plays hadn't been too sharp, and we made other mistakes. I thought that one mistake I made was Kenny Stabler. I should have really disciplined him, but I didn't, and we went downhill from there.

Of course there were other problems. Campuses across the country were rebelling. Students were protesting all over the land and football players in most of the schools had to be handled with more care, less iron-like discipline.

1969

In the opening game of the 1969 season, with junior quarterback Scott Hunter firing passes to sophomore Johnny Musso and George Ranager, Alabama slipped by Virginia Tech, 17–13. One week later, Hunter combined flawless passing with the great running of Musso and Pete Moore to swamp Southern Mississippi, 63–14.

Then, in a game that was a thriller from the opening gun, Alabama and Scott Hunter faced Archie Manning and a great Ole Miss eleven at Birmingham. Finally, with the clock winding down, the Tide struggled to a 33–32 win. Manning completed thirty-three passes, while Hunter hit on twenty-two in what was one of the great individual passing battles ever seen on any gridiron.

But on succeeding weeks, Vanderbilt and Tennessee defeated the Crimson Tide, and suddenly a season that began so brilliantly now stood at 3–2. Then the Tide regrouped as Scott Hunter picked apart the Clemson defense and Johnny Musso ripped the Tiger line for a big 38–13 win.

The following week, Musso scored two last-period touchdowns to give Alabama a win over Mississippi State, 23–19, but then LSU ground out a 20–15 triumph for the Tide's third loss. With scouts from the Peach and Liberty Bowl in the box seats at Tuscaloosa, Alabama, behind the great play-making of Musso and Hunter, won an invitation to the Liberty Bowl by ripping the Miami Hurricanes 42–6. But in the final game of the regular season, Auburn's Tigers ripped Alabama's defense for forty-nine points to hand the Tide its fourth loss.

Alabama closed out the season in a Liberty Bowl classic that was as wild and free-wheeling as any football game ever played. Colorado scored sixteen points in the first and second periods, before Hunter, Musso, and Ranager could crank up the Tide, and at halftime the Buffaloes led 31–19. Then Hunter and Musso scored touchdowns to bring Alabama back in the third period, but only to run out of gas. Colorado pushed over sixteen points in the final quarter to give them an exciting 47–33 victory.

Despite the Liberty Bowl appearance, Alabama's 6–5 season record was its most disappointing in several years.

1970

Southern California traveled to Birmingham for the opening game of the 1970

Johnny Musso's great running led the Tide in '69, '70, and '71.

season, and according to Coach Bryant, "It was a hell of a way to start a new year and a new season. Southern California beat us 42–21." Like the year before, 1970 would prove to be a rollercoaster, with the team up one week and down the next.

In the second game of the season against Virginia Tech, Alabama righted itself as quarterbacks Neb Hayden and Scott Hunter directed a diversified attack that led to a seven-touchdown rout and a 51–18 victory. Tommy Wade, injured for two years, returned to his peak form as he took a VPI punt and returned it seventy-one yards for a touchdown. Then in the first home game of the year, Alabama romped over Florida, 46–15, as Hunter and Hayden tossed passes for three touchdowns while Johnny Musso raced for 139 yards. But just when the Tide thought it was rolling, Mississippi devastated Alabama the next week, 48–23.

After a win over Vanderbilt, the Tide was shut out by the Tennessee Vols, 24–0, the first time since 1959 that Alabama had not scored a point in a game. But the Crimson Tide came back a week later to beat Houston, 30–21, in a nail-biter. Steve Higginbotham, 165-pound defensive back, intercepted a Houston pass and dashed eighty yards for a touchdown with but two minutes to play.

Johnny Musso bore the brunt of the Alabama attack as he rushed for three touchdowns in a fine win over a stubborn Mississippi State eleven, 35–6, but then LSU handed Alabama its fourth defeat of the season, 14–9. Against Miami the next week, Jerry Cash, a fine flanker, caught a pass for a touchdown in the final seconds of the first half, and with just twenty-five seconds to play in the game, he caught another pass for a touchdown as Alabama rolled, 32–8.

Once again it was time to face the hard-fighting Auburn Tiger. Alabama started the game as if it would demolish its old rival,

running up a 17–0 lead in the first period. Then Pat Sullivan went to work for Auburn and burned Alabama with twenty-two completions and four touchdowns. In what many fans of the Auburn-Alabama rivalry consider one of the greatest games in the series, Auburn prevailed, 33–28.

The Alabama players had voted to go to El Paso and the Sun Bowl, but only if they would face a worthy opponent. When the Bluebonnet Bowl Committee offered Oklahoma, 'Bama said yes, and the game proved to be superlative—a 24–24 tie that left the crowd gasping.

In the fourth period, Musso took a handoff, stopped, fired a great pass to Scott Hunter, and Scott dashed over for a touchdown that gave Alabama a 24–21 lead. Then, with just fifty-nine seconds left in the game, Oklahoma's Bruce Derr booted a remarkable 42-yard field goal to tie the game at 24, and the clock ran out on one of the great contests of the year.

But for Alabama, it was another disappointing season: six wins, five losses, and a tie.

6

YEARS OF GLORY

1971–1982

BEAR BRYANT –

In the late 1960s Darrell Royal told me about his new offense he was installing at Texas. He called it the wishbone because the backs line up in the shape of one. He told me all about the system and how he was going to use it, and pretty soon it became a wonderful and simple offense for a college team . . . a team that didn't have a great drop-back passer. We had the best in Trammell, Namath, Stabler, Sloan, and Hunter, but now we didn't have the kind of back I needed, and anyway it was time to move on to something new and exciting. And that was what the wishbone offense had.

The one major difference in lining up a wishbone is that you have to have your best athlete as the quarterback. He has to judge whether to pass or to run. And with Terry Davis we had that kind of athlete at quarterback in 1971.

In the opening game in Los Angeles against Southern California, the sportswriters favored Southern Cal by at least two, perhaps three touchdowns. But they had not counted on the brilliance of Johnny Musso, who scored on touchdown sprints of eight and thirteen yards. Bill Davis kicked a great 37-yard field goal, and Alabama had one of the biggest upset victories of the season, 17–10.

Southern Cal's coach, John McKay, said it best: "Alabama outhit us, outran us and completely outplayed us to win."

Johnny Musso was given the game ball, but he in turn presented it to Coach Bryant, saying, "Coach, you deserve this. It's your 200th victory."

In what was primarily a warm-up game at home, the Tide whipped Southern Mississippi, 42–6. Then, against Florida, Johnny Musso was unstoppable as he raced across the Gators' goal line for four touchdowns in a spectacular display, and

Bear during the glorious '70s.

the Tide swamped Florida, 38–0. The thrashing continued against Ole Miss, 40–6, and Vanderbilt went down under an avalanche of touchdowns, 42–0.

Surprisingly, the Tide had romped to five straight wins, and it wasn't through yet. Tennessee, winners of the last four games against the Tide, suffered a sound beating, 32–15, as Terry Davis ran for two scores and tossed a pass for a third. Houston fell, 34–20, and against stubborn Mississippi State the Tide exploded in the fourth quarter for a 41–10 victory.

LSU showed its great defensive strength, holding Alabama to two field goals and a 6–0 lead. But a touchdown and a two-point conversion gave Alabama a hotly contested 14–7 win. Wilbur Jackson, Steve Bisceglia and David Knapp did a wonderful job in subbing for injured Tide stars Musso, Ellis Beck, and Joe LaBue as the Tide ran over, around and through the Miami Hurricanes, 31–3.

Then it was on to Birmingham, and national TV, as the fifth-ranked Auburn Tigers, with a 9–0 record, met undefeated Alabama, the number-two team in the nation. It had all the hoopla and hysteria of a National Championship as both teams dug in for two strenuous weeks of preparation, and by Thanksgiving Day the suspense was unbelievable. When it was announced that Auburn's Pat Sullivan had won the Heisman Trophy, the excitement escalated a couple more notches. A crowd estimated at 75,000 jammed every inch of old Legion Field as the two undefeated teams finally squared off.

Auburn won the toss of the coin and received the kickoff but failed to gain. On fourth down, Auburn's Dave Beverly tried to kick the ball from his 20-yard line, but the kick was smothered by the entire Alabama line, and the Tide recovered. On first down, Terry Davis lost a couple of yards. Then

Musso ran for five, and Davis broke away for ten yards and a first down on Auburn's eight. Davis then faked a pass and darted in for Alabama's first score. Bill Davis converted and it was 7–0, Alabama.

On their second possession, Alabama drove steadily from their own 20-yard line to the Tiger twenty-eight. Then, from the Wishbone, Terry Davis faked a pass, ducked under two Tiger tacklers and sprinted in for the second 'Bama score and a 14–0 lead.

A wonderful 40-yard pass from Sullivan to Terry Beasley netted forty-five yards to the 'Bama 29-yard line. Then Sully handed off to Harry Unger, and Unger lofted a pass to Beasley for the Tigers' first score. Jeff Gardner converted, and it was Alabama 14–Auburn, 7 at the half.

In the third period, Bill Davis kicked a clutch 42-yard field goal for a 17–7 Alabama

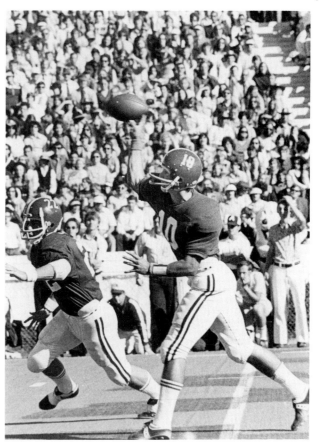

For great athlete Terry Davis, Bryant installed the wishbone offense.

lead, and shortly thereafter, Chuck Strickland intercepted a Sullivan Pass and returned it to the Tigers' 7-yard line. Musso rammed the ball over for another Alabama touchdown and a 24–7 advantage. Another interception, by Jeff Rouzie, and another touchdown by Musso concluded the scoring: Alabama 31, Auburn 7.

With its eleventh victory of the season, Alabama won the SEC Championship for the tenth time. Musso, Hannah, Tom Surlas, Robin Parkhouse, David Bailey, Jim Grammer, Steve Higginbotham, and Jim Krapf were all named to the All-SEC team.

The Orange Bowl contest that pitted Alabama and the top-rated Nebraska Cornhuskers was a dream game, probably made in coaches' heaven, but the dream became a nightmare for the Tide. The Nebraska backs, led by Johnny Rodgers, romped to a 38–6 victory. Evidently the huge Auburn game had taken all the starch out of 'Bama.

Nevertheless, it was a tremendous year, one that returned Alabama to its wonted place of pre-eminence in the college football ranks.

1972

Prospects for the 1972 season were bright. Returning stars included guard John Hannah, end Johnny Mitchell, center Jim Krapf, Terry Davis, Greg Gantt, Wayne Wheeler, superb linebacker Chuck Strickland, tackle Buddy Brown, defensive back Bob McKinney.

Alabama opened against Duke, a team that had not faced Alabama since a 1945 Sugar Bowl battle when the Blue Devils eked out a 29–26 upset. This time, however,

quarterback Terry Davis made mincemeat of the Devils, and the Tide ground out a 35–12 victory. Kentucky was the next victim, as Davis tossed touchdown passes and ran for a third score in a 35–0 rout. The fun continued for the next three weeks, as the Tide steamrolled over Vanderbilt, 48–21, swept past Georgia, 25–7, and scored three second-half touchdowns to blow out Florida.

Apparently, Tennessee had the upset of the season in its game against Alabama. The Vols led 10–3 with less than two minutes left to play. But two sensational touchdowns, by Terry Davis and Steve Bisceglia, gave the Tide fourteen points and a cardiac-arresting 17–10 win. Two more overwhelming wins, over Southern Mississippi, 48–11, and then over Mississippi State, 58–11, and Alabama had an 8–0 record.

Next, on national television, Alabama defeated LSU with two thrilling, last minute drives. Terry Davis flashed for forty-three yards before Steve Bisceglia scored from the 1-yard line, and Joe LaBue sprinted fifty-two yards to give Alabama a hard-fought 35–21 victory, its ninth straight.

In the locker room after the LSU game, Coach Bryant faced the nation's sports press and talked about Terry Davis: "I don't know how you go about considering the Heisman Award winner, but he's done it all. He has never lost a regular season game in two years."

Some 48,000 Alabama spectators saw the Crimson Tide drench Virginia Tech in a shower of touchdowns for a 52–13 victory in Tuscaloosa. Wilbur Jackson scored twice, Terry Davis and his sub Gary Rutledge each scored once, and Randy Billingsley and Steve Bisceglia also scored touchdowns. Jackson, a six-two junior from Ozark, Alabama, and one of Bryant's first black recruits, carried the ball only three times,

Two-time All-American John Hannah.

but was the best ground gainer with 131 yards.

Then it was time for the dramatic Auburn game on December 2, a game that no Auburn fan will ever forget. The Tigers were behind by a 16–3 margin with only five and a half minutes left in the game.

Then lightning struck. Auburn blocked a punt, recovered the ball, and took it over the goal line. Alabama 16, Auburn 10.

It couldn't happen, but lightning struck again. Another blocked punt and another Auburn score, and it was Auburn 17, Alabama 16.

The Cotton Bowl provided a similarly distressing scenario. Alabama led Texas 13–3 at the half, but Alan Lowry scored a touchdown in the third period, added another via a bootleg play of thirty-four yards late in the fourth period, and Texas had a 17–13 win.

Despite the Auburn win, Alabama won the SEC Championship, second in a row and eleventh in its history. Hannah, Mitchell, Krapf, Gantt, Davis, Wheeler, Buddy Brown, Bob McKinney and Chuck Strickland were named to the all SEC team.

1973

It was obvious early in 1973 that it would take a great eleven to beat the Tide, for Coach Bear Bryant, starting his sixteenth season, had one of the finest, best-balanced teams in his coaching career.

The Tide had two outstanding quarterbacks, the red-headed junior Gary Rutledge and the multi-talented Richard Todd; Wayne Wheeler, a six-two, 200-pound receiver said to be as fast and as elusive as the immortal Don Hutson; Wilbur Jackson, a smashing halfback who led the SEC with seven yards per carry in 1972; linebacker

Woody Lowe, who was being compared to the great Lee Roy Jordan; defensive end, Mike Dubose, a fierce hitter who loved to play all the time; offensive guard Buddy Brown; tackle, Mike Raines; and cornerback Mike Washington.

The former Clemson head coach Frank Howard, witnessing a couple of early season games said, "I've never seen a better balanced, more versatile team in my coaching life."

Thus, on the night of September 15, there was more than the ordinary interest in the opening game of the season. It seemed as though all eyes were on Alabama as it took the field in Birmingham to face the University of California eleven. The huge crowd had hardly settled into their seats before Alabama had a 14–0 lead on two touchdown passes by Todd and Rutledge. Coach Bryant was already using his second and third stringers in the third period as the Tide pulled away to a stunning 66–0 win.

On week two, Kentucky Wildcats surprised Alabama and built up a 14–0 lead at half time, but that lead vanished in the third period as Alabama struck back ... dramatically. Halfback Willie Shelby took the kickoff to start the period, got by two Kentucky tacklers, dodged and fought his way to the sidelines, and sped through the entire Kentucky team ... for a 100-yard touchdown sprint. The stunned Wildcats made only one first down in the second half as Alabama scored twenty-one points in the third period and another touchdown in the fourth for a 28–14 win.

Then in rapid succession, the Tide defeated Vanderbilt, 44–0; survived a scare by Georgia but managed to score fifteen points in the final period to win, 28–14; and trounced Florida, 35–14.

Tennessee became Alabama's sixth victim as they fell under a 21-point barrage in

Wilbur Jackson on a 35-yard TD sprint against California in 1973.

the final five minutes of the game to lose 42–21. But the Tide offense was still warming up. The following week, against Virginia Tech in Tuscaloosa, Alabama's offense rolled for eleven touchdowns in a 77–6 rout. Coach Bryant used every one of the players on the squad as the Crimson Tide amassed 828 yards running and passing to set a new NCAA record.

Still in high gear, 'Bama cruised over Mississippi State, 35–0, and subdued the Hurricanes of Miami, 43–13. Then, in a nationally televised contest, Alabama had to battle all the way to defeat a solid LSU eleven, 21–7. Once again quarterback Gary Rutledge was outstanding as he ran for one touchdown and passed for two more, including a spectacular 77-yarder to end Wayne Wheeler.

In the final game of the regular season, a fired-up Alabama eleven, determined to avenge the one-point, 1972 loss, annihilated the Auburn Tigers, 35–0. Halfback Wilbur Jackson scored once, and his great broken-

field running kept Auburn off balance throughout the game. Gary Rutledge scored on two runs of one and three yards as the Tide ended the season with an 11–0 record.

Six teams finished the 1973 season undefeated: Alabama, Penn State, Notre Dame, Michigan, Oklahoma, and Ohio State. But Alabama was voted the number-one team in the nation by the United Press and was matched against number-three Notre Dame in the Sugar Bowl in New Orleans, December 31. This was the first-ever meeting between the two giants of collegiate football, and the game proved to be everything any football fan would ever wish to see.

An overflowing crowd of 85,000 sat with bated breath as Notre Dame, in a tremendous defensive display, held the Crimson Tide offense without a single yard during the first quarter. Meanwhile, Tom Clements of Notre Dame proceeded to fill the air with his passes: nineteen yards to Casper, twenty-six more to Casper, and then Wayne Bullock capped a 64-yard drive for an Irish touchdown and a 6–0 lead.

But Alabama came right back in the second period, sustaining an offensive drive until Randy Billingsley smashed into the Irish line and drove across for an Alabama score. Bill Davis converted and it was 7–6, Alabama. Still in the second period, Notre Dame's Al Hunter took a kickoff on his 7-yard line and sprinted downfield ninety-three yards for a touchdown. The Irish completed a two point conversion and it was Notre Dame 14, Alabama 7. Bill Davis then kicked a 39-yard field goal and it was 14–10, Notre Dame at half time.

The teams swapped touchdowns in the third period, Alabama pulling ahead, 17–14, and then the Irish surging back up, 21–17. Then Alabama recovered a Notre Dame fumble, and on the first play Richard Todd handed off to Mike Stock. Stock circled to his right, stopped, and then lofted a high, arching pass to a wide-open Todd, who raced in untouched for an Alabama score. Davis missed the crucial conversion, and

the score now stood at Alabama 23, Notre Dame 21.

The Irish responded quickly and drove the ball to the Alabama 15-yard line. Then Coach Ara Parseghian sent in his kicking specialist, Bob Thomas, and Thomas promptly booted a three-pointer to give the Irish a 24–23 victory and the Associated Press version of the National Championship.

1974

In 1974, Coach Bryant's seventeenth season as Alabama's head coach, the Tide once again rolled through a perfect regular season, but with a couple of scares along the way. After opening with wins over Maryland, Southern Mississippi, Vandy and Ole Miss, an over-confident 'Bama entertained a Florida State team with a record of seventeen consecutive losses. But the Seminoles played their hearts out and were leading

1973 National Champions: *Front row:* B. Davis, Pizzitola, Boles, Pappas, Gantt, Ridgeway, Rutledge, Todd, O'Rear, Sharpless, Bolden, McMakin, R. Davis, Odom, Perry, Riley, Spivey, Marcello. *Second row:* Billingsley, Taylor, Ford, Shelby, Prudhomme, Stock, Culliver, Washington, Beck, Strickland, Dawson, P. Harris, Murphy, Stokes, King, Rhodes, Dean, Lowe, Cary, Hall. *Third row:* Hannah, Smith, Hubbard, Dubose, Robertson, Callaway, Duncan, Lambert, Croom, Hunt, Rogers, Hall, Montgomery, Whitley, B. Brown, Turpin, Yelvington, White, Eckenrod. *Back row:* Ruffin, Patterson, Kubelius, Szubinski, Norman, Hanrahan, Maxwell, Sprayberry, Jackson, J. Brown, Wheeler, Croyle, J. Harris, Dyar, Pugh, Raines, Watkins, Kulback, Barnes, Cook.

Richard Todd led the Tide in '74 and '75.

Alabama 7–5 with just 1:27 left to play in the game. Then it was Bucky Berrey kicking a last-second 36-yard field goal to give Alabama an 8–7 win . . . as the gun sounded to end the game. The game against Florida State marked the first game that Alabama had been held without a touchdown since 1970.

Richard Todd and Willie Shelby started the Alabama offense revving, and the Tide blew by its next five opponents—Tennessee, Texas Christian, Mississippi State, LSU, and Miami.

Then, in the final game of the season, it was Alabama, the nation's number-two team, versus seventh ranked Auburn in a nationally televised contest, and Auburn battled Alabama right down to the final gun. There were just seven minutes left to play in the game when Auburn's Phil Gargis cracked through the Crimson Tide line for a touchdown to make it Alabama 17, Auburn 13. Auburn tried for a two-point conversion, but missed, and the Tide held on for a huge win over the Tigers.

The Orange Bowl Committee was delighted with Alabama's unbeaten season and, given the thrilling game versus Notre Dame a year previous, wasted no time inviting both teams back again. The Miami venue was packed with a crowd of more than 72,000 shreiking fans who were up and out of their seats from the opening kickoff.

Both teams seemed jittery and anxious in the opening moments, and the Tide made the first big mistake. The Irish recovered a fumble on the 'Bama 4-yard line, and on the first play Irish fullback Wayne Bullock burst through for the touchdown and an early 7–0 lead. Then, in the second period, the Irish drove seventy-seven yards for a second touchdown with Mark McLane diving across from the 5-yard line. The missed extra point gave the Tide

faithful a flicker of hope. Alabama's Dan Ridgeway kicked a 21-yard field goal late in the second period to give Alabama its first points, and at the half it was 13–3, Notre Dame.

After a scoreless third period, Willie Shelby broke loose to the Irish 49-yard line, and then Richard Todd fired a perfect strike to Russ Schamun for an Alabama touchdown. Then Todd hit George Pugh for a two-point conversion to close the score to Notre Dame 13, Alabama 11.

The game ended with Alabama fighting desperately to get within field goal range. Todd almost managed to pull the game put, but his final pass was intercepted on the Irish 10-yard line, and one of the most dramatic bowl games in history went to the Irish of Notre Dame.

1975

As the '75 season got underway, Bear Bryant carefully checked the candidates for his varsity squad and turned to senior quarterback Richard Todd. "Looks like we might have something special this year," he said, "with all the veterans returning. Just have to be careful that you all don't get too cocky out there."

"No chance, Coach. This is the last year for a lot of us and we're not going to blow anything away. Got to win the Championship this year."

But something most unexpected did happen in the very first game of the season. Missouri completely outplayed Alabama in a nationally televised game at Birmingham that had a great crowd of 65,000 reeling in astonishment.

Missouri scored ten points in the first quarter, ten more in the second, and held the Crimson Tide helpless until late in the fourth period. Then Richard Todd tossed a pass to Ozzie Newsome for a touchdown, but it was too little too late. The game was practically over at that point and an amazing Missouri Tiger had beaten nationally ranked Alabama 20–7.

The Tide had a two-week respite before facing tough Clemson, and Bryant drove the squad through a series of merciless drills that had the players gasping. But the work paid off. Alabama scored in every period to overwhelm the Tigers, 56–0, and rolled on to crushing victories over Vanderbilt, 40–7; Mississippi, 32–6; Washington, 52–0; Tennessee, 30–7; and Texas Christian, 45–0.

Mississippi State fought hard before falling, 21–10, and the Tide struggled to defeat stubborn LSU, 23–10. Then, after a routine 27–6 win over Southern Mississippi, it was once again time for Auburn.

This year, however, the brilliance of Richard Todd overwhelmed the Tigers. By scoring twice and passing for a third touchdown, Todd once again proved that he was one of the finest quarterbacks in the nation. The Crimson Tide closed out a most memorable season with ten successive wins after a loss to Missouri.

Alabama was invited to meet Penn State in the first Sugar Bowl to be played in the new Super Dome in New Orleans, and on December 31, 1975, thousands of Alabama's faithful headed west for the game.

Alabama scored a field goal in the first period to take a 3–0 lead over Joe Paterno's Nittany Lions, and that score held until Penn State's Chris Bahr tied it with a field goal in the third period.

Then in the final quarter, Richard Todd tossed a sensational 55-yard aerial to Ozzie Newsome to the 11-yard line, and on the next play Mike Stock burst in from the 11-yard line for a touchdown. Chris Bahr

Ozzie Newsome emerges as one of Todd's great receivers.

kicked a Penn State field goal to make it 10–6, but Dan Ridgeway returned the favor to give Alabama a hard-earned 13–6 win. This was Alabama's first post-season victory in eight games as well as an unprecedented fifth SEC Championship in succession.

1976

The 1976 campaign began inauspiciously, with the Tide dropping its first conference game since 1972. It was a tough 10–7 loss to Ole Miss, but Bryant and his staff let the players know that he was thoroughly dissatisfied with his team's poor play.

The following week, a chastened Tide, behind quarterback Jack O'Rear, swamped Southern Methodist, 56–3. Jeff Rutledge, Ozzie Newsome, Pete Cavan, and Bob Baumhower also starred for the Tide.

In the third game of the season, against Vanderbilt, Jack O'Rear sprinted fifty-two yards for a touchdown the first time Alabama had the ball, but sprained his ankle on the play. Jeff Rutledge replaced him and guided the Crimson Tide to an impressive 42–14 win. But a week later at Athens, Georgia's Bulldogs played an inspired game to defeat Alabama, 21–0. Georgia had dedicated the Alabama game to one of their star linemen, Hugh Hendrix, who had died during the summer of a rare blood infection, and the Bulldogs simply controlled the game from start to finish.

"Our students partied and celebrated all week and classes had to be called off,"

All-American linebacker Barry Krauss made ten tackles, eight assists, and returned an interception for a TD in the '76 Liberty Bowl.

recalled Coach Vince Dooley. "To beat Alabama as we did was unheard of in those days."

The Tide quickly rebounded with successive wins over Southern Mississippi, Tennessee, Louisville, Mississippi State, and LSU, and then was ready for the battle against Notre Dame at South Bend, November 13. It was the first-ever regular season game between the two bitter rivals, and the 'Bama squad entered Notre Dame Stadium to be greeted by a roar from the more than 60,000 fans.

After a scoreless first period, Irish quarterback Rick Slager tossed a magnificent, 65-yard scoring pass to Dan Kelleher, and the Irish took a 7–0 lead. But the Tide stayed right with them, and Notre Dame held a slight 21–18 lead with three minutes left to play. Then Jeff Rutledge, with Pete Cavan wide open in the right corner of the endzone, threw an interception toward double-covered Ozzie Newsome, and the game ended with Notre Dame the winner.

The following week, Jeff Rutledge and Tony Nathan starred for the Crimson Tide as they easily defeated hated rival Auburn by 38–7. Quarterback Rutledge hit on six of eight passes for one touchdown, while Nathan, a flashy sophomore, ripped off two great touchdown sprints. The victory gave Alabama an 8–3 season record and an invitation to play UCLA in the Liberty Bowl, Alabama's eighteenth straight post-season appearance.

Barry Krauss, a six-three, 235 pound linebacker from Pompano Beach, played one of the finest defensive games in Alabama history in that Liberty Bowl game. Krauss made ten tackles and eight assists and sparked the Crimson Tide by intercepting a pass and then scrambling forty-four yards for the first score of the game. Krauss's play inspired the rest of the Tidesmen, and Alabama scored in every period to

Captain Ozzie Newsome led the Tide to a superb 11–1 record in 1977.

bury UCLA, 36–6. Bob Baumhower, Ozzie Newsome, Davis Gerasimchuk and Charley Hannah were named to the All-SEC team, but the Tide's five-year reign as king of the conference had come to an end.

1977

Alabama's 1977 varsity squad consisted of some of the most talented and versatile people to ever wear the Crimson, and Coach Bryant, beginning his twentieth season, had reason for high expectations.

Among the returning veterans were Marty Lyons, a huge, 6-5, 250-pound tackle; Barry Krauss, MVP in the Liberty

In 1977 and '78, quarterback Jeff Rutledge set a 'Bama record with 100 straight passes without an interception.

Bowl game in 1976; the third member of the great Hannah brothers, David, at 6–3 and 240 pounds. On the offense, Bryant had Tony Nathan, one of the most talented halfbacks in Alabama football, and senior quarterback Jeff Rutledge, who broke his wrist on the final day of the 1977 spring practice, then went on to gain 3518 yards in total offense.

But the '77 campaign proved to be no stroll through the park. After a routine opening-day win over Ole Miss, the Tide traveled to Lincoln, Nebraska, and got shucked by the Cornhuskers in a 31–24 upset. The Cornhuskers had scouted the Alabama offense thoroughly and intercepted quarterback Jeff Rutledge an incredible five times. Rutledge would not throw another interception until the second game of 1978, setting a new Alabama record with 100 straight passes without an interception.

During the following three weeks, Ala-

bama defeated Vanderbilt, 24–12, struggled to an 18–10 victory over Georgia, and struggled even harder to prevail over Southern Cal, 21–20. After 'Bama withstood a furious last-quarter rally, including stopping a two-point conversion attempt in the final seconds, an exhausted Bryant had this to say: "I think we got a little bit of help from the man upstairs. We were lucky to get out with a win. I've never seen a team come back so strong as they did."

The great win over Southern California sparked the Crimson Tide to victories over their next six opponents: Tennessee, Louisville, Mississippi State, LSU, Miami and Auburn were all soundly beaten to give Alabama a satisfying 10–1 season, along with its sixth SEC title in seven years.

The Sugar Bowl Committee selected Ala-

bama to meet Ohio State in the annual New Year's day game, pitting two of the nation's legendary coaches, Bear Bryant and Ohio State's Woody Hayes.

After a scoreless, defense-dominated first period, the Tide suddenly found an opening, and Jeff Rutledge hurled a 27-yard scoring strike to Bruce Bolton. Then, after an exchange of kicks, Alabama drove to the Ohio State 1-yard line, and Tony Nathan burst through for a second score. The Tide continued to pour it on in the second half, as MVP Rutledge led his offense to a huge 35–6 victory.

Alabama fans thought such a decisive win over the Buckeyes would be enough to earn the Tide voted the National Championship. But their hopes were dashed when Notre Dame was voted National Champions.

Tony Nathan crashes through the Buckeye line for a TD in the Sugar Bowl, January 1, 1978.

1978

It was Charley Thornton, Alabama's outstanding public relations director, who, after thumbing through the NCAA records, one day in 1978 casually mentioned to Bear Bryant that he was within reach of the immortal Amos Alonzo Stagg's record for the most victories in a coaching career. Thornton saw the record as an incentive that might be valuable after a decade of unparalleled success. The Bear saw it as a way of resolving the question of when he would retire, a question other schools had used against him in recruiting.

Meanwhile, even as younger coaches left the game, Bear continued to search for new ways to reach his players. What other coach would have written Ann Landers for help as Bryant did in that period?

He wrote Landers and asked her to reprint a column about a fictional teenager who drives the family car too fast, crashes, and sees himself declared dead and buried. "Most of these boys [his players] are seventeen and eighteen," wrote Bryant. "I hope your column does something to them. It might save somebody some day."

Thousands of Ann Landers fans wrote Bryant in appreciation.

The '78 season began with three games against powerful intra-sectional opponents. First, the Tide got sweet revenge against Nebraska, 20–3, then came back to defeat surprisingly tough Missouri, 38–20. Then Southern California traveled to Birmingham September 23, determined to avenge the stunning defeat Alabama had given the Trojans a year earlier. And they did just that, scoring in every period but the third to hand Alabama a 24–14 defeat. The

Trojans held the vaunted Crimson Tide offense scoreless in the first half.

Then, after a win over Vanderbilt, 'Bama prepared for another tough intra-sectional foe — the Washington Huskies. Alabama was rocked back on its heels as Tom Porres, the Huskies' quarterback, tossed a 74-yard bomb to Spider Gaines and a Mike Lansford field goal gave the Huskies a 10–0 lead. But then halfback Major Ogilvie took command,

Major Ogilvie breaks loose for a TD versus Mississippi State.

capping a 53-yard drive with a 15-yard burst into the end zone. Tony Nathan scored the go-ahead touchdown for the Tide in the third period, and Rutledge passed thirty-six yards to Rick Neal in the final period to give Alabama a nail-biting 20–17 win.

The Tide followed the win over Washington with five straight less nerve-racking victories: 23–12 over Florida; 30–17 over Tennessee; a 35–0 rout of Virginia Tech; 35–14 over Mississippi State; and 31–10 over LSU. Then, on December 2, it was time for Auburn.

The two rivals met head-on before a record crowd of more than 79,000 fans, and both teams began the game with fumbles. The players were so geared up for the game they had trouble executing. Then 'Bama got the big break and capitalized. Marty Lyons recovered an Auburn fumble at the Tiger's 40-yard line, and Rutledge immediately connected with Bruce Bolton for thirty-three yards and an Alabama score. Undaunted, Auburn went on the attack, driving to the Tide's 32-yard line. Then Auburn pulled a surprise. The Tigers lined up for a field goal attempt, but holder Foster Christy shoveled the ball back to William Andrews, who scooted to the 15-yard line before he was stopped. Joe Cribbs carried the ball four straight times and finally smashed across the goal line. The kick was good for a 7–7 tie.

Alabama scored ten more points in the half, but Auburn scored after a Rutledge fumble to stay close, 17–13 at half time. However, the second half was all Alabama as the Tide ripped and tore the Tigers' defense apart. Rutledge tossed for two touchdowns and McElroy kicked a beauty of a 39-yard field goal for seventeen points and a 34–16 Alabama victory.

Alabama finished the season ranked second only to Penn State, and both teams were invited to meet in the Sugar Bowl at New Orleans, January 1, for the National Championship. On the day of the showdown, Coach Bear Bryant commented that his secondary had been slowed by numerous injuries and that the team was to go under the gun against Penn State's Chuck Fusina, whom Coach Joe Paterno called the best passer he ever had. "And," said Bryant, "rushing the passer is the thing we do worst."

Then, in about as thorough a demonstra-

Billy Jackson on an 87-yard burst against Florida.

tion of defensive scratch-and-harry as you've ever seen, the Crimson Tide not only shut down Fusina, but rushed him to distraction every time he got set to throw the ball. In addition, Wayne Hamilton, E. J. Junior, Marty Lyons, Byron Baggs, Curtis McGriff, Ricky Gilliland, and the tough Barry Krause took turns stuffing Penn's runners like a sausage. The result was that Alabama had almost exclusive control of the ball in the first half and drove into the lead when Rutledge fired a 30-yard touchdown pass to Bolton.

But Penn State retaliated in the third quarter. Pete Harris leaped high into the air to intercept a Rutledge pass on the 'Bama 48-yard line, and then Fusina came alive. He tossed for twenty-five yards to Guman, then hit Scott Fitzkee on a 17-yard pass to tie the score at 7–7.

1978 National Champions: *Front row:* Umphrey, Chapman, Pugh, Jacobs, McElroy, Neal, Harris, Shealy, Rutledge, K. Jones, Crumbley, Tucker, Legg. *Second row:* Haney, Nathan, Perrin, J. Jones, Coleman, Sutton, Spencer, McNeil, Ikner, Bolton, Jackson, Allman, Turpin, Wingo, Haynes, Junior. *Third row:* Ferguson, Ogilvie, Clements, Hill, Whitman, Braggs, Scott, DeNiro, Smith, Barnes, Hufstetler, McCarty, Stephenson, Palmer, Boothe, Robbins. *Fourth row:* Allison, Bunch, Boler, Cowell, Searcey, Brock, Sebastian, McCombs, Hannah, Krauss, Aydelette, Faust, Clark, Sanderson (tr.), Thomas (mgr.). *Back row:* Vines, Mauro, Booker, Kraut, Travis, Parker, Boyd, Lyles, Gilliand, Lyons, Hamilton, Inman, McGriff, Rumley, Theis, Lancaster.

Then, after an exchange of possession, Lou Ikner took a Penn State punt and twisted, turned, and spun for sixty-two yards to the State eleven. Rutledge took the pass from center, faked to his fullback, and pitched the ball to Major Ogilvie, and the Major went over for Alabama's winning touchdown.

When the Bowl Games were done with, the Associated Press voted Alabama the National Championship.

1979

Major Ogilvie, the talented running back from Birmingham put Alabama's attitude toward the 1979 season in perspective: "Alabama's approach to each season comes right to the point. We have a great winning tradition. Our object is to win. There is no pretending that winning doesn't matter. We start each season with the single goal of winning the National Championship. And I like that."

In 1979, the Crimson Tide had good reason to feel they could go all the way. Returning were eight starting veterans on offense, six on defense. And up front where the coaches say games are won and lost, Alabama would return nine of ten starters.

Offensively, Alabama had Jim Bunch, Vince Blothe, Dwight Stephenson, Mike Brock, and Bud Aydelette. In the backfield, Steadman Shealy was the number-one quarterback; Tim Travis, Bart Krout, Keith Pugh, and Tim Clark were the receivers. Alan McElroy was back to handle the place-kicking and Woody Umphrey was the punter.

Defensively, the Tide had E.J. Junior, Warren Lyles, Byron Baggs, Wayne Hamilton, David Hannah, and John Mauro for front-line duties. Randy Scott and Tom Boyd were the linebackers, while Don McNeal, Mike Clements, Tommy Wilcox, Ricky Tucker, and Jim Bob Harris made up the secondary. This was an all-star lineup that would give every Alabama opponent sleepless nights in 1979.

The Crimson Tide warmed up with a 30–6 whipping of Georgia Tech on national television, then clobbered Baylor, 45–0, and routed Vanderbilt, 66–3. Now rolling, the Tide methodically downed Wichita State, 38–0; Florida, 40–0; Tennessee, 27–17; Virginia Tech, 31–7; and Mississippi State, 24–7.

On November 10 in a driving rain, a hard-nosed, aggressive LSU Tiger squad

Steadman Shealy became the starting quarterback in '79 and led the Tide to another National Championship.

his Arkansas Razorbacks in New Orleans on January 1.

Halfback Major Ogilvie, the game's MVP, turned in a great first-half performance as the Tide ran up a 17–3 lead. The Major carried the ball fourteen times for sixty-nine yards and touchdowns of twenty-two and one yard. He also returned a punt fifty yards to set up still another score. And when the Tide had its back against its own goal line, Ogilvie got off a quick-kick of forty-five yards that set the Razorbacks back into their territory. Credit also a tremendous display by the Alabama defensive line which stopped Arkansas whenever they appeared to be threatening. Final score: Alabama 24–Arkansas 9.

In the Rose Bowl contest, USC took a squeaker from favored Ohio State, leaving Alabama the only undefeated, untied team in the nation. The next day, after the bowl games, the Associated Press, United Press, Football Writers, and Coaches Associations voted Alabama National Champions.

held the Tide even for the better part of three periods, then Alan McElroy kicked a dandy 27-yard field goal to give Alabama the only points of the game. A week later, Miami fell, 30–0, to give Alabama its longest winning streak in years, nineteen in a row. Miami Coach Howard Schnellenberger, a former Bryant aide at Alabama, said, "Alabama is the toughest team we've played this year. I'm happy not to play them again."

Despite four costly fumbles in the third period, Alabama defeated chief rival Auburn on December 1, by a 25–18 margin. This victory was the eleventh straight of the season and assured the Crimson Tide of a Sugar Bowl match-up with Lou Holtz and

Major Ogilvie was the Sugar Bowl MVP as the Tide clinched the 1979 Championship.

1979 National Champions. *Front row:* Holt, Umphrey, Pugh, Jacobs, McElroy, Sprinkle, Harris, Shealy, Coley, Landrum, Gary, Wilcox, Reeves, Tucker, Castille, Simon. *Second row:* Haney, Perrin, J. Jones, Spencer, McNeal, Orcutt, White, Jackson, Blue, Fagan, Rozzell, Collins, Williams, Junior, Ferguson, M. Ogilvie, Clements, Hill, Whitman, Miller (tr.). *Third row:* Connor (mgr.), Braggs, Nix, Bobby Smith, DeNiro, Scott, Barry Smith, Barnes, Mott, Dasher, Robbins, Allison, Bunch, Holcombe, Cowell, Bramblett, Searcy, Brock, Cayavec, McCombe, Hannah, Cates (mgr.). *Back row:* Collins, Aydelette, Clark, Pitts, Marks, Brown, Mauro, Beazley, R. Ogilvie, Kraut, Travis, Wood, Boyd, Lyles, Homan, McGriff, R. Jones, Cline, Lancaster.

1980

Bear Bryant had set a coaching mark with 103 victories in a single decade. He had won Coach of the Year honors and conference and national championships. Now there was the mark set back in the 1940's by the immortal Amos Alonzo Stagg, head coach at the University of Chicago, when the Maroons were the very best in the land. Stagg coached at Chicago for fifty-seven years, then at the University of the Pacific and at Susquehanna until he was ninety-six years of age.

His record of 314 coaching wins had been considered impossible to surpass.

Now, in 1980, Bear Bryant of Alabama had a record of 296 wins, and the countdown had began in earnest. In newspapers, magazines, on radio and television, sportscasters and fans were talking about the Bear and number 314.

Bryant kept aw-shucksing about the record, but no one doubted that it was this goal that he wanted very much ... kept

him going. He cut down on smoking. He would no longer jump in a plane to speak at a Touchdown Club somewhere or visit a new recruit. He simply did not have the strength it took.

In August, just before the first game of the season against Georgia Tech, Bryant's doctors had ordered him into the hospital. He had suffered a stroke, though it was never officially announced. They put him on medication and didn't let him out of bed for six days. He lost twenty-one pounds but was back on the field in time to open his thirty-fifth season as head coach.

The 1980 team had no franchise player, but the talent ran so deep that Bear would send players out in waves — a true Crimson Tide. On opening day against Tech, Bryant used eleven running backs as the Tide romped to a 26–3 victory. The next week the Tide's depth was again evident as Major Ogilvie contributed two touchdowns and running backs Bill Jackson and Lin Patrick each rushed for more than 100 yards in a 59–35 win over Ole Miss. The Tide then crushed Vanderbilt, 41–0, and Kentucky, 45–0, for Coach Bryant's 300th victory.

After an excruciating 17–13 win over

Some of 'Bama's bowl game MVPs from the '70s: Jeff Rutledge (11), Rich Wingo (36), Tony Nathan (22), Barry Krauss (77), and Marty Lyons (93).

Rutgers in Giants Stadium, followed by routine victories over Tennessee and Southern Mississippi, a miracle occurred in Jackson, Mississippi. On November 1 the Mississippi State Bulldogs defeated the seemingly invincible Crimson Tide, 6–3, in as wild and exciting game as had ever been seen in that town. Alabama had won twenty-eight straight games, the longest streak in the nation and was a prohibitive favorite to win.

Two minutes remained as Alabama, behind 6–3, drove down to the Bulldogs' 3-yard line. Quarterback Don Jacobs tried to circle right end for the winning score, but was hit by end Tyrone Keys of Mississippi State and fumbled the ball. Mississippi recovered the ball and ran out the clock for State's first win over Alabama since 1957.

The Tide bounced back to beat LSU, 28–7, but then lost again—this time in a bitter struggle against nemesis Notre Dame, 7–0.

There was some consolation, however, in beating Auburn the following week. Freshman quarterback Walter Lewis sprinted seventy-three yards for one touchdown, then set up another score to lead Alabama to a 34–18 triumph.

The Tide was invited to the Cotton Bowl to face Baylor University, touted for the best offense in the southwest conference. But an inspired Crimson Tide rolled up five times as much yardage as Baylor to take a 30–2 victory. Major Ogilvie led his team in rushing and scored on a 1-yard plunge, making him the first player ever to run for a touchdown in four bowl games. Peter Kim kicked three field goals, and guard Warren Lyles was voted the game's MVP.

The win was the 306th career win for Bryant, leaving him just eight short of Amos Alonzo Stagg's record. It also was the Tide's twenty-second consecutive bowl appearance as Alabama finished the season at 10–2.

1981

In 1981 Bear Bryant began his twenty-fourth year as Alabama's head coach. He was trying to be more patient, more grandfatherly, with his players, he said. But in the first several days of practice, a number of players, including a very promising halfback, Linnie Patrick, could not run the mile in the time prescribed by Bryant. He barred those players until they could qualify.

In the season opener, September 5, a nationally televised game against LSU, the Tide offense came ready to roll. Behind fleet halfback Kenny Simon, 'Bama scored seventeen first-quarter points. Then quarterback Ken Coley sprinted for gains of fifty-one and forty-two yards, and Walt Lewis, a flashy halfback, scored on a trick-keeper play. Peter Kim booted a 20-yard field goal to make it a 24–7 victory, as Alabama's great defensive unit held LSU scoreless until the final three minutes of the game.

An inspired Georgia Tech squad rolled into Birmingham a week later, determined to defeat Alabama for the first time since it won in 1962 by a 7–6 margin. Coached by Bill Curry, Tech managed to hold the Crimson Tide to a 13–7 half time lead, then broke loose for seventeen points and defeated Alabama in a tense battle, 24–21. Three Alabama fumbles led to Alabama's demise.

The Tide settled down after the loss to Georgia Tech and defeated Kentucky, 19–10, on four Peter Kim field goals; Vanderbilt, 28–7; and Ole Miss, 38–7. Then, in another shocker, Southern Mississippi scored ten points in the final few minutes of their game to tie Alabama 13–13.

Then, as the season moved into October, Alabama defeated Tennessee, Rutgers, and, with the aid of a fourth-quarter field goal, defeated Mississippi State, 13–10, for the 313th victory of Coach Bryant's career.

At Penn State the following week, a record crowd of more than 85,000 turned out for one of the biggest games of any year. In addition to the national television coverage, more than 350 sportswriters and commentators were on hand to witness the historic game.

Bob Hope pays his respects to the man about to become the winningest coach in college football history.

The Alabama players were more excited than the outwardly calm Bryant, but just as the team left the locker room, Bryant urged them with these words: "Go out there and play like it was the last game of your lives. Play every moment as if this was your last play, play like you're behind."

Alabama took a 7–0 lead after eleven minutes of the period, when quarterback Walter Lewis broke away from State tacklers and tossed a 37-yard pass to Jesse Bendross

for a touchdown, then ran up seventeen points in the second period to take a 24–3 lead at half time. State outscored Alabama 13–7 in the second half, but it was not enough to prevent the inspired, proud Crimson Tide from winning number 314 for Coach Bryant.

"This was the biggest game anyone on this team ever played," said quarterback Walt Lewis, whose two touchdown passes, supported by a tenacious Alabama defense, made the big difference.

In the locker room after the game, Coach Bryant was overwhelmed by the legion of reporters who vied to record one of the most memorable, magical moments in college football history. Badgered to make a statement, Bryant said, "I really haven't had time to think about it. I really didn't tie the record. There have been multiple people with a hand in it, and I'm grateful to all of them."

Finally, after two weeks of steadily mounting media pressure, the big day arrived, November 28, and Auburn. On this historic day the two teams produced perhaps the most unforgettable game in their long and illustrious history.

After an interception by Tommy Wilcox, Alabama took over and moved the ball out to their own 30-yard line. Then quarterback Alan Gray turned left end, and raced sixty-three yards to the Tigers' twenty-three. Five plays later Gray sneaked over from the 3-yard line for an early 7–0 lead. But the Tigers roared back. Fullback George Peoples banged through the Alabama line and was off and running for a 63-yard touchdown and a 7–7 tie at half time.

Alabama regained the lead in the third period, as Ken Coley pitched a short pass to Jesse Bendross, and Jess scampered across the goal line from the 21-yard mark. But before 'Bama could draw an easy breath, Joey Jones fumbled a Tiger punt, and

Despite Joey Jones' 69-yard kickoff return, the Tide lost to Texas in the '82 Cotton Bowl.

on to the Cotton Bowl, where Alabama would play a University of Texas team Bryant had never beaten in a bowl game and only once in eight tries. Nor would Coach Bryant add to his total of victories on New Year's Day, 1982. Alabama blew a 10-point lead as Texas scored all of their fourteen points in the final period. The game ended with the band playing, "The Eyes of Texas" and the living legend walking slowly to the locker room, uniformed troopers on either side of him. He never looked back.

1982

Alabama started the 1982 season as they had so many recent ones, with the look of eagles. The Tide won its first five games, four of them by wide margins: Georgia Tech fell, 45–7; Mississippi went down, 42–14; Vanderbilt took a tough 24–21 loss; Arkansas State got trounced, 34–7; and Joe Paterno's Penn State eleven, ranked one of the best in the East, was humbled, 42–21. Now, as October dawned, Alabama fans had visions of another National Championship.

But then Tennessee, with one of their great teams, topped the Crimson Tide, 35–28, in a struggle that went right down to the final minutes of the game.

After two more hard-fought victories, over Cincinnati and Mississippi State, an aggressive LSU outplayed the Tide to win 20–10. It was another tough loss, and after the game Coach Bryant dropped broad hints that this was his final season.

Then Southern Mississippi surprised Alabama with a 38–29 upset in a home game at Tuscaloosa, the first loss suffered by Alabama at home since 1963. And to make matters worse, the regular season ended with a bitter 23–22 defeat by Alabama's

Auburn recovered on the Tide 2-yard line. Two plays later Lionel James of Auburn scored the tying touchdown. Then Auburn took a 17–14 lead on a field goal by Al Del Greco, and the Auburn fans went wild. The sky reverberated with the thunder of their cheers.

But Walt Lewis quickly silenced them. Two quick passes to Bendross gave 'Bama a 21–17 lead, and three minutes later Alabama broke the game open as Linnie Patrick broke away for a clinching touchdown.

And Bear Bryant, the kid from Moro Bottom, was getting phone calls from President Ronald Reagan and ex-President Jimmy Carter, congratulating him on being the winningest coach in the history of college football.

To conclude the historic season, it was

The Bear announces his retirement.

ancient rival Auburn. The win was Auburn's first since 1972, when the Tigers won by one point, 17–16. Alabama finished the regular season with three straight losses, four in the last six games: it all added up to a 7–4 record, the poorest in twelve years.

On December 15, two weeks before his team would face Illinois in the Liberty Bowl, Bryant made the dreaded official announcement that he was retiring as football coach.

When Bryant made his retirement statement to the press his voice stumbled, as though he didn't want to read his own handwriting. He didn't seem sad or even sentimental . . . just very tired. He would stay on as athletic director, but he had in

effect fired himself as the coach because Alabama in 1982 had played, he said, only "four or five games like a Bryant-coached team should."

"There comes a time in every profession when you have to hang it up," he said, "and that time has come for me as head football coach at the University of Alabama."

At the same time, his successor was announced: Ray Perkins, one of his great Alabama players, a star receiver with the Baltimore Colts, most recently head coach of the New York Giants.

After the drama and excitement of the run for the record, the 1982 season had turned out to be an anticlimax for Bryant. But now the Liberty Bowl would take on new significance — the Bear's last game.

The game opened with the teams sparring like two fighters maneuvering for an opening, but Alabama, jabbing at the Illini line, drove to the 5-yard line. Fullback Ricky Moore dove across the goal line and Kim kicked the point for a 7–0 Alabama lead as the quarter ended. In the second period, Curtis of Illinois punched across the Tide goal and it was 7–6, Alabama, at the half.

But the Tide pulled away in the second half. Jesse Bendross barreled across the Illini goal for a third-period score, and Craig Turner scored the decisive touchdown in the final period to give Alabama a hard-earned 21–15 victory.

When the final gun went off, Bryant's players tried to lift the coach onto their shoulders, but his bulk and their anxiety couldn't make it happen, so they formed a tight cordon to escort him off the field.

Bryant strolled off into retirement with a coaching record of 323 wins, 85 losses and 17 ties. And as he left the field, the scoreboard lights blinked:

GOODBYE BEAR, WE'LL MISS YOU.

Bear Bryant suffered from coronary artery disease, commonly known as hardening or narrowing of the arteries. He survived a stroke in 1980, but his doctor, William Hill, prescribed a powerful stimulant and he was back on the field in a week.

In 1981, according to Dr. Hill, Bryant suffered a light stroke with paralysis on the right side of the body. It wasn't clear that anyone outside his family knew about this setback. Again, after a week or two he was back on the field.

"He made a remarkable recovery from the stroke," said Dr. Hill. "I was relieved when he announced his retirement."

In the early evening of Tuesday, January 25, just six weeks after he announced his retirement, Bryant felt violent chest pains. He was at the home of Jimmy Hinton, his partner in land and meatpacking deals. Bryant seemed to have a capacity for collapsing among friends.

He was rushed to Druid City Hospital where tests disclosed no massive heart damage. He spent a restful night, and in the morning had a relaxed visit with Sam Bailey, his associate athletic director, and Ray Perkins.

But at 12:24 p.m. Bryant's breathing became labored. Ten or fifteen seconds later his heart stopped beating, and a code-blue alarm sounded throughout the coronary unit. The medical staff swung into action to try to save his life, and for a few brief moments they raised a weak heartbeat. Then it was gone. A great heart had stopped. At 1:30 p.m. Paul William Bryant was pronounced dead.

Over the next several hours the news spread like wildfire. Radio, television, and newspaper editors called for confirmation, then went on the air to announce the passing of a great American hero.

The small First Methodist Church, where

the services for Bryant were held, seated only a few hundred people, and some of Bryant's former players and coaches had to stand outside in a crowd estimated at 10,000, listening to the eulogy over loudspeakers.

Following the services, the longest funeral procession in the history of Tuscaloosa passed through the town to the Elmwood Cemetery in Birmingham. It was estimated that more than 100,000 people stood in tribute along the highway from Tuscaloosa to Birmingham, and at the cemetery the area was packed by more than 7,000 friends, players, coaches, and family. And then it was over and the Bear was at rest.

YEARS OF GLORY

7

PASSING THE TORCH

1983–1990

Ray Perkins hails from Mount Olive, Mississippi and was born November 6, 1941, with the proverbial football in his mouth. At Petal High School Ray was an All-American fullback and was offered a football scholarship to Alabama in 1962.

For the Crimson Tide, Perkins became one of the leading receivers in college football. A favorite receiver for quarterbacks Joe Namath, Steve Sloan, and Kenny Stabler, Perkins caught a then-record nine passes against Ole Miss in a 1966 Tide victory. Also in 1966, Ray was elected Co-Captain of an Alabama team that went undefeated in eleven games, and his nine receptions in the Sugar Bowl game against Nebraska is still an Alabama record.

After a five-year pro career with Baltimore, Perkins coached at Mississippi State in 1973. Then he joined the New England Patriots for four years and in 1979 was named head coach of the New York Giants. In 1981 Perkins led the Giants to the NFL playoffs for the first time in eighteen years.

In 1983, the Crimson Tide ushered in the "Ray Perkins era" with an impressive 20–7 win over Georgia Tech at Legion Field in Birmingham before a sellout crowd of more than 77,000 fans. Before the game began, Perkins led the Alabama players in a pre-game prayer in Coach Bryant's memory. The huge crowd stood in a moment of silence before the kickoff. The players wore hound's-tooth decals on their helmets, and Perkins wore a decal on the left side of his collar.

"I wanted to win this game more than any football game I've ever been associated with," Perkins said.

'Bama followed Perkins' first victory with three more big wins in a row: a 40–0 rout of Ole Miss, an exciting 34–17 comeback over Vanderbilt, and a 44–13 Homecoming party over Memphis State. Tide faithful were confident that they had found the right man to carry the Bryant torch.

Ray Perkins, Bryant's successor.

PASSING THE TORCH

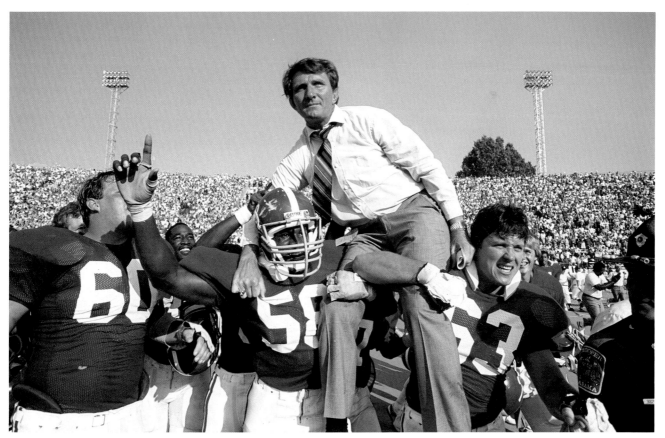
Coach and players celebrate Perkins' first win, 20–7 over Georgia Tech.

At State Park, Pennsylvania, however, Alabama faced a hungry Nittany Lion and dropped behind 34–7 after three periods. It looked as if the game was over, but suddenly the Alabama offense began to click. Kerry Goode scored from Penn's 1-yard line, and on the next possession Alabama drove sixty-nine yards in four plays and scored on a Lewis pass to Jesse Bendross. Then it was another Lewis to Bendross touchdown play, with the crowd on their feet shouting on every play. The Tide rolled down the field once more, to a first down on the State 6-yard line, and Lewis appeared to have thrown the tying touchdown to Preston Gothard, but the official ruled him out of the back of the end zone.

Perkins had a second taste of defeat a week later when a tough Tennessee eleven defeated Alabama, 41–34, in a high-scoring game that was not over until the final gun sounded. The Tide then put together successive wins over Mississippi State, LSU and, Southern Mississippi, but on November 25 at Foxboro, Boston College took a hard-fought win over Alabama, 30–13.

The first Alabama-Auburn game of the Perkins era was such a thriller that it had a crowd of 77,000 fans standing through the entire third and fourth periods. Both teams marched up and down the rain-drenched field, trying to deliver the knock-out punch, but when the gun sounded, the Tide was on the short end, 23–20.

Some consolation came in the fiftieth anniversary of the Sun Bowl, against a favored SMU eleven rated one of the best teams in the Southwest. The Tide shocked sports experts with a convincing 28–7 victory.

In Ray Perkins' first year as head coach, Alabama won eight games and lost four. "And with a bit of luck here and there, we could have won at least two other games," said Perkins. "But we'll do better as we get along in our program."

1984

In Ray Perkins' second season as coach of the Crimson Tide, he had high hopes for an outstanding season. Forty-one lettermen were returning for the 1984 season, including nine starters on defense and six on offense.

The offense, where Perkins had shelved Bear Bryant's wishbone and installed his own pro-set formation, would have such talented quarterbacks as Mike Shula and Vince Sutton, and Perkins had great expectations that they would uphold 'Bama's tradition of outstanding quarterbacks. The big gun on offense was Rickey Moore, a husky powerful runner and second-team All-American in 1983. Moore, along with such standouts as halfback Kerry Goode and receivers Greg Richardson, Joe Smith, and Preston Gothard would give the Tide a powerful offensive unit. Key linemen included Wes Neighbors, son of former All-American linebacker Billy Neighbors, guards John McIntosh and Mike White, and tackles Willard Scissum, Gary Otten and Hardy Walker.

But the season's bright promise was quickly tarnished. In the season opener, an amazing Doug Flutie—aided by a disastrous season-ending injury to Goode—led Boston back from a 31–14 deficit to a stunning 38–31 victory in Birmingham. And one week later a spirited crew from Georgia Tech upset Alabama 16–6 in a nationally televised game at Atlanta. In the first home game of the year, Paul Ott Carruth scored three smashing touchdowns against Southwest Louisiana and only then did the Crimson Tide roll to its first win of the season.

After two more tough losses, to Vanderbilt and Georgia, 'Bama's record stood at a dismal 1–4. A huge 6–0 win over Penn State looked like a new beginning, but Tennessee handed the Tide a bitter 28–27 defeat. Alabama defeated Mississippi State, 24–20, lost a heartbreaker to LSU by a 16–14 margin, then beat Cincinnati 29–17.

Alabama partially redeemed a poor season with a come-from-behind, dramatic 17–15 win over favored Auburn. A heroic goal-line stand stopped Auburn's halfback Brent Fullwood as he attempted to sweep the right end for what would have been the winning touchdown.

Nonetheless, Alabama finished the season with a poor 5–6 record and, after twenty-five bowl games in a row, was not invited to post-season play.

1985

The year before, Bobby Humphrey had been selling Coca-Cola at Alabama's football games in Birmingham and wondering what it would be like to wear a Crimson Tide uniform and be playing on Legion Field. Gene Jelks of Gadsden, Alabama, was a frequent visitor in the stands, hoping against hope that perhaps he, too, would be wearing an Alabama football uniform soon.

It all came about sooner than either young man suspected.

Bobby Humphrey became a starter after five games in 1985, and the six-one, 190-pounder from Glenn High School wound up with 502 yards on 99 carries and ran for four touchdowns. He had fifteen receptions for three additional scores. Jelks, a five-eleven, 175-pound speedster, became Alabama's number-one rusher with 588 yards in 93 carries and five touchdowns.

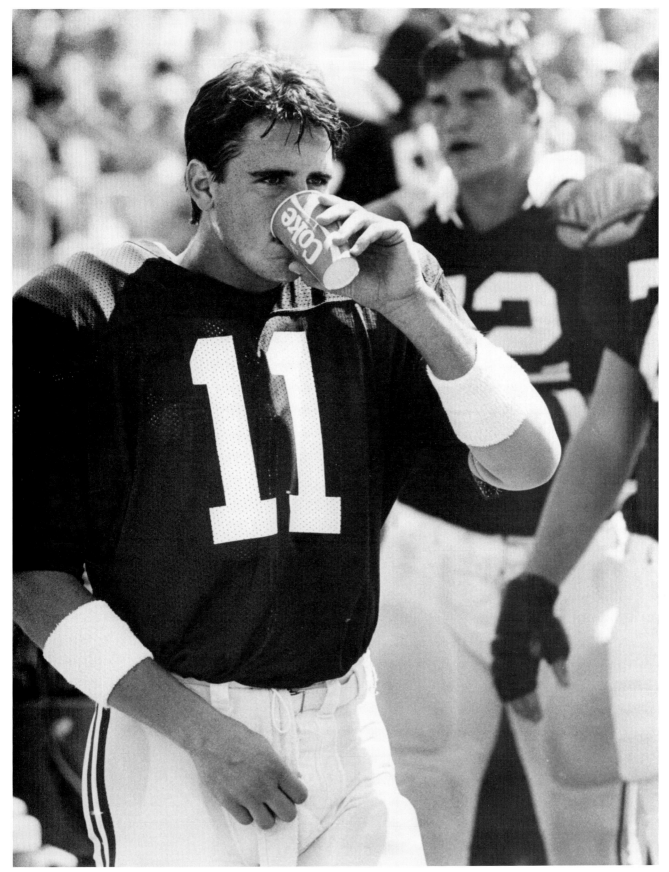

Quarterback Mike Shula led the Tide in '84, '85, and '86.

In the opening game of the season against Georgia, Alabama was nursing a 13–9 lead with a minute to play when a Tide punt was blocked and the ball rolled to the 'Bama 5-yard line. But Georgia's Cal Ruff batted the ball into the end zone and fell on the ball for a touchdown that gave Georgia a 16–13 lead. But Alabama, playing like a veritable fury, began a 75-yard drive with

fifty seconds left to play. Mike Shula completed four successive passes and then capped the drive with a 17-yard pass to Al Bell for the winning touchdown.

The Tide followed this auspicious debut with three more wins—over Texas A & M, Cincinnati, and Vanderbilt—before traveling to State College, Pennsylvania. Penn State's Matt Knizer entered the game late in

All-American Bobby Humphrey stiff-arms a would-be Auburn tackler.

Offensive huddle at the 1985 Aloha Bowl: Shula (11), Humphrey (26), Greg Richardson (17), Al Bell (1), and Doug Allen (46).

the fourth period and threw just one pass, but it was good enough to give the Nittany Lions a touchdown and an 19–10 lead. Alabama mounted a furious drive with just fifteen seconds left in the game and scored a touchdown to make it 19–17. But time ran out, and the Tide had lost for the first time this year.

A second loss came the next week, though, in a nationally televised game at Birmingham. Tennessee's Carlos Reveiz kicked three field goals to eke out a tense, 16–14 win in one of the season's biggest upsets. 'Bama bounced back with wins over Memphis State, 28–9, and Mississippi State, 44–28, and then, after a last-minute touchdown, elected to kick the extra point for a tie with LSU, 14–14.

The Tide finished the regular season with a win over Southern Mississippi and a huge upset over a highly rated Auburn team, 25–23, in a thriller that left a crowd of 75,000 limp with exhaustion. Gene Jelks carried for 192 yards in the game, including a 74-yard touchdown dash.

The win over Auburn gave Alabama a season record of eight wins, two losses, and a tie, and earned them an invitation to meet Southern California in the Aloha Bowl in Honolulu, Hawaii, December 28.

After a 3–3 tie at half time, 'Bama took control of the game and dominated the tough Trojans, 24–3. In a game that seemed to return the Tide to its rightful place in college football's upper echelon, Gene Jelks was named offensive MVP while Cornelus Bennett was honored as the defensive player of the game.

1986

The eyes of the nation watched as Alabama, ranked fourth, and Ohio State, ranked eighth, faced each other in the 1986 "Kickoff Classic" at Giants Stadium in East Rutherford, New Jersey. It was one of the most difficult and emotional games that the Crimson Tide had ever played, for two fine Alabama players, George Scruggs and Willie Ryles, had been killed before the season started. Two miniature black helmets adorned the Alabama helmets as a tribute to the two departed men.

Two field goals by Van Tiffin gave 'Bama the early lead, but Ohio State answered midway in the second quarter when Jamie Holland scored on a reverse to give the Buckeyes a 7–6 edge.

The Buckeyes took a 10–6 lead in the thrid period, but the fourth quarter was all

Gene Jelks breaks for daylight.

Alabama's. Mike Shula tossed a short touchdown pass to Al Bell to give the Tide a 13–10 margin, and Tiffin kicked his third field goal of the night to give Alabama a 16–10 win.

Back home at Tuscaloosa, ten days after the Kickoff Classic, Jelks and Humphrey sparked the Tide to a 42–10 rout of Vanderbilt, followed by successive wins over Southern Mississippi and Florida. Then came October 5, 1986, a day that will live in infamy at Notre Dame University. Alabama, with quarterback Mike Shula passing for three touchdowns and Cornelius Bennett crunching Irish quarterback Steve Buerlein, humbled an outstanding Irish eleven in a nationally televised game at Birmingham by a 28–10 score. This was the first-ever Alabama win over the Irish, and for Mike Shula, one of his finest games in a Tide uniform.

The Tide rolled on over Memphis State, 37–0, and Tennessee, 56–28, before stumbling against a heralded Penn State team, 23–3. In its next three games, 'Bama sandwiched a tough 14–10 loss to LSU between wins over Mississippi State and Temple and carried a fine 9–2 record into their last regular season game against Auburn — a nationally televised ABC-TV Special.

Mike Shula tossed for two touchdowns to take a 14–0 lead in the second period, but Brent Fullwood scored on an 18-yard drive to end the half with Alabama on top 14–7.

After Van Tiffin connected on a 29-yard field goal to give the Tide a short-lived 17–7 lead, Fullwood and Lawyer Tillman made the big plays as Auburn roared back for the victory, 21–17.

On December 25, Alabama and the University of Washington met in the annual Sun Bowl Classic at El Paso, in what would prove to be Ray Perkins' last game as the Alabama coach.

As far as the Huskies were concerned, it

After starting 27 games in a row, Mike Shula ended his great career with a win over Washington in the '86 Sun Bowl.

All-American linebacker Cornelius Bennett won the coveted Lombardi Trophy as the outstanding defensive player of 1986.

was too much Bobby Humphrey and too much Mike Shula. Humphrey cantered sixty-four yards for one of his three touchdowns, and Shula threw completions at will. The 28–6 victory gave the Tide an outstanding 10–3 season.

1987

Late on the night of December 29, 1986, at a Birmingham hotel, Tampa Bay Buccaneers Owner Hugh Culverhouse and Ray Perkins shook hands on a deal whereby Perkins would become Tampa Bay's new head coach. The contract was "one that I simply could not refuse," said Perkins, "as it made me general manager and vice president of the club."

As soon as news of Perkins' departure was released to the public, Alabama's president Dr. Joab Thomas hired Steve Sloan, a former Alabama star quarterback, as the athletic director and Bill Curry as the new head coach. Curry, a former pro-Bowl center, had been the head Coach at Georgia Tech for seven years. He was named the ACC Coach of the Year after the 1985 season as Tech posted a 9–2–1 record, including a tremendous win over Michigan State in the All-American Bowl.

Alabama opened the 1987 season under Bill Curry in an auspicious manner, romping to a 38–6 victory over Southern Mississippi in Birmingham. "Quarterback David Smith was phenomenal," said Coach Curry, as he completed 13 of 21 passes for 147 yards and two touchdowns. And All-American Bobby Humphrey picked right up where he had left off, scoring three opening-day touchdowns.

After a great 24–13 win at Penn State the following week, 'Bama lost to a snapping

Florida Gator, 23–14. Freshman halfback Emmett Smith ran for 224 yards and two touchdowns to dominate the game.

A week later, Alabama defeated Vanderbilt, 30–23, on a last-minute touchdown by Bobby Humphrey. Next, in the big Homecoming game at Birmingham, Alabama roughed up Southwestern Louisiana, 38–10, scoring in every period to win easily. But the following week, Memphis State provided the shocker as they defeated Alabama 13–10. Alabama made several miscues and played poorly overall to present State with the huge upset win.

'Bama then put together its longest winning streak of the year — trouncing Tennessee, 41–22; squeezing past Mississippi State, 21–18; and subduing the Tigers of LSU, 22–10. But a trip to South Bend ended the streak decisively with a 37–6 loss to Notre Dame.

Then, in the final game of the regular season, an aggressive, inspired Auburn Tiger defeated Alabama 10–0 in a brutal defensive struggle. It was the first time that an Alabama team had failed to score since 1980, when Notre Dame held the Tide scoreless.

A last-minute touchdown by Michigan in the Hall of Fame Bowl overshadowed a brilliant 149-yard, two touchdown performance by Bobby Humphrey and closed out Bill Curry's first season with seven wins and five losses.

1988

Coach Curry had high hopes for the 1988 season — and why not? After all, All-American Bobby Humphrey, a leading candidated for the Heisman Trophy, was back to spark the powerful Tide offense.

The season opened with a trip to Philadelphia where, after a defense-dominated first half, 'Bama blew out the Temple Owls, 37–0. At home two weeks later, it was a 44–10 rout of Vandy, but a dark cloud hung over the Tuscaloosa sky. Bobby Humphrey broke a bone in his foot, and Alabama's brightest star was out for the rest of the year.

In the third game of the season, a fighting Kentucky Wildcat squad completely dominated Alabama for more than three quarters and led the Tide 20–7, but suddenly the Tide turned and fought back.

Playing for injured David Smith, Vince Sutton took command and fired two late-game touchdown passes to give Alabama a sensational 31–27 victory. However, there was to be no Homecoming celebration at Tuscaloosa on October 8. The Ole Miss Rebels scored two touchdowns within the final four minutes of the game to break 'Bama's heart 22–12. The next week against Tennessee, quarterback David Smith, injured in practice earlier in the year, re-entered the fray in the third period and directed two touchdown drives that

Captain Derrick Thomas harasses Penn State quarterback Tony Sacca.

PASSING THE TORCH

gave Alabama a 28—20 win.

Next, 'Bama fought a tremendous defensive battle against Penn State. Alabama's Derrick Thomas was the big difference. He crashed through the Lions' defense time after time to harry the quarterback Tony Sacca, sacked three times, and made tackles all over the field as Alabama prevailed, 8–3.

The next week the Tide played well against Mississippi State, running for a 53–34 win as David Smith passed for 290 yards and David Casteal scored four touchdowns. But at home the following week against LSU's Tigers, Alabama led until the final minute of the game only to see a 34-yard field goal by Dave Browndyke give LSU a 19–18 upset win.

During the next three weeks, Alabama defeated Southwest Louisiana, 17–0, lost to a Sugar Bowl-bound Auburn, 15–10, in a bruising defensive struggle, and then closed out the regular season with a flourish, thrashing Texas A & M, 30–10.

Before the Texas A & M game, Alabama's president Dr. Roger Sayers conducted a press conference to discount the mounting rumor that Coach Curry's job was in jeopardy. Of course, there had been Curry detractors from day one, and they made Curry's life most unhappy. But President Sayers' declaration of support for Curry and his program put all those rumors to rest . . . for a time.

Alabama and Army were named as the contestants in the Sun Bowl Game, December 24 at El Paso, Texas, and the record crowd was treated to an amazing spectacle. In the third period, after the unbelievable Derrick Thomas blocked two field goal tries by Army, David Smith led the Tide the length of the field and tossed a scoring pass to Greg Payne to give 'Bama a 20–14 lead. But then Mayweather, Army's great halfback, scored on a 3-yard smash to put the

Army in front, 21–20. Army scored again on a 57-yard run after an interception to lead by 28–20.

Philip Doyle closed the gap with a 23-yard field goal, and then David Casteal scored a touchdown from two yards out to give Alabama an incredible one-point triumph over the Black Knights.

Coach Curry's second season concluded with a fine 9–3 record and gave every indication that the Curry program was well on its way to re-establishing Alabama as a powerhouse in collegiate football circles.

1989

For Siran Stacy, a young halfback just out of Coffeyville Junior College, the afternoon of September 16, 1989, must have been something out of a dream, for in the opening game of the season against Memphis State, the twenty-year-old Stacy wrote his name in bold letters across the pages of Alabama's football story. The first time Stacy got the ball, he scored on a 6-yard dash. In the third period, as the Crimson Tide struggled against a stubborn Memphis defense, Stacy flashed forty-six yards for his second touchdown and gave Alabama some breathing space with a 21–7 lead. In the fourth period, it was Stacy once again on a short 2-yard burst for his third touchdown, and in the final few minutes of the game, Stacy slashed through the State line and raced sixty-four yards for his fourth touchdown in a 35–7 Alabama victory.

With that opening-day win the Tide was launched on a roll the likes of which it had not seen in many a moon. In week two, behind the rugged defensive play of Willie Wyatt and Phil Doyle's three field goals,

Siran Stacy led the Tide's rushing attack in 1989.

'Bama beat Kentucky, 15–3. Vanderbilt fell the next week, 20–14, and in week four Gary Hollingsworth tossed a record five touchdown passes to spark the Crimson Tide to a smashing 62–27 win over Ole Miss. In the big Homecoming game at Tuscaloosa, the Tide pulled out a close one from Southwestern Louisiana, 24–17, for the fifth win of the year.

In game six Siran Stacy flashed for four touchdowns and Gary Hollingsworth unleashed a record thirty-two pass completions as Alabama defeated a Tennessee eleven that had won ten straight games.

It was do-or-die the next week at Penn State, with scouts from every major bowl in attendance. The score was Alabama 17, Penn State 16, and State had the ball on the 1-yard line and in position for the winning field goal. Thomas Rayam timed his leap perfectly and deflected the kick to help his team win as thrilling a game as ever had been seen at Penn State.

The winning streak hit eight as 'Bama defeated Mississippi State in a fierce defensive battle, 23–10. Number nine came against the Tigers from LSU, as Siran Stacy broke the game open with a sensational 72-yard run at the start of the third period. Then, in the final home game of the sea-

Quarterback Gary Hollingsworth tossed five TD passes versus Ole Miss in 1989, a Tide record.

son, Alabama easily defeated Southern Mississippi by a 37–14 margin as quarterback Gary Hollingsworth led the Tide attack with a total of 248 yards passing for two touchdowns.

But eleven proved to be the unlucky number. The Tigers of Auburn defeated Alabama 30–20 to close out the regular season with a nevertheless outstanding record of ten wins and one loss.

On January 1, 1990, the Miami Hurricanes took a 7–0 lead in the first quarter of the Sugar Bowl battle against Alabama and scored twice more in the second period. But two touchdown passes by Gary Hollingsworth and a 45-yard field goal by Phil Doyle gave the Tide seventeen points in the second period, and the teams left the field at half time with the score 20–17, Miami. However, Craig Erikson, Miami's quarterback, threw two scoring passes in the second half to out-duel Hollingsworth, and the final score read Miami 33, Alabama 25.

1990

A number of important changes in the administrative and coaching positions in the Alabama football program began in June 1989, when Dr. Joab Thomas resigned as President of the University to return to the classroom. His successor was Dr. Roger Sayers, a geneticist with a brilliant record of more than twenty-seven years of service to the university.

It was Dr. Thomas who selected former Alabama quarterback Steve Sloan to handle the difficult job as Director of Athletics. When Sloan resigned, in 1989, Sayers appointed former Alabama gridster Hootie Ingram as the new AD. However, Coach Bill Curry, unhappy with the new contract he was offered, resigned to take a similar post at the University of Kentucky, and Dr. Sayers and Ingram interviewed several former Alabama players for the coaching post.

Their choice was Gene Stallings, and the official announcement was made by Hootie Ingram at a press conference on January 11, 1989.

Gene Stallings' portrait, if you want to sketch it, would be red, white, and blue. He's a ramrod-straight Texan, a man of sharp beliefs and principles. He does not smoke, rarely drinks, keeps his language clean, and rises at 5:00 a.m. He espouses downhome values and loves his family, his ranch, and his football team.

"I'm the kind of person," says Stallings, "that if I go to a restaurant ten times, I'm liable to order the same food ten times."

Gene "Bebes" Stallings was born in Paris, Texas, in 1935 and attended Paris High School, where he became one of the area's top football and baseball stars, winning all-district honors in both sports.

Gene attended the Texas A & M, where he played under the toughest football training program in the school's history. The program was directed by Coach Bear Bryant.

"The training program was so tough," said Stallings, "that we went to camp in three buses, and only one came back."

At age twenty-three, Gene was named an assistant coach under Bryant at Alabama and remained there until 1965, when he was named head coach at his alma mater. During his seven seasons at A & M, one of his most memorable moments came in 1968, when his Aggies took on Bryant and the Crimson Tide in the Cotton Bowl and defeated the Bryant-coached team 20–16.

Stallings then took a post with Tom Landry and the Dallas Cowboys and remained there for fourteen magnificent seasons. In 1986 Stallings was named head coach of the St. Louis Cardinals.

But the Stallings era at Alabama started slowly. The Tide not only lost its opener to Southern Mississippi, it also lost star running back Siran Stacy for the season. Two more tough losses—to Florida, 17–13, and Georgia, 17–16—and the Tide was in a deep hole.

But on September 29 at Tuscaloosa the doors of sweet victory finally opened for the Crimson Tide, as 'Bama buried the Vanderbilt Commodores under a barrage of thirty-one points in the first period. One week later Alabama defeated Southwestern Louisiana 25–6 as Phil Doyle set an Alabama record by kicking six field goals in the game.

In the sixth game of the year at Knoxville, third-ranked Tennessee faced an Alabama team that refused to be awed by the polls. 'Bama held the Vols to just two field goals, while the magnificent foot of Phil Doyle again prevailed. Doyle kicked three field goals for a hard-fought 9–6 win.

The seventh game of the season proved to be another bitter defensive battle, but this time Alabama came up short. Penn State held the aggressive Alabama offense to just six yards rushing as they took a 9–0 victory back to State College.

The next three weeks produced wins for Stallings—a 22–0 shutout of Mississippi State; a 24–3 win over LSU, with freshman Chris Anderson scoring twice; and a 45–7 thrashing of Cincinnati. Then it was time: Alabama versus Auburn.

Most experts were picking Auburn, but on this day the experts were wrong. The Alabama defense completely stymied Auburn's aggressive backs and held Auburn to just fifty-two yards rushing. Time after time Alabama's great defense, led by Efrum Thomas, George Thornton, and Johnny Sullins stopped the Tigers' defense, allowing just one touchdown all day. Alabama defeated its bitterest foe, 16–7, and Gene Stallings became the first head coach to

Reigning Alabama coach Gene Stallings.

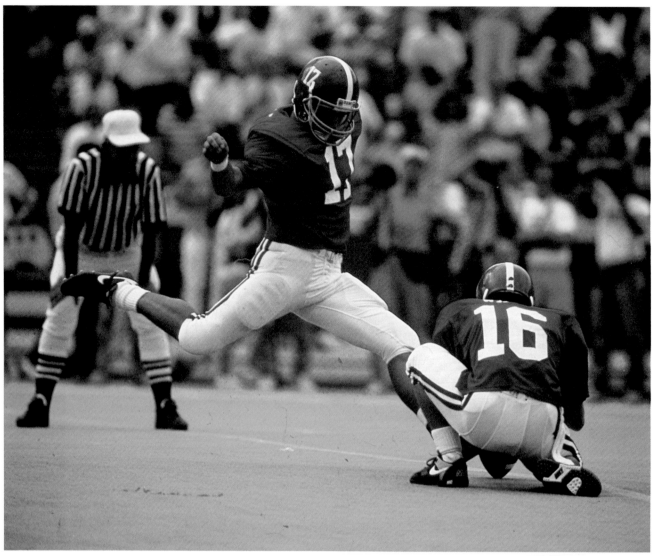

1990 All-American place-kicker Philip Doyle.

beat Auburn in his first season since W. H. Pollard in 1906.

Stallings took his first team to the Fiesta Bowl to face an overpowering Louisville passing unit quarterbacked by 6'-5" Browning Nagle, described by his coach Howard Schnellenberger as "better than Jim Kelly." Sure enough on this day Louisville's offense took matters in hand, scoring twenty-five points in the first period and defeating the Crimson Tide by a 34–7 margin.

"I don't think our team was really prepared to play with all the hoopla and media coverage," said Alabama's coach Gene Stallings, "and our play indicated that."

"But for 1991 and into the future," Stallings continued with a smile, "I think we'll have a few nice surprises for our opponents. We've some of the finest young talent returning, and if we can keep them healthy, we will do very well. And if Siran Stacy's knee is sound, we'll have an ace in the hole. He's one of the best backs I've ever coached. Then there's Craig Sanderson, also injured last year, and John Sullins, and Robert Stewart. In 1991 we'll have a fine team, one that will represent all of the great ideals and traditions of the Crimson Tide as we prepare for the 100th year of Alabama football."

PASSING THE TORCH

University of Alabama Football Lettermen– (1892-1990)

A

ABBOTT, Eli (T)
Tuscaloosa, Ala., 1892-93
ABNEY, Larry (SE)
Slidell, La., 1984-85-86-87
ABRAMS, Charlie (TE)
Demopolis, Ala., 1986-87-89
ABRUZZESE, Raymond (HB)
Philadelphia, Pa., 1960-61
ABSTON, Bill (RH)
Peterson, Ala., 1948-49
ADAMS, George (E)
Montgomery, Ala., 1935
ADCOCK, Mike (OT)
Huntsville, Ala., 1981-82-83
ADKINSON, Wayne (HB)
Dothan, Ala., 1970-71-72
ALAND, Jack (T)
Birmingham, Ala., 1942
ALBRIGHT, George (HB)
Tuscaloosa, Ala. 1944
ALLEN, Charles G. (T)
Athens, Ala., 1957-58-59
ALLEN, Doug (FB)
Cantonment, Fla., 1985-86-87
ALLEN, John (T)
Birmingham, Ala., 1907
ALLEN, Steve (G)
Athens, Ala., 1961-62-63
ALLISON, Scott (OT)
Titusville, Fla., 1978-79-80
ALLMAN, Phil (DB)
Birmingham, Ala., 1976-77-78
AMELONG, William (LB)
Los Angeles, Calif., 1988-89
ANDERSON, Andy (OG)
Lithia Springs, Ga., 1986
ANDREWS, Mickey (HB)
Ozark, Ala., 1963-64
ANGELICH, James Dykes (HB)
Indiana Harbor, Ind., 1933-34-35
ARANT, Hershel W. (G)
Notasulga, Ala., 1908
ARTHUR, Paul (E)
Birmingham, Ala., 1949
ATKINS, Sam (OT)
Mobile, Ala., 1988
AUGUST, Johnny (HB)
Shadyside, Ohio, 1942-46-47
AUSTILL, Huriescsco (E)
Springhill, Ala., 1904
AUSTILL, Jere (B)
Springhill, Ala., 1908
AVERITTE, Warren (C)
Greenville, Miss., 1938-39-40
AVINGER, Clarence "Butch" (QB)
Montgomery, Ala., 1948-49-50
AYDELETTE, William Leslie
"Buddy" (TE)
Mobile, Ala., 1977-78-79
AYERS, Calvin (RB)
Decatur, Ala., 1989

B

BAILEY, David (SE) All-SEC
Bailey, Miss., 1969-70-71
BAKER, George (T)
Cleveland, Ohio, 1921
BALLARD, Clarence Bingham (T)
Birmingham, Ala., 1901-02
BANKHEAD, M. H. (B)
Fayette, Ala., 1895
BANKHEAD, Wm. Brockman (FB)
Fayette, Ala., 1892-93
BANKS, R. R. (G)
Columbus, Miss., 1901
BARKER, Troy (G)
Lineville, Ala., 1931-32-33
BARNES, Emile "Red" (HB) All-
SEC, Grove Hill, Ala., 1925-26
BARNES, Ronnie Joe (DE)
Abbeville, Ala., 1973-74
BARNES, W. A. (T)
Dothan, Ala., 1912
BARNES, Wiley (C)
Marianna, Fla., 1978-79
BARNETT, Henry Herndon (C)
Fitzpatrick, Ala., 1911
BARRON, Marvin (G-T)
Troy, Ala., 1970-71-73
BARRON, Randy (DT)
Dadeville, Ala., 1966-67-68
BARRY, Dick (FB)
Cordele, Ga., 1951
BARTLETT, Charles (HB)
Marlin, Texas, 1920-21
BASWELL, Ben (T)
Pell City, Ala., 1935
BATES, C. F. (B)
Mobile, Ala., 1914
BATES, Tim (LB)
Tarrant, Ala., 1964-65
BATEY, Joseph Dwight "Bo" (OG)
Jacksonville, Ala., 1976
BATTLE, Bill (E)
Birmingham, Ala., 1960-61-62
BATTLE, Marco (WR)
Phenix City, Ala., 1987-88-89
BATY, William C., Jr. (HB)
Bessemer, Ala., 1921-22
BAUGHMAN, Bill (C)
Jeanette, Pa., 1946
BAUMHOWER, Robert Glenn
(DT), All-SEC,
Tuscaloosa, Ala.,74-75-76
BEALLE, Sherman "Bucky" (E)
Elyria, Ohio 1929
BEAN, Dickie (HB)
Childersburg, Ala., 1966
BEARD, Jeff (DT)
Bessemer, Ala., 1969-70-71
BEARD, Ken (T)
Bessemer, Ala., 1963
BEARD, Silas "Buddy" (HB)
Guntersville, Ala., 1937-38
BEAZLEY, Joe (DT)
Woodbridge, Va., 1979-80-81-82
BECK, Ellis (HB)
Ozark, Ala., 1971-72-73
BECK, Willie (E)
Northport, Ala., 1956-57

BEDDINGFIELD, David (QB)
Gadsden, Ala., 1969
BEDWELL, David (DB)
Cedar Bluff, Ala., 1965-66-67
BELL, Albert (F) All-SEC
Los Angeles, Calif., 1985-86
BELL, Stanley (E)
West Anniston, Ala., 1959
BENDROSS, Jesse (SE)
Hollywood, Fla., 1980-81-82-83
*BENNETT, Cornelius (OLB)
All-SEC
Birmingham, Ala., 1983-84-85-86
BENTLEY, Edward K., Jr. (DB)
Sylacauga, Ala., 1970
BENTLEY, Jeff (OG)
Alabaster, Ala., 1986-87
BERREY, Fred Benjamin "Bucky" (K)
Montgomery, Ala., 1974-75-76
BETHUNE, George (LB-DE)
Ft. Walton Beach, Fla., 1986-87-88
BEVELLE, Willis (S)
Bessemer, Ala., 1989
BIBLE, Tom (T)
Piedmont, Ala., 1961
BILLINGSLEY, Randy (HB)
Sylacauge, Ala., 1972-73-74
BIRD, Ron (T)
Covington, Ky., 1963
BIRES, Andy (E)
Ambridge, Pa., 1942
BISCEGLIA, Steve (FB)
Fresno, Calif., 1971-72
BLACKMON, Sumpter (QB)
Columbus, Ga., 1941
BLACKWELL, Gene (E)
Blytheville, Ark., 1937-38-39
BLACKWOOD, J. E. (G)
Birmingham, Ala., 1921
BLAIR, Bill (DB)
Nashville, Tenn., 1968-69-70
BLAIR, Elmer (B)
Birmingham, Ala., 1917
BLAIR, J. W. (T)
Clayton, Ala., 1897
BLALOCK, Ralph (E)
Cullman, Ala., 1956-57
BLEVINS, James Allen (T)
Moulton, Ala., 1957-58-59
BLITZ, Jeff (DB)
Montgomery, Ala., 1972
BLUE, Al (DB)
Maitland, Fla., 1981-82
BOBO, Mike (FB)
Crossville, Ala., 1985
BOLDEN, Ray (DB)
Tarrant, Ala., 1974-75
BOLER, Clark (T)
Northport, Ala., 1962-63
BOLER, Thomas (OT)
Northport, Ala., 1980
BOLES, John "Duffy" (HB)
Huntsville, Ala., 1973-75
BOLTON, Bruce (SE)
Memphis, Tenn., 1976-77-78

BOMAN, T. D. (T)
Heflin, Ala., 1914-15
BOOKER, David (SE)
Huntsville, Ala., 1979
BOOKER, Steve (LB)
Huntsville, Ala., 1981-82-83
BOONE, Alfred Morgan "Dan" (E)
Samantha, Ala., 1917-18-19
BOONE, Isaac M. "Ike" (E)
Samantha, Ala., 1919
BOOTH, Baxter (E)
Athens, Ala., 1956-57-58
BOOTHE, Vince (OG)
Fairhope, Ala., 1977-78-79
BOOZER, Young (HB)
Dothan, Ala., 1934-35-36
BORDERS, Tom (T)
Birmingham, Ala., 1939
BOSCHUNG, Paul (DT)
Tuscaloosa, Ala., 1967-68-69
BOSTICK, Lewis (G)
Birmingham, Ala., 1936-37-38
BOSWELL, Charley (HB)
Ensley, Ala., 1938-39
BOWDOIN, James L. "Goofy" (G)
Coffee Springs, Ala., 1927-28
BOWDOIN, Jimmy (HB)
Elba, Ala., 1954-55-56
BOWMAN, Steve (FB) All-SEC
Pascagoula, Miss., 1963-64-65
BOX, Jimmy (E)
Sheffield, Ala., 1960
*BOYD, Thomas (LB) All-SEC
Huntsville, Ala., 1978-79-80-81
BOYKIN, Gideon Frierson (G)
Brewton, Ala., 1894
BOYKIN, Dave (FB)
Parrish, Ala., 1928-29
BOYLE, R. E. (G)
Birmingham, Ala., 1893
BOYLES, J. V. (E)
Thomasville, Ala., 1904
BOYLSTON, Robert W. "Bobby" (T)
Atlanta, Ga., 1959-60
BRADFORD, James J. "Jim" (OG)
Montgomery, Ala., 1977
BRADFORD, Vic (QB)
Memphis, Tenn., 1936-37-38
BRAGAN, Dale (LB)
Birmingham, Ala., 1976
BRAGGS, Byron (DT) All-SEC
Montgomery, Ala., 1977-78-79-80
BRAGGS, Chester (RB)
Greensboro, Ala., 1983-84-85-86
BRAMBLETT, Dante (OLB)
Morrow, Ga., 1984
BRAMBLETT, Gary (OG)
Dalton, Ga., 1979-80-81-82
BRANNAN, Troy Crampton (FB)
Mobile, Ala., 1914
BRANNEN, Jere Lamar (E)
Anniston, Ala., 1957-58
BRASFIELD, Davis (HB)
Birmingham, Ala., 1927

BREWER, Richard (SE)
Sylacauga, Ala., 1965-66-67
BRITT, Gary (LB)
Mobile, Ala., 1977
BROCK, Jim (OG)
Montgomery, Ala., 1981
BROCK, Mike (OG) All-SEC
Montgomery, Ala., 1977-78-79
BROOKER, Johnny (PK)
Demopolis, Ala., 1982
BROOKER, Wm. T. "Tommy" (E)
Demopolis, Ala., 1959-60-61
BROOKS, Wm. S. "Billy" (C)
Tuscaloosa, Ala., 1954-55-56
BROWN, Bill (DB)
DeKalb, Miss., 1982
BROWN, Billy (HB)
Dothan, Ala., 1928
BROWN, Carl Abercrombie (G)
Birmingham, Ala., 1898-99
BROWN, Dave (HB)
Birmingham, Ala., 1940-41-42
•BROWN, Halver "Buddy" (G)
All-SEC, Tallahassee, Fla., 71-72-73
BROWN, Jack (QB)
Selma, Ala., 1948-49-50-51
BROWN, Jerry (TE)
Fairfax, Ala., 1974-75
BROWN, Johnny Mack (HB) All-SC
Dothan, Ala., 1923-24-25
BROWN, Larry (TE)
Pembroke Pines, Fla., 1979-80-81-82
BROWN, Marshall (FB)
Ladysmith, Wis., 1955-56-57
BROWN, Phillip (LB)
Birmingham, Ala., 1983-86
BROWN, Randy (T)
Scottsville, N.Y., 1968
BROWN, Robert C. (B)
Ensley, Ala., 1916-17
BROWN, Tolbert "Red" (HB)
Dothan, Ala., 1926-27
BROWN, T. L. (T)
Jasper, Ala., 1919-20
BROWN, Randall R. (B)
Tuscaloosa, Ala., 1908-09
BRUNGARD, David A. (FB)
Youngstown, Ohio, 1970
BRYAN, Richard (DT)
Verona, N.J., 1972-74
BRYANT, Paul W. "Bear" (E)
Fordyce, Ark., 1933-34-35
BUCHANAN, Richard Woodruff
"Woody" (FB)
Montgomery, Ala., 1976
BUCK, Oran (K)
Oak Ridge, Tenn., 1969
BUCKLER, Wm. E. "Bill" (G) All-SC
St. Paul, Minn., 1923-24-25
BUMGARDNER, Robert H. (E)
Besemer, Ala., 1909-10
•BUNCH, Jim (OG) All-SEC
Mechanicsville, Va., 1976-77-78-79
BURKHART, C. T. (E)
Hanceville, Ala., 1920
BURKETT, Jim (FB)
Dothan, Ala., 1949-50
BURKS, Auxford (HB)
Tuscaloosa, Ala., 1903-04-05
BURKS, Basil Manly (T)
Tuscaloosa, Ala., 1913-14
BURKS, Henry Thomas (T)
Tuscaloosa, Ala., 1906-07-08

BURNETT, Hunter Tennille (B)
Tuscaloosa, Ala., 1914-15
BURNS, Harmon Theron (B)
Wedowee, Ala., 1901-02
BURR, Borden (B)
Talladega, Ala., 1893-94
BUSBEE, Kent (DB)
Meridian, Miss., 1967
BUSBY, Max (OG)
Leeds, Ala., 1977
BUSH, Jeff (B)
Tuscaloosa, Ala., 1933-34
BUSH, Jim (G)
Columbus, Ga., 1945-46
BUTLER, Clyde (OT)
Scottsboro, Ala., 1970
C
CADENHEAD, Billy (RH)
Greenville, Miss., 1946-47-48-49
CAIN, Jim (E)
Eudora, Ark., 1945-46-47-48
•CAIN, Johnny (FB) All-SEC
Montgomery, Ala., 1930-31-32
CALDWELL, Blackie (B)
Tallassee, Ala., 1936
CALDWELL, Herschel (HB) All-SC
Blytheville, Ark., 1925-26
CALLAWAY, Neil (LB-DE)
Macon, Ga., 1975-77
CALLIES, Kelly (DT)
Fairhope, Ala., 1977
CALVERT, John (G) All-SEC
Cullman, Ala., 1965-66
CALVIN, Tom (FB)
Athens, Ala., 1948-49-50
CAMP, Joseph "Pete" (T)
Manchester, Ala., 1923-24-25
CAMPBELL, John (QB)
Durant, Miss., 1928-29-30
CAMPBELL, Mike (DB)
Pinson, Ala., 1988
CAMPBELL, Tilden "Happy" (QB)
Pine Bluff, Ark., 1934-35
CANTERBURY, Frank (HB)
Birmingham, Ala., 1964-65-66
CARGILE, C. J. (B)
Bessemer, Ala., 1914
CARRIGAN, Ralph (C)
Oak Park, Ill., 1951-52-53
CARROLL, Jimmy (C)
Enterprise, Ala., 1965-66
CARRUTH, Paul Ott (RB)
Summit, Miss., 1981-82-84
CARTER, Joe (RB)
Starkville, Miss., 1980-81-82-83
CARY, Robert H., Jr. "Robin" (DB)
Greenwood, S.C., 1972-73
CASH, Danny (OT)
Spartanburg, S.C., 1987-89
CASH, Jerauld Wayne "Jerry" (E)
Bogart, Ga., 1970-71
CASH, Steve (LB)
Huntsville, Ala., 1980
CASHIO, Gri (G)
Gadsden, Ala., 1947
CASSIDY, Francis (T)
Neff, Ohio, 1944-45-46-47
CASSIMUS, John (DB-RB-WR)
Birmingham, Ala., 1987-88-89
CASTEAL, David (HB)
Eglin AFB, Fla., 1986-87-88
•CASTILLE, Jeremiah (DB) All-SEC
Phenix City, Ala., 1979-80-81-82

CAVAN, Peter Alexander (HB)
Thomaston, Ga., 1975-76-77
CAUSEY, Joe (HB)
Douglas, Ariz., 1931
CAYAVEC, Bob (OT) All-SEC
Largo, Fla., 1980-81-82
CHAFFIN, Phil (FB)
Huntsville, Ala., 1968-69-70
CHAMBERS, Jimmy (C)
Fort Payne, Ala., 1967
CHANDLER, Thornton (TE)
Jacksonville, Fla., 1983-84-85
CHAPMAN, Herb (C)
Elmore, Ala., 1947
CHAPMAN, Roger (K)
Hartselle, Ala., 1977-78
CHAPPELL, Howard (B)
Sylacauga, Ala., 1931-32-33
CHATMAN, Terrill (OT) (All SEC)
Childersburg, Ala., 1987-88-89
CHATWOOD, David (FB)
Fairhope, Ala., 1965-66-67
CHILDERS, Morris (B)
Birmingham, Ala., 1960
CHILDS, Bob (LB)
Montgomery, Ala., 1966-67-68
CHIODETTI, Larry (LH)
Philadelphia, Pa., 1950-51
CHRISTIAN, Knute Rockne (C)
Tuscaloosa, Ala., 1954-55
CIEMNY, Richard (K)
Anthony, Kan., 1969-70
CLARK, Cotton (HB)
Kansas, Ala., 1961-62
CLARK, Frank Barnard (B)
Mobile, Ala., 1903-04
CLARK, Phil (G)
Columbus, Ga., 1956
CLARK, Tim (SE)
Newnan, Ga., 1978-79-80-81
CLAY, Hugh Stephen (G)
Gadsden, Ala., 1969
CLEMENS, Al (E) All-SC
Scottsboro, Ala., 1921-22-23
CLEMENT, C. B. "Foots" (T)
Rower, Ark., 1928-29-30
CLEMENTS, Mike (DB)
Center Point, Ala., 1978-79-80
CLINE, Jackie (DT)
McCalla, Ala., 1980-81-82
CLONTS, Steve (C)
Rome, Ga., 1989
CLORFELINE, Julius (G)
Anotpol, Russia, 1911
COCHRAN, Bob (LH)
Hueytown, Ala., 1947-48-49
COCHRAN, Chris (LB)
Germantown, Tenn., 1989
COCHRAN, Donald G. (G)
Birmingham, Ala., 1957-58-59
COCHRAN, Ralph (QB)
Hueytown, Ala., 1949
COCHRANE, David (B)
Tuscaloosa, Ala., 1931
COCHRANE, Henry (QB)
Paducah, Ky., 1937
COHEN, Andy (B)
El Paso, Texas, 1923-24
COKELY, Donald (T)
Chickasha, Okla., 1970-71
COLBURN, Rocky (DB)
Cantonment, Fla., 1982-83-84

•COLE, Richard (DT)
Crossville, Ala., 1965-66
COLE, Tommy (NG-DT)
Jasper, Ala., 1985-86-87-88
COLEMAN, Michael (SE)
Anaheim, Calif., 1978
COLEY, Ken (DB-QB)
Birmingham, Ala., 1979-80-81-82
COLLINS, Danny (DE)
Birmingham, Ala., 1976-77
COLLINS, Earl (FB)
Mobile, Ala., 1980-81
COMPTON, Ben E. (LG)
Greensboro, Ala., 1923-24-25
COMPTON, Charley (T)
Sylacauga, Ala., 1942-46-47
COMPTON, Joe (FB)
Sylacauga, Ala., 1949-50-51
COMSTOCK, Charles Dexter (B)
Birmingham, Ala., 1895-96
COMSTOCK, Donald (HB)
Lincoln, Neb., 1956
CONDON, Bill (OG) All-SEC
Mobile, Ala., 1984-85-86-87
CONNOR, Don (C)
Gadsden, Ala., 1955
CONWAY, Bob (RH)
Fort Wayne, Ind., 1950-51-52
CONWAY, William P. "Bill" (G)
Birmingham, Ala., 1944
COOK, Elbert (LB)
Jacksonville, Fla., 1960-61-62
•COOK, Leroy (DE) All-SEC
Abbeville, Ala., 1972-73-74-75
COOK, Ted (E)
Birmingham, Ala., 1942-46
COOK, Wayne (TE)
Montgomery, Ala., 1964-65-66
COOPER, Britton (DB)
Mobile, Ala., 1983-84-85-86
COOPER, Ernest "Shorty" (T)
St. Stephens, Ala., 1921-22-23
COPE, Robert (RG)
Union Springs, Ala., 1892-93
CORBITT, James "Corky" (RH)
Nashville, Tenn., 1945-46
COSTIGAN, Chris (SE)
Danville, Calif., 1989
COUCH, L. B. (C)
Alexander City, Ala., 1949-50
COUNTESS, C. C. (C) All-SC
Duncanville, Ala., 1907-08
COURTNEY, Earlando (DB)
Thomasville, Ala., 1986-87
COWELL, Vince (OG) All-SEC
Snellville, Ga., 1978-79-80
COX, Allen (OT)
Satsuma, Ala., 1972
•COX, Carey (C)
Bainbridge, Ga., 1937-38-39
COX, Tony (LB)
LaGrange, Ga., 1988
COYLE, Dan Joseph, Jr. (E)
Birmingham, Ala., 1954-55
CRAFT, Russ (HB)
Beach Bottom, W.Va., 1940-41-42
•CRANE, Paul (C-LB) All-SEC
Prichard, Ala., 1963-64-65
CRENSHAW, Curtis (T)
Mobile, Ala., 1961
CREEN, Cecil L. (B)
Anniston, Ala., 1916

*CROOM, Sylvester (C) All-SEC
Tuscaloosa, Ala., 1972-73-74
CROSS, Andy (LB)
Birmingham, Ala., 1972
CROSS, Howard (TE)
New Hope, Ala., 1985-86-87-88
CROW, John David, Jr. (HB)
El Cahon, Calif., 1975-76-77
CROWSON, Roger (FB)
Jackson, Miss., 1968
CROYLE, John (DE)
Gadsden, Ala., 1971-72-73
CRUMBLEY, Allen (DB)
Birmingham, Ala., 1976-78
CRYDER, Robert J. (OG)
O'Fallon Township, Ill., 1975-76-77
CULLIVER, Calvin (FB)
East Brewton, Ala., 1973-74-75-76
CULPEPPER, Ed (T)
Bradenton, Fla., 1951-52-53-54
CULWELL, Ingram (HB)
Tuscaloosa, Ala., 1961-62
CUMMINGS, Joe (E)
Muleshoe, Texas 1952-53
CUNNINGHAM, E. A. "Jim" (T)
Winfield, Ala., 1955-56
CURTIS, Joe (E)
Birmingham, Ala., 1950-51-52
CURTIS, Nathan Stephenson (B)
Carrollton, Ala., 1906
D
DARE, Charlie (OG)
Enterprise, Ala., 1989
DASHER, Bob (OG)
Plymouth, Miss., 1981
DAVIS, Alvin "Pig" (FB)
Green Forest, Ark., 1937-38
DAVIS, Bill (K)
Columbus, GA., 1971-72-73
DAVIS, Charley (RH)
Uniontown, Pa., 1948-49
DAVIS, Fred (T) All-SEC
Louisville, Ky., 1938-39-40
DAVIS, Fred, Jr. (T)
Louisville, Ky., 1964
DAVIS, Jim (LG)
Hamilton, Ala., 1951-52-53
DAVIS, John (R)
Dallas, Texas, 1987-89
DAVIS, Johnny Lee (FB)
Montgomery, Ala., 1975-76-77
DAVIS, Mike (K)
Columbus, Ga., 1975
DAVIS, Ricky (S) All-SEC
Bessemer, Ala., 1973-74
DAVIS, Steve (K)
Columbus, Ga., 1965-66-67
DAVIS, Terry Ashley (QB) All-SEC
Bogalusa, La., 1970-71-72
DAVIS, Terry Lane (E)
Birmingham, Ala., 1970
DAVID, Tim (K)
Columbus, Ga., 1961-62-63
DAVIS, Vantreise (LB)
Phenix City, Ala., 1986-87-88-89
DAVIS, Wayne (LB)
Gordo, Ala., 1983-84-85
DAVIS, William (DT)
Fort Deposit, Ala., 1978
DAVIS, William "Junior" (T)
Birmingham, Ala., 1967-68
DAVIDSON, James Lafayette (C)
Centreville, Ala., 1900

DAWSON, Jimmy Dale (LB)
Excel, Ala., 1973
DEAN, Louis (DB)
Foley, Ala., 1984
DEAN, Mike (DB)
Decatur, Ga., 1967-68-69
DEAN, Steve (HB)
Orlando, Fla., 1972-73
DeLAURENTIS, Vincent (C)
Hammonton, N.J., 1952-53
DEMOS, Joe (OG)
Clearwater, Fla., 1989
DEMPSEY, Benny (C)
Brantley, Ala., 1956-57
DEMYANOVICH, Joe (FB)
Bayonne, N.J., 1932-33-34
DeNIRO, Gary (DE)
Youngstown, Ohio, 1978-79-80
DeSHANE, Charley (QB)
Grand Rapids, Mich., 1940
DICHIARA, Ron (K)
Bessemer, Ala., 1974
DILDY, Jim (T)
Nashville, Ark., 1931-32-33
DILDY, Joe (C)
Nashville, Ark., 1933-34
DILL, Jimmy (E)
Mobile, Ala., 1962-63
DISMUKE, Joe (OT)
Gadsden, Ala., 1982-83
DIXON, Dennis (TE)
Orange, Calif., 1967-68
DOBBS, Edgar (E)
Collinsville, Ala., 1928-30
*DOMNANOVICH, Joe (C) All-SEC
South Bend, Ind., 1940-41-42
DONALD, Joseph Glenn (C)
Marion Junction, Ala., 1905-06
DONALDSON, Paul (E)
Florala, Ala., 1954
DORAN, Stephen Curtis (TE)
Murray, KY., 1969-70
DOTHEROW, Autrey (E)
Brooksville, Ala., 1930-31
*DOWDY, Cecil (OT) All-SEC
Cherokee, Ala., 1964-65-66
DOYLE, Philip (PK) All-SEC
Birmingham, Ala., 1987-88-89
DRENNEN, Earl (QB)
Birmingham, Ala., 1900-01
DRINKARD, Reid (OG)
Linden, Ala., 1968-69-70
DUBOSE, Mike (DE)
Opp, Ala., 1972-73-74
DUKE, Jim (DT)
Columbus, Ga., 1967-68-69
DUNCAN, Conley (LB) All-SEC
Hartselle, Ala., 1973-74-75
DUNCAN, Jerry (OT)
Sparta, N.C., 1965-66
DUNN, Jeff (QB)
Greensboro, N.C., 1987-88
DURBY, Ron (T)
Memphis, Tenn., 1963-64
DYAR, Warren E. (TE)
Florence, Ala., 1972-73
DYE, George (C)
Birmingham, Ala., 1927
DYESS, Johnny (RB)
Elba, Ala., 1981
DYESS, Marlin (HB)
Elba, Ala., 1957-58-59

E
EBERDT, JESS (c)
Blytheville, Ark., 1929-30
ECKENROD, Michael Lee (C)
Chattanooga, Tenn., 1973
ECKERLY, Charles (G)
Oak Park, Ill., 1952-53-54
EDWARDS, Bryant B. (RE)
Union Springs, Ala., 1906
EDWARDS, Marion "Buddy" (T)
Attalla, Ala., 1944
EDWARDS, Randy (DT)
Marietta, Ga., 1980-81-82-83
ELDER, Venson (LB)
Decatur, Ga., 1982-83
ELIAS, Johnny (MG)
Columbus, Ga., 1981-82
ELLARD, Butch (Mgr.)
Tuscaloosa, Ala., 1982
ELLETT, Alvin (T)
Owen Cross Roads, Ala., 1955
ELLIS, Raiford (C)
Birmingham, Ala., 1934
ELLIS, Billy (B)
Florence, Ala., 1928
ELMORE, Albert, Sr., (E)
Reform, Ala., 1929-30
ELMORE, Albert, Jr. (QB)
Troy, Ala., 1953-54-55
ELMORE, Grady (K-HB)
Ozark, Ala., 1962-63-64
EMERSON, Ken (DB)
Columbus., Ga., 1969-70
EMMETT, J. H. (HB)
Albertville, Ala., 1919-20-21-22
EMMONS, James Thomas (T)
Atmore, Ala., 1954
ENIS, Ben (E)
Fayette, Ala., 1926
EPPS, Craig (OLB)
Miami, Fla., 1984-85-86-87
F
FAGAN, Jeff (RB)
Hollywood, Fla., 1979-80-81-82
FAUST, Donald W. (FB)
Fairhope, Ala., 1975-76-77
FAUST, Douglas (DT)
Fairhope, Ala., 1972
FEDAK, Frank (HB)
Short Creek, W.Va., 1945
FELDER, Shannon (DB)
Willis, Tex., 1985-87
FERGUSON, Burr (LE)
Birmingham, Ala., 1892-93
FERGUSON, Charles M. (OG)
Cuthbert, Ga., 1968-69
FERGUSON, Hill (B)
Birmingham, Ala., 1895-96
FERGUSON, Mitch (RB)
Augusta, Ga., 1977-79-80
FERGUSON, Richard (OG)
Fort Payne, Ala., 1969
FICHMAN, Leon (T)
Los Angeles, Calif., 1941-42
FIELDS, Paul (QB)
Gardendale, Ala., 1982-83
FIELDS, William H. (E)
Nashville, Tenn., 1944
FILIPPINI, Bruno (G)
Powhatan Point, Ohio,
1944-45-46-47
FINKLEY, Donnie (WR)
Fairhope, Ala., 1989

FINLAY, Louis Malone (T)
Pollard, Ala., 1909-10
FINNELL, Edward Judson (B)
Tuscaloosa, Ala., 1911
FLANAGAN, Thad (SE)
Leighton, Ala., 1974-75-76
FLETCHER, Maurice (QB)
Clarksdale, Miss., 1937
FLORENCE, Craige (DB)
Enterprise, Ala., 1981-82
FLORETTE, Anthony Raymond (E)
Cleveland, Ohio, 1920
FLOWERS, Dick (T)
Mobile, Ala., 1946-47
FLOWERS, Lee (T)
Mobile, Ala., 1945
FORBUS, Roy (E)
Alexander City, Ala., 1956
FORD, Danny (OT) All-SEC
Gadsden, Ala., 1967-68-69
FORD, Mike (DE) All-SEC
Tuscaloosa, Ala., 1966-67-68
FORD, Steven (DB)
Tuscaloosa, Ala., 1973-74
FORMAN, James R. (T)
Ashville, Ala., 1901-02
FORTUNATO, Steve (G)
Mingo Junction, Ohio, 1946-47-48
FOSHEE, Jess (G)
Clanton, Ala., 1937-38
FOWLER, Conrad (SE)
Columbiana, Ala., 1966-67-68
FOWLER, Les (DB)
Hartselle, Ala., 1976
FRACCHIA, Mike (FB) All-SEC
Memphis, Tenn., 1960-61-63
FRALEY, Robert (QB)
Winchester, Tenn., 1974-75
FRANCIS, Kavanaugh "Kay" (C)
Timson, Ala., 1934-35
FRANK, Milton (G)
Huntsville, Ala., 1958-59
FRANK, Morris
Huntsville, Ala., 1962
FRANKLIN, Arthur (RT)
Greensboro, N.C., 1906
FRANKO, Jim (G)
Yorkville, Ohio, 1947-48-49
FRAZER, Thomas Sydney (B)
Union Springs, Ala., 1893
*FREEMAN, Wayne (OG) All-SEC
Fort Payne, Ala., 1962-63-64
FRENCH, Buddy (K)
Decatur, Ala., 1963-64
FREY, Calvin (G)
Arkadelphia, Ark., 1931-32-33
FRUHMORGEN, John (OG)
Tampa, Fla., 1986-87-88
FUHRMAN, Darrel (OLB)
Gadsden, Ala. 1987
FULLER, Jimmy (T)
Fairfield, Ala., 1964-65-66
FULLER, Leon (HB)
Nederland, Texas, 1959-60
G
GAGE, Fred Harrison (B)
Hampton, N.H., 1916
GAMBRELL, D. Joe (C)
Talladega, Ala., 1945-46
GAMMON, George (HB)
Cullman, Ala., 1941-42
GANDY, Joseph Maury (T)
Pell City, Ala., 1912-13

GANDY, Ralph (E)
  Birmingham, Ala., 1932-33-34-35
GANTT, Greg (K) All-SEC
  Birmingham, Ala., 1971-72-73
GARDNER, Charles (DB)
  Carson, Calif., 1988-89
GARRETT, Broox Cleveland (E)
  Thomasville, Ala., 1909
GARRETT, Coma, Jr. (E)
  Thomasville, Ala., 1905-06
GAY, Stan (DB)
  Tuskegee, Ala., 1981-82-83
•GELLERSTEDT, Sam (NG) All-
  SEC, Montgomery, Ala., 1968
GERASIMCHUK, Davis (OG) All-
  SEC, Lomita, Calif., 1975-76
GERBER, Elwood (G)
  Napierville, Ill., 1940
GERMANOS, Nicholas "Nick" (E)
  Montgomery, Ala., 1954-55
GETCHELL, Billy (SE)
  Queens, N.Y., 1984
GIBBONS, James Booth (T)
  Tuscaloosa, Ala., 1914
GIBSON, Richard (E)
  Mobile, Ala., 1945
GILBERT, Danny (DB)
  Geraldine, Ala., 1968-69-70
GILBERT, Greg (LB)
  Decatur, Ala., 1985-86-87-88
GILDER, Andrew (FB)
  Elmore, Ala., 1983
GILLILAND, Rickey (LB)
  Birmingham, Ala., 1976-77-78
GILLIS, Grant (QB) All-SC
  Grove Hill, Ala., 1924-25
GILMER, Creed (DE) All-SEC
  Birmingham, Ala., 1964-65
GILMER, David (OG)
  Attalla, Ala., 1984-85
•GILMER, Harry (HB) All-SEC
  Birmingham, Ala., 1944-45-46-47
GODFREE, Newton (T)
  Alexander City, Ala., 1930-31-32
GODWIN, Joe (LB)
  New Brocton, Ala., 1984-85-86
GOODE, Chris (DB)
  Town Creek, Ala., 1986
GOODE, Clyde (CB)
  Town Creek, Ala., 1989
GOODE, Kerry (RB)
  Town Creek, Ala., 1983-86-87
GOODE, Pierre (WR)
  Town Creek, Ala., 1987-88-89
GORNTO, Jack "Red" (E)
  Valdosta, Ga., 1938
GOSSETT, Don Lee (MG)
  Knoxville, Tenn., 1969
GOTHARD, Andrew "Andy" (DB)
  Alexander City, Ala., 1975-76
GOTHARD, Preston (TE)
  Montgomery, Ala., 1983-84
GRAHAM, Glen W. (C)
  Florence, Ala., 1955-56
GRAMMER, James W. (C) All-SEC
  Hartselle, Ala., 1969-71
GRAMMER, Richard (C)
  Hartselle, Ala., 1967-68-69
GRANADE, James Napoleon (E)
  Frankville, Ala., 1898-99
GRANT, Fred (FB)
  Christianburg, Va., 1944-45-46

GRANTHAM, Jim (E)
  Plano, Texas, 1945-46
GRAVES, Bibb
  Montgomery, Ala., 1892-93
GRAY, Alan (QB)
  Tampa, Fla., 1979-80-81
GRAY, Charles (E)
  Pell City, Ala., 1956-57-58
GRAYSON, David Allison (RE)
  Gurley, Ala., 1892-93
GREEN, Jack (G)
  Centre, Ala., 1945
GREEN, Louis E. (OG)
  Birmingham, Ala., 1974-76-77
GREENE, Edgar D. (RT)
  Waverly, Ala., 1907-08
GREENWOOD, Darren (CB)
  Lanett, Ala., 1989
GREER, Charles West (B)
  Marion, Ala., 1910-11
GRESHAM, Owen Garside (T)
  Prattville, Ala., 1908-09
GROGAN, Jay (TE)
  Cropwell, Ala., 1981-82-83
GRYSKA, Clem (HB)
  Steubenville, Ohio, 1947-48
GUINYARD, Mickey (RB)
  Atlanta, Ga., 1981-82-83
GWIN, James C. C. (C)
  East Lake, Ala., 1903
H
HAGLER, Ellis (C)
  Blue Springs, Ala., 1927-28
•HALL, Mike (LB) All-SEC
  Tarrant, Ala., 1966-67-68
HALL, Randy Lee (DT)
  Huntsville, Ala., 1972-73-74
HALL, Wayne (LB)
  Huntsville, Ala., 1971-72-73
HAMER, Norris (DE)
  Tarrant, Ala., 1967-68
HAMILTON, Wayne (DE) All-SEC
  Okahumpka, Fla., 1977-78-79
HAMMOND, Spencer (LB)
  Rome, Ga., 1987-88-89
HAMNER, Robert Lee (B)
  Fayette, Ala., 1925-26-27
•HAND, Jon (DT) All-SEC
  Sylacauga, Ala., 1982-83-84-85
HAND, Mike (LB-OG)
  Tuscumbia, Ala., 1968-69-70
HANEY, James (RB)
  Rogersville, Ala., 1979
HANNAH, Charles (DT) All-SEC
  Albertville, Ala., 1974-75-76
HANNAH, David (OT) All-SEC
  Albertville, Ala., 1975-77-78-79
HANNAH, Herb (G)
  Athens, Ga., 1948-49-50
•HANNAH, John (OG) All-SEC
  Albertville, Ala., 1970-71-72
HANNAH, William C. (T)
  Indianapolis, Ind., 1957-58-59
HANNON, Emile "Chick"
  Montgomery, Ala., 1907
HANRAHAN, Gary (OG)
  Pompano Beach, Fla., 1973
HANSEN, Cliff (T)
  Gary, Ind., 1940-41
HANSON, John (FB)
  Roanoke, Ala., 1939-40

HARKINS, Grover (G)
  Gadsden, Ala., 1937-38
HARKNESS, Fred (MG)
  Winfield, Ala., 1980
HARPOLE, Allen "Bunk" (DG)
  Columbus, Miss., 1965-66-67
HARRELL, Billy (HB)
  Opelika, Ala., 1940
HARRIS, Charles (DE)
  Mobile, Ala., 1965-66-67
HARRIS, Craig (RB)
  Panama City, Fla., 1989
HARRIS, Don (DT)
  Vincent, Ala., 1968-69-70
HARRIS, Hudson (HB)
  Tarrant, Ala., 1962-63-64
HARRIS, Jim Bob (DB) All-SEC
  Athens, Ga., 1978-79-80-81
HARRIS, Joe Dale (SE)
  Uriah, Ala., 1975
HARRIS, Paul (DE)
  Mobile, Ala., 1974-75-76
HARRISON, Bill (DT)
  Ft. Walton Bch., Fla., 1976
HARRISON, Stacy (DB)
  Atlanta, Ga., 1988-89
HARSH, Griffin R. (QB)
  Birmingham, Ala., 1914
HARSH, William L. (HB)
  Birmingham, Ala., 1914-15
HAYDEN, Neb (QB)
  Charlotte, N.C., 1969-70
HEARD, Victor John (B)
  Camp Hill, Ala., 1910
HEARD, Vigil Willis (B)
  Camp Hill, Ala., 1910-11
HEATH, Donnie (C)
  Anniston, Ala., 1960
HECHT, George (G)
  Chicago Heights, Ill., 1940-41-42
HELMS, Sandy (G)
  Tuscaloosa, Ala., 1949-50
HELTON, Rodney (LB)
  Knoxville, Tenn., 1989
HENDERSON, Josh (DB)
  Panama City, Fla., 1982
HENDERSON, Wm. T. "Bill" (TE)
  Tuscaloosa, Ala., 1975-77
HENDERSON, S. W.
  Talladega, Ala., 1892
HENRY, Butch (E)
  Selma, Ala., 1961-62-63
HEWES, Willis (C)
  Russellville, Ark., 1931-32
HICKERSON, Ed (G)
  Venture, Calif., 1938-40
HICKS, Billy (QB)
  Abilene, Texas, 1928-29
HICKS, J. W. (G)
  Ozark, Ala., 1912-13
HIGGINBOTHAM, Robert (DB)
  Hueytown, Ala., 1967-68
HIGGINBOTHAM, Steve (DB) All-
  SEC, Hueytown, Ala., 1969-70-71
HILL, John (RB)
  Centre, Ala., 1979-80
HILL, Marvin "Buster" (QB)
  Huntsville, Ala., 1952-54
HILL, Murry (RB)
  Atmore, Ala., 1988-89
HILL, Roosevelt (LB)
  Newnan, Ga., 1982-83

HILMAN, R. G. (E)
  Epes, Ala, 1895
HINES, Edward T. (DE)
  LaFayette, Ala., 1970-72
HINTON, Robert Poole (B)
  Uniontown, Ala., 1922-23
HITE, John H. (HB)
  Nashville, Tenn., 1944
HOBBS, Sam (G)
  Selma, Ala., 1907
HOBSON, Clell (QB)
  Tuscaloosa, Ala., 1950-51-52
HODGES, Bruce (DE-T)
  Sarasota, Fla., 1977
HODGES, Norwood (FB)
  Hueytown, Ala., 1944-45-46-47
HOLCOMBE, Danny (OG)
  Marietta, Ga., 1980-81-82
HOLDBROOKS, Byron (DT)
  Haleyville, Ala., 1987-88-89
HOLDER, Harry (B)
  Birmingham, Ala., 1927
HOLDNAK, Ed (G) All-SEC
  Kenvil, N.J., 1948-49
HOLLEY, Hillman D. (B)
  Tuscaloosa, Ala., 1930-31-32
HOLLINGSWORTH, Gary (QB)
  All-SEC, Hamilton, Ala., 1989
HOLLIS, William C. (HB)
  Biloxi, Miss., 1954-55
•HOLM, Bernard "Tony" (FB) All-
  SEC, Ensley, Ala., 1927-28-29
HOLM, Charlie (FB) All-SEC
  Ensley, Ala., 1937-38
HOLMES, Gordon "Sherlock" (C)
  All-SEC, Springville, Ala.,
  1924-25-26
HOLOMAN, Desmond (LB)
  Hampton, Va., 1985-86
HOLSOMBACK, Roy (G)
  West Blocton, Ala., 1959-60
HOLT, Darwin (LB)
  Gainesville, Texas, 1960-61
HOLT, James Jay "Buddy" (P)
  Demopolis, Ala., 1977-79
•HOMAN, Dennis (SE) All-SEC
  Muscle Shoals, Ala., 1965-66-67
HOMAN, Scott (DT)
  Elkhart, Ind., 1979-80-81-82
HOOD, Bob (T)
  Gadsden, Ala., 1946-47-48
HOOD, E. P. (T)
  Woodlawn, Ala., 1919-20
HOOD, SAMMY (DB)
  Ider, Ala., 1982-83
HOPPER, Mike (E)
  Huntsville, Ala., 1961-62-64
HORSTEAD, Don (HB)
  Elba, Ala., 1982-84-85
HORTON, Jimmy (DE)
  Tarrant, Ala., 1971
HOUSTON, Ellis "Red" (C)
  Bessemer, Ala., 1930-31-32
HOUSTON, Martin (FB)
  Centre, Ala., 1989
HOVATER, Dexter Louis (B)
  Russellville, Ala., 1914-15
HOVATER, Jack (E)
  Russellville, Ala., 1919-20-21
HOVATER, Walter E. (RH)
  Russellville, Ala., 1917-18-19
HOWARD, Frank (G)
  Barlow Bend, Ala., 1928-29-30

150

HOWARD, Johnny (OT)
  Bessemer, Ala., 1989
*HOWELL, Millard "Dixie" (HB)
  All-SEC, Hartford, Ala., 1932-33-34
HOWLE, G. D. (FB)
  Wetumpka, Ala., 1907
HUBBARD, Colenzo (LB)
  Mulga, Ala., 1974-75-76
*HUBERT, A. T. S. "Pooley" (FB)
  All-SEC, Meridian, Miss.,
  1922-23-24-25
HUDSON, Ben A. (E)
  Montgomery, Ala., 1923-24-25
HUDSON, H. Clayton (E)
  Montgomery, Ala., 1921-22
HUFSTETLER, Thomas R., Jr. (C)
  Rossville, Ga., 1977-78
HUGHES, Hal (QB)
  Pine Bluff, Ark., 1937-38
HUGHES, Howard (T)
  Little Rock, Ark., 1941
HUGHES, Larry (B)
  Tuscaloosa, Ala., 1931-32-33
HUMPHRIES, Marvin (OLB)
  Montgomery, Ala., 1984
*HUMPHREY, Bobby (HB) All-SEC
  Birmingham, Ala., 1985-86-87-88
HUNDERTMARK, John (T)
  Washington, Pa., 1933
HUNT, Ben (G)
  Scottsboro, Ala., 1920-21-22
HUNT, Morris Parker (OT)
  Orlando, Fla., 1972-73
HUNT, Travis (T)
  Albertville, Ala., 1950-51-52
HUNTER, Scott (QB)
  Prichard, Ala., 1968-69-70
*HUPKE, Tom (G) All-SC
  East Chicago, Ind., 1931-32
HURL, Clarence S. (E)
  Bessemer, Ala., 1908-09
HURLBUT, Jack (QB)
  Houston, Texas, 1962-63
HURST, Tim (OT)
  DeArmandville, Ala., 1975-76-77
HURT, Cecil A. (E)
  Chattanooga, Tenn., 1927-28-29
HUSBAND, Hunter (TE)
  Nashville, Tenn., 1967-68-69
HUSBAND, Woodward A.
  "Woodie" (LB)
  Nashville, Tenn., 1969-70
*HUTSON, Don (E) All-SEC
  Pine Bluff, Ark., 1932-33-34

I
IKNER, Lou (RB)
  Atmore, Ala., 1977-78
INGRAM, Cecil "Hootie" (DB)
  All-SEC, Tuscaloosa, Ala.,
  1952-53-54
ISRAEL, Jimmy Kent (QB)
  Haleyville, Ala., 1966
ISRAEL, Thomas Murray (G)
  Haleyville, Ala., 1969
IVY, Hyrle, Jr. (E)
  Fort Wayne, Ind., 1951-52
IVY, Jim (DT)
  Birmingham, Ala., 1983-84

J
JACKSON, Billy (RB) All-SEC
  Phenix City, Ala., 1978-79-80
JACKSON, Bobby (QB)
  Mobile, Ala., 1957-58

JACKSON, Mark (C)
  Houston, Texas, 1981-82-83
JACKSON, Max (T)
  Notasulga, Ala., 1930-31
JACKSON, Wilbur (HB) All-SEC
  Ozark, Ala., 1971-72-73
JACOBS, Donald (QB)
  Scottsboro, Ala., 1979-80
JAMES, Kenneth Morris (T)
  Columbus, Ga., 1969-70
JARVIS, Curt (NG) All-SEC
  Gardendale, Ala., 1983-84-85-86
JELKS, Gene (HB-DB)
  Gadsden, Ala., 1985-86-87-88-89
JENKINS, John Felix (E)
  Camden, Ala., 1894-95
JENKINS, Jug (E)
  Eufaula, Ala., 1949-50-51
JENKINS, Tom "Bobby" (FB)
  Talladega, Ala., 1942
JILLEBA, Pete (FB)
  Madison, N.J., 1967-68-69
*JOHNS, Bobby (DB) All-SEC
  Birmingham, Ala., 1965-66-67
JOHNSON, Billy (C)
  Selma, Ala., 1965-66-67
JOHNSON, Comell (HB)
  High Point, N.C., 1959-60
JOHNSON, D. B.
  DeSotoville, Ala., 1892
JOHNSON, Forney (QB)
  Birmingham, Ala., 1899
JOHNSON, Harold (C)
  Greensboro, Ala., 1951
JOHNSON, Hoss (OT)
  Huntsville, Ala., 1984-85-86
JOHNSON, James (HB)
  Tuscaloosa, Ala., 1924-25
JOHNSON, Donny (HB)
  Birmingham, Ala., 1966-69
JOHNSTON, J. Goree (FB)
  Wetumpka, Ala., 1915-16
JOHNSTON, Sidney (G)
  Athens, Ala., 1919-20
JOHNSTON, Wm. McDow (HB)
  Meridian, Miss., 1914
JONES, Amos (RB)
  Aliceville, Ala., 1980
JONES, Brice Sidney (E)
  Tuscaloosa, Ala., 1906-07
JONES, Bruce (RG)
  Jasper, Ala., 1923-24-25
JONES, H. H. (T)
  Centreville, Ala., 1901
JONES, Howard Criner (LG)
  Huntsville, Ala., 1914
JONES, Joe (RB)
  Thomaston, Ga., 1978-79-80
JONES, Joey (SE)
  Mobile, Ala., 1980-81-82-83
JONES, Kevin (QB)
  Louisville, Ky., 1977-78
JONES, Paul B. (RHB)
  Selma, Ala., 1907
JONES, Ralph (E)
  Florence, Ala., 1944
JONES, Ralph Lee (G)
  Jones Mills, Ala., 1917-18-19
JONES, Raymond Wm. (E)
  Huntsville, Ala., 1912
JONES, Robbie (LB)
  Demopolis, Ala., 1979-80-81-82

JONES, Robert (RB)
  Birmingham, Ala., 1989
JONES, Terry Wayne (C)
  Sandersville, Ga., 1975-76-77
JOPLIN, Charles West (QB-HB-E)
  Gurley, Ala., 1911-12
*JORDAN, Lee Roy (LB) All-SEC
  Excel, Ala., 1960-61-62
JORDAN, Lint (E)
  Monticellow, Ga., 1950-51
*JUNIOR, E. J. III (DE) All-SEC
  Nashville, Tenn., 1977-78--79-80

K
*KEARLEY, Dan (DT) All-SEC
  Talladega, Ala., 1962-63-64
KELLER, Phillip Brooks (LG)
  Montgomery, Ala., 1911
KELLER, Thomas B. "Red" (LE)
  Cullman, Ala., 1937
KELLEY, Joe (QB)
  Ozark, Ala., 1966-67-68
KELLEY, Leslie (FB)
  Cullman, Ala., 1964-65-66
KELLEY, Max (FB)
  Cullman, Ala., 1954-55-56
KELLY, William Milner (E)
  Birmingham, Ala., 1920-21
*KENDRICK, Kermit (S)
  Meridian, Miss., 1985-86-87-88
KENNEDY, President John F.
  (Honorary) Washington, D.C.,1961
KENT, William (RB)
  Rome, Ga., 1988
KERR, Dudley (K)
  Reform, Ala., 1966-67
*KILGROW, Joe (HB) All-SEC
  Montgomery, Ala., 1935-36-37
KILLGORE, Terry (C)
  Annandale, Va., 1965-66-67
KILROY, William (FB)
  Philadelphia, Pa., 1952
KIM, Peter (KS)
  Honolulu, Hi., 1980-81-82
KIMBALL, Morton (G)
  South Bend, Ind., 1941
KINDERKNECHT, Donald H. (FB)
  Hays, Kansas, 1955-56
KING, Emanuel (DE)
  Leroy, Ala., 1982-83-84
KING, Joe (OT)
  Gadsden, Ala., 1985-86-87
KING, Tyrone (DB) All-SEC
  Docena, Ala., 1972-73-74-75
KIRBY, Lelias E. (HB)
  Albertville, Ala., 1920-21
KIRKLAND, B'Ho (G)
  Columbia, Ala., 1931-32-33
KNAPP, David (HB)
  Birmingham, Ala., 1970-71-72
KNIGHT, William (HB)
  Homewood, Ala., 1957
KRAMER, Michael T. (DB)
  Mobile, Ala., 1975-76-77
*KRAPF, James Paul (C) All SEC
  Newark, Del., 1970-71-72
*KRAUSS, Barry (LB) All-SEC
  Pompano Beach, Fla., 1976-77-78
KROUT, Bart (TE) All-SEC
  Birmingham, Ala., 1978-79-80-81
KUBELIUS, Skip (DT)
  Morrow, Ga., 1972-73
KULBACK, Steve Joseph (DT)
  Clarksville, Tenn., 1973-74

KYZER, G. H. (E-RH)
  Richmond, Ala., 1893
L
LaBUE, John (RB)
  Memphis, Tenn., 1976
LaBUE, Joseph II (HB)
  Memphis, Tenn., 1970-71-72
LAMBERT, Buford (OT)
  Warner Robins, Ga., 1976
LAMBERT, Jerry (E)
  Alabama City, Ala., 1952
LAMBERT, Randolph (C)
  Athens, Ga., 1973-74
LANCASTER, John (DE)
  Tuscaloosa, Ala., 1979
LANGHORNE, Jack (T)
  Uniontown, Ala., 1922-23-24
LANGDALE, Noah (T)
  Valdosta, Ga., 1940-41
LANGSTON, Griff (SE)
  Birmingham, Ala., 1968-69-70
LANIER, M. B. (B)
  Birmingham, Ala., 1905
LARY, Al (E) All-SEC
  Northport, Ala., 1948-49-50
LARY, Ed (E)
  Northport, Ala., 1949-50-51
LASLIE, Carney (T)
  Charlotte, N.C., 1930-31-32
LASSIC, Derrick (RB)
  Haverstrow, N.Y., 1989
LAUER, Larry (C)
  Wilmette, Ill., 1948-49-50
LAW, Phil (OT)
  Montgomery, Ala., 1971
LAWLEY, Lane (SE)
  Citronelle, Ala., 1970
LAYTON, Dale (E)
  Sylacauga, Ala., 1962
LAZENBY, K. J. (OT)
  Monroeville, Ala., 1974-75-76
LEACH, Foy (E)
  Siloam Springs, Ark., 1931-32-33
*LEE, Bill (T) All SEC
  Eutaw, Ala., 1932-33-34
LEE, Harry C. (G-LB)
  Birmingham, Ala., 1951-52-53-54
LEE, Mickey (FB)
  Enterprise, Ala., 1968-69
LEE, Shon (DB)
  Deatsville, Ala., 1985-86
LEETH, Wheeler (E)
  Boaz, Ala., 1941-42
LEGG, Murray (DB) All-SEC
  Homewood, Ala., 1976-77-78
LENOIR, David (DE-TE)
  Memphis, Tenn., 1987-88-89
LENOIR, E. B. "Mully"
  Marlin, Texas, 1917-18-19
LEON, Tony (G)
  Follansbee, W.Va., 1941-42
LETCHER, Marion (C)
  Shorter, Ala., 1893-94
LETT, Frank Montague (G)
  Good Hope, Ala., 1901-02
LEWIS, Al (G)
  Covington, Ky., 1961-62-63
LEWIS, Butch (C)
  Mobile, Ala., 1985-87-88
LEWIS, Tommy (FB)
  Greenville, Ala., 1951-52-53
LEWIS, Walter (QB) All-SEC
  Brewton, Ala., 1980-81-82-83

LITTLE, Poc (FB)
Birmingham, Ala., 1920
LITTLE, W. G. (G)
Livingston, Ala., 1892-93
LOCKRIDGE, Doug (C)
Jasper, Ala., 1948-49
LOFTIN, James (HB)
Dothan, Ala., 1956-57
LOMBARDO, John (DB)
Birmingham, Ala., 1984
LONDON, Antonio (LB)
Tullahoma, Tenn., 1989
LONG, Charles Allen (B)
Bessemer, Ala., 1913-14
LONG, Leon (HB)
Haleyville, Ala., 1929-30-31
LOPEZ, Alan (PK)
Dothan, Ala., 1987
LOVE, Henry Benton (G)
New Market, Ala., 1912
LOWE, Eddie (LB)
Phenix City, Ala., 1980-81-82
•LOWE, Woodrow (LB) All-SEC
Phenix City, Ala., 1972-73-74-75
LOWMAN, Joseph Allen (E)
Birmingham, Ala., 1916-17
LUMLEY, Wade H. (RG)
Stanton, Ala., 1907
LUMPKIN, Billy Neal (HB)
Florence, Ala., 1955
LUNA, Robert K. "Bobby" (HB)
Huntsville, Ala., 1951-52-53-54
LUSK, Thomas Joseph III (DE)
Clarksville, Tenn., 1970-72
LUTZ, Bill (TE)
Tuscaloosa, Ala., 1987
LUTZ, Harold "Red" (E-K)
Clinton, Iowa, 1949-50-51
LYLES, Warren (NG) All-SEC
Birmingham, Ala., 1978-79-80-81
LYNCH, Curtis R. (E)
Wadley, Ala., 1953-54-55
LYON, Samuel Hamilton (T)
Meridian, Miss., 1934-35
•LYONS, Martin A. "Marty" (DT)
All-SEC
St. Petersburg, Fla., 1977-78

M
MACHTOLFF, Jack (C)
Sheffield, Ala. 1937
MADDOX, Sam H. (TE)
Orlando, Fla., 1976-77
MALCOLM, Charles (FB)
Birmingham, Ala., 1952
MALLARD, James (SE)
Tampa, Fla., 1980
•MANCHA, Vaughn (C) All-SEC
Birmingham, Ala., 1944-45-46-47
•MANGUM, John (DB) All-SEC
Magee, Miss., 1986-87-88-89
MANLEY, Harold (E)
Winfield, Ala., 1950-51
MANN, Frank (K)
Birmingham, Ala., 1968-69-70
MANNING, Thomas (C)
Talladega, Ala., 1910-11
MARCELLO, Jerry (DB)
McKeesport, Pa., 1973
MARCUS, Van J. (T)
Birmingham, Ala., 1950-51-52
MARDINI, Georges (PK)
Damascus, Syria, 1980

MARLOW, Bobby (HB) All-SEC
Troy, Ala., 1950-51-52
MARKS, Keith (SE)
Tuscaloosa, Ala., 1979-82
MARR, Charles (G) All-SEC
Pine Bluff, Ark., 1933-34
MARSH, Griffith (QB)
Birmingham, Ala., 1913-14-15
MARSH, William "Bill" (LH)
Birmingham, Ala., 1915-16
MARSHALL, Fred H. (C)
Montgomery, Ala., 1970-71
MARTIN, Darrell (T)
Blountsville, Ala., 1987
MARTIN, Gary (HB)
Dothan, Ala., 1961-62-63
MARTIN, Kenny (FB)
Hemet, Calif., 1966-67
MASON, George L. (T)
Langdale, Ala., 1952-53-54
MAURO, John (DE)
South Bend, Ind., 1978-79-80
MAXWELL, Raymond Edward (OT)
Flat Rock, Ala., 1973-74-75
MAY, Walter (B)
Mobile, Ala., 1949
MAYFIELD, Dave (T)
Jacksonville, Fla., 1949-50
MAYNOR, E. W. (C)
Oneonta, Ala., 1915-16
MELTON, James "Bimbo" (HB)
Wetumpka, Ala., 1949-50-51
MERRILL, Walter (T)
Andalusia, Ala., 1937-38-39
MERRILL, William Hoadley (G)
Eufaula, Ala., 1910
MIKEL, Bobby (DE)
Ft. Walton Bch., Fla., 1976
MILLER, Andrew McMurray (C)
Nanafalia, Ala., 1914
MILLER, Floyd (T)
Oneonta, Ala., 1948-49
MILLER, Hugh (G)
Round Mountain, Ala., 1929-30
MILLER, John (G)
Hazelhurst, Miss., 1928-29-30
MILLER, Noah Dean (LB)
Oneonta, Ala., 1973
MIMS, Carl (HB)
Sylacauga, Ala., 1941
MIMS, Fred (G)
Birmingham, Ala., 1951-52
MITCHELL, David Dewey (LB)
Tampa, Fla., 1975-76-77
•MITCHELL, John (DE) All-SEC
Mobile, Ala., 1971-72
MITCHELL, Ken "Tank" (G)
Florence, Ala., 1964
MITCHELL, Lydell (LB)
Prichard, Ala., 1985-86-87
MITCHELL, Ripp (DB)
Mobile, Ala., 1989
MIZERANY, Mike (G) All-SEC
Birmingham, Ala., 1948-49-50
MOHR, Chris (P)
Thomson, Ga., 1985-86-87-88
MONTGOMERY, Greg (LB)
Macon, Ga., 1972-73-74-75
MONTGOMERY, Robert M. (DE)
Shelbyville, Ky., 1970
MONTGOMERY, Wm. Gabriel (T)
Birmingham, Ala., 1920-21

•MONSKY, Leroy (G) All-SEC
Montgomery, Ala., 1936-37
MOODY, Farley (B)
Tuscaloosa, Ala., 1912
MOODY, Wash (RG)
Tuscaloosa, Ala., 1906
MOONEYHAM, Marlin (FB)
Montgomery, Ala., 1962
MOORE, Harold (FB)
Chattanooga, Tenn., 1965-66
MOORE, Jimmy (E)
Anniston, Ala., 1928-29-30
MOORE, John (HB)
Montgomery, Ala., 1962
MOORE, Mal (QB)
Dozier, Ala., 1962
MOORE, Pete (FB)
Hopkinsville, Ky., 1968-69
MOORE, Randy (TE)
Montgomery, Ala., 1970-73
MOORE, Ricky (FB) All-SEC
Huntsville, Ala., 1981-82-83-84
MOORE, Robert "Bud" (E)
Birmingham, Ala., 1958-59-60
MOORER, Jefferson (G)
Evergreen, Ala., 1953-54
MORGAN, Ed (FB)
Hattiesburg, Miss., 1966-67-68
MORRISON, Duff (HB)
Memphis, Tenn., 1958-59-61
MORRISON, William (FB)
Selma, Ala., 1926
MORROW, Bob Ed (G)
Selma, Ala., 1934
MORROW, Hugh (QB)
Birmingham, Ala., 1944-45-46-47
MORROW, Hugh (B)
Birmingham, Ala., 1893
MORTON, Farris (E)
Sardis, Ala., 1962
MORTON, L. D. (E)
Birmingham, Ala., 1916
MOSELEY, Elliott (C)
Selma, Ala., 1960
MOSELEY, Frank "Chesty" (B)
Montgomery, Ala., 1931-32-33
MOSLEY, Herschel "Herky" (B)
Blytheville, Ark., 1937-38-39
MOSLEY, John (HB)
Thomaston, Ala., 1964-65-66
MOSLEY, Norman "Monk" (HB)
Blytheville, Ark., 1942-46-47
MOSLEY, Russ (HB)
Blytheville, Ark., 1942
MOSS, Stan (LE)
Birmingham, Ala., 1965-66-67
MOTT, Steve (C)
New Orleans, La., 1980-81-82
MOYLE, Lamar (C)
Decatur, Ala., 1934-35-36
MUDD, Joseph Paul (B)
Birmingham, Ala., 1908-09
MURPHY, Philip (HB)
Anniston, Ala., 1973
•MUSSO, Johnny (HB) All-SEC
Birmingham, Ala., 1969-70-71

Mc
MacAFEE, Ken (E)
North Easton, Mass., 1951
MacCARTEE, Allen Graham (HB)
Washington, D.C., 1922-23
McALPINE, Frank (FB)

Boligee, Ala., 1944
McBEE, Jerry (HB)
Birmingham, Ala., 1955
McCAIN, George (HB)
Clanton, Ala., 1950-51
McCANTS, A. G. (RH)
Meridian, Miss., 1892-94
•McCANTS, Keith (LB) All-SEC
Mobile, Ala., 1988-89
McCLENDON, Frankie (T)
Guntersville, Ala., 1962-63-64
McCLINTOCK, Graham (E)
Laurel, Miss., 1925-27
McCOLLOUGH, Gaylon (C)
Enterprise, Ala., 1962-63-64
McCOMBS, Eddie (OT)
Birmingham, Ala., 1978-79-80
McCONVILLE, John (E)
Wheeling, W.Va., 1944
McCORQUODALE, John C. (LT)
Salitpa, Ala., 1902
McCORVERY, Gessner T. (B)
University, Ala., 1900-01
McCRARY, Tom (DT)
Scottsboro, Ala., 1982-83-84
McDONALD, James T. (T)
Sylacauga, Ala., 1927
McDOWELL, Holt Andrews (B)
Ensley, Ala., 1911-12
McELROY, Alan (PK)
Tuscaloosa, Ala., 1978-79
McGAHEY, T. A. "Son" (T)
Columbus, Miss., 1934-35
McGEE, Barry (OG)
Birmingham, Ala., 1975
McGILL, Larry (HB)
Panama City, Fla., 1962-63
McGRIFE, Curtis (MG)
Cottonwood, Ala., 1977-78-79
McINTOSH, John (OG)
Dalton, Ga., 1983-84-85
McINTYRE, David (OT)
Columbus, Miss., 1975-76
McKEWEN, Jack, (T)
Birmingham, Ala., 1941-42
McKEWEN, Jack II (T)
Birmingham, Ala., 1968
McKINNEY, Robert B., Jr. (DB)
All-SEC, Mobile, Ala., 1970-71-72
McKOSKY, Ted (G)
Monessen, Pa., 1941-42-46
McLAIN, Rick (TE)
Walnut Hill, Fla., 1974-75
McLEOD, Ben (DE)
Pensacola, Fla., 1965
McLEOD, Ben W. (HB)
Leeksville, Ala., 1934-35-36
McMAKIN, David (DB) All-SEC
Tucker, Ga., 1971-72-73
McMILLIAN, Thomas E. (E)
Brewton, Ala., 1933
•McNEAL, Don (DB) All-SEC
McCullough, Ala., 1977-78-79
McQUEEN, Mike (OT)
Enterprise, Ala., 1981-82-83
McRAE, Scott (LB)
Huntsville, Ala., 1982-83-84
McRIGHT, Ralph (HB)
Mt. Hope, Ala., 1928-29-30
McWHORTER, Jim (QB)
Athens, Ga., 1942

N

*NAMATH, Joe Willie (QB) All-SEC
Beaver Falls, Pa., 1962-63-64
NATHAN, R. L. (QB)
Sheffield, Ala., 1912-13
NATHAN, Tony (HB)
Birmingham, Ala., 1975-76-77-78
NEAL, Rick (TE)
Birmingham, Ala., 1976-77-78
*NEIGHBORS, Billy (T) All-SEC
Northport. Ala., 1959-60-61
NEIGHBORS, Sidney (T)
Northport, Ala., 1956-57
*NEIGHBORS, Wes (C) All-SEC
Huntsville, Ala., 1983-84-85-86
NELSON, Benny (HB) All-SEC
Huntsville, Ala., 1961-62-63
NELSON, Charles (QB)
Opp, Ala., 1956
NELSON, Jimmy (HB) All-SEC
Live Oak, Fla., 1939-40-41
NELSON, Rod (K)
Birmingham, Ala., 1974-75-76
NESMITH, C. C. (HB)
Vernon, Ala., 1892-93-94
NEWBERRY, Gene (TE)
Blytheville, Ark., 1988
NEWMAN, Hal (E)
Birmingham, Ala., 1938-39
*NEWSOME, Ozzie (SE) All-SEC
Leighton, Ala., 1974-75-76-77
NEWTON, Tom (E)
Birmingham, Ala., 1920-21-22
NICHOLS, Mike (SE)
Andalusia, Ala., 1988
NISBET, James "Bubba" (FB)
Bainbridge, Ga., 1934-35-36
NIX, Mark (RB)
Altoona, Ala., 1979-80-81
NOLAND, John Phillip
Tuscaloosa, Ala., 1917-18
NOOJIN, Augustus Young (B)
Gadsden, Ala., 1908
NOONAN, L. W. "Red" (FB)
Mobile, Ala., 1945-47-48-49
NORMAN, Haywood Eugene
"Butch" (DE)
Luverne, Ala., 1973
NORRIS, Lanny S. (DB)
Russellville, Ala., 1970-71-72
NORTHINGTON, M. P. (G)
Prattville, Ala., 1893

O

OATES, W. C. (G)
Montgomery, Ala., 1906
O'DELL, Richard (E)
Lincoln, Ala., 1959-60-62
O'CONNOR, J. T.
St. Louis, Mo., 1919-20
ODEN, Derrick (LB)
Tuscaloosa, Ala., 1989
ODOM, Ernest Lavont (E)
Birmingham, Ala., 1973
OGDEN, Ray (HB)
Jesup, Ga., 1962-63-64
OGILVIE, Morgan Oslin "Major"
(RB) All-SEC
Birmingham, Ala., 1977-78-79-80
OLENSKI, Mitchell (T)
Vestal, N.Y., 1942
O'LINGER, John (C)
Scottsboro, Ala., 1959-60-61

OLIVER, William (HB)
Panola, Ala., 1952-53
OLIVER, William "Brother" (DB)
Livingston, Ala., 1960-61
OLIVER, W. S. "Country" (B-T)
Panola, Ala., 1925
ORCUTT, Ben (RB)
Arlington Heights, Ill., 1981
O'REAR, Jack (QB)
Tarrant, Ala., 1974-76-77
OSER, Gary (C)
New Orleans, La., 1976
O'STEEN, Robert "Gary" (FB)
Anniston, Ala., 1957-58-59
O'SULLIVAN, Pat (LB) All-SEC
New Orleans, La., 1947-48-49-50
O'TOOLE, Mike (DB)
Palmerdale, Ala., 1982
OTTEN, Gary (OT)
Huntsville, Ala., 1983-84-86
OWEN, Wayne (LB)
Gadsden, Ala., 1966-67-68
OWENS, Donald (E)
Memphis, Tenn., 1956-57
OZMINT, Lee (DB) All-SEC
Anderson, S.C., 1986-87-88-89

P

PAGET, Manchester (LG)
El Paso, Texas, 1920
PALMER, Dale (LB)
Calera, Ala., 1978
PALMER, Thomas W. (B)
Tuscaloosa, Ala., 1908-09
PAPIAS, Julius (HB)
Hammond, Ind., 1941
PAPPAS, Peter George (SE)
Birmingham, Ala., 1973
PARKER, Calvin (DE)
Eastoboga, Ala., 1976-78
*PARKHOUSE, Robin (DE) All-SEC
Orlando, Fla., 1969-70-71
PARSONS, Don (G)
Houston, Texas, 1958
PATRICK, Linnie (RB)
Jasper, Ala., 1980-81-82-83
PATTERSON, Jim (OG)
Annandale, Va., 1971
PATTERSON, Steve (OG)
Omaha, Neb., 1972-73-74
PATTERSON, Trent (OG)
Syracuse, N.Y., 1987-88-89
PATTON, David Dane (C)
Coatopa, Ala., 1898-99-1900
PATTON, James "Jap" (E)
Tuscumbia, Ala., 1959-61
PATTON, William Pratt (E)
Fosters, Ala., 1906-07
PAYNE, Brian (LB)
Enterprise, Ala., 1989
PAYNE, Greg (SE)
Montgomery, Ala., 1984-87-88
PAYNE, Leslie (T)
Bay Minette, Ala., 1925-26-27
PEARCE, Clarke "Babe" (T)
Winfield, Ala., 1926-27-28
PEARL, James H. (E)
Connellsville, Pa., 1944
PEAVY, John Roberts (T)
Thomasville, Ala., 1902-03-04
PEEBLES, Emory Bush (QB)
Vienna, Ala., 1908-10
PELL, Charles B. (T)
Albertville, Ala., 1960-61-62

PEPPER, Raymond W. (FB)
Albany, Ala., 1926-27
*PERKINS, Ray (E) All-SEC
Petal, Miss., 1964-65-66
PERRIN, Benny (DB)
Decatur, Ala., 1980-81
PERRY, Anthony "Lefty" (DB)
Hazel Green, Ala., 1973
PERRY, Claude (T)
Jasper, Ala., 1925
PETER, G. F.
Brierfield, Ala., 1892
PETERS, William E. (G)
Hammond, Ind., 1936-37
PETTEE, Robert A. "Bob" (G)
Bradenton, Fla., 1960-61-62
PETTUS, Gordon (HB)
Birmingham, Ala., 1945-46-48
PHARO, Edward (FB)
Birmingham, Ala., 1952-56
PHILLIPS, Gary (G)
Dothan, Ala., 1958-59-60
PICKETT, Darryl (LB)
Montgomery, Ala., 1988-89
PICKHARD, Frederick (T) All-SC
Mobile, Ala., 1926-27
PIERCE, Billy (DB)
Crossett, Ark., 1983-84
PIPER, Billy (HB)
Poplar Bluff, Mo., 1960-62-63
*PITTS, Mike (DE) All-SEC
Baltimore, Md., 1979-80-81-82
PITTMAN, Alex Noel (LB)
New Orleans, La., 1970
PIVER, Mike (LB)
Chapel Hill, N.C. 1989
PIZZITOLA, Alan (DB) All-SEC
Birmingham, Ala., 1973-74-75
POOLE, John Paul (E)
Florence, Ala., 1955-58
POPE, Herman "Buddy" (OT)
Bradenton, Fla., 1973-74-75
POTTS, Douglas (G)
Evergreen, Ala., 1954-55-56
POWE, Frank Houston (E)
Talladega, Ala., 1899-1900-01
POWELL, Harold Mustin (T)
Birmingham, Ala., 1910-11
PRATT, Derrill B. (E)
Pell City, Ala., 1908-09
PRATT, G. W. (G)
Pell City, Ala., 1907-09
PRATT, Henry Merrill (RG)
Prattville, Ala., 1892-93-94
PRESTWOOD, Thomas A. (DE)
Chattanooga, Tenn., 1975
PROPST, Clyde "Shorty" (C)
Ohatchee, Ala., 1922-23-24
PROPST, Eddie (DB)
Birmingham, Ala., 1966-67
PRITCHETT, James P. (E)
Birmingham, Ala., 1955
PROM, John (G)
Jacksonville, Fla., 1951
PRUDHOMME, John Mark (DB)
Memphis, Tenn., 1973-74-75
PUGH, Ed (TE)
Opelika, Ala., 1984
PUGH, George (TE)
Montgomery, Ala., 1972-73-74-75
PUGH, Keith Harrison (SE)
Evergreen, Ala., 1977-78-79

Q

QUICK, Cecil Van (DE)
Collins, Miss., 1970

R

RABURN, Gene (FB)
Jasper, Ala., 1965-66
RADFORD, James Solomon (T)
Hartford, Ala., 1935-36
RAINES, Billy (G)
Moulton, Ala., 1956-57
RAINES, James Patrick (C)
Montgomery, Ala., 1970-71-72
RAINES, Vaughn Michael (DT),
All-SEC
Montgomery, Ala., 1972-73
RAMIL, Mike (DT)
Corona, Calif., 1988-89
RANGER, George (SE)
Meridian, Miss., 1968-69-70
RANKIN, Carlton (QB)
Piedmont, Ala., 1962
*RAST, Holt (E) All-SEC
Birmingham, Ala., 1939-40-41
*RAY, David (SE-K) All-SEC
Phenix City, Ala., 1964-65
RAYAM, Thomas (DT)
Orlando, Fla., 1987-88
REAVES, Pete (G)
Bessemer, Ala., 1958
REDDEN, Guy (G)
Sulligent, Ala., 1904-05
REDDEN, Jake (G)
Vernon, Ala., 1937-38
REED, Wayne (Mgr.) 1981
REIDY, Thomas (LHB)
Boston, Mass., 1907-08
REILLY, Mike (DG)
Mobile, Ala, 1966-67-68
REITZ, John David (DE-OT)
Morristown, Tenn., 1965-66-67
REESE, Kenny (HB)
El Dorado, Ark., 1942
RHOADS, Wayne R. (DE)
Jackson, Miss., 1969-70
RHODEN, Steve (K)
Red Bay, Ala., 1981
RHODES, D. Wayne, Jr. (DB)
All-SEC, Decatur, Ga., 1973-74-75
RICE, William J. "Bill" (E)
Troy, Ala., 1959-60-61
RICH, Jerry (HB)
Attalla, Ala., 1959
RICHARDSON, Greg (WR)
Mobile, Ala., 1983-84-85-86
RICHARDSON, Jesse (G)
Philadelphia, Pa., 1950-51-52
RICHARDSON, Ron (DB)
Columbus, Ga., 1971
RICHARDSON, Todd (DB-WR)
Syracuse, N.Y., 1986-87-88
RICHARDSON, W. E. (HB)
Jasper, Ala., 1959-60-61
RICHESON, George (T)
Russellville, Ala., 1942
RICHESON, Ray (T)
Russellville, Ala., 1946-47-48
RIDDLE, Charles D. (C)
Talladega, Ala., 1912-13
RIDGEWAY, Danny Howard (K)
Fyffe, Ala., 1973-74-75
*RILEY, Joe (HB) All-SEC
Dothan, Ala., 1934-35-36

RILEY, Mike (DB)
Corvallis, Ore., 1974
RIPPETOE, Benny (QB)
Greenville, Tenn., 1971
ROBBINS, Joe (C)
Opp, Ala., 1978-79-80
ROBERTS, James "Babs" (E)
Blytheville, Ark., 1940-42
ROBERTS, Johnny (FB)
Birmingham, Ala.,1937
ROBERTS, Kenneth (C)
Anniston, Ala., 1956-57-58
ROBERTS, Larry (DT)
Dothan, Ala., 1982-83-84-85
ROBERTS, Rob (C)
Birmingham, Ala., 1984-85
ROBERTSON, James (HB)
Scottsboro, Ala., 1944-45-46
ROBERTSON, Ronald Dale (LB)
Signal Mtn., Tenn., 1973-74
ROBINETTE, Chris (OG)
Enterprise, Ala., 1988-89
ROBINSON, Carlos (FB)
Enterprise, Ala., 1986-87
ROBINSON, Freddie (DB) All-SEC
Mobile, Ala., 1983-84-85-86
ROCKWELL, Bragg (OLB)
Daphne, Ala., 1989
ROCKWELL, Randy (OLB)
Daphne, Ala., 1984-85-86-87
RODDAM, J. D. (HB)
Pinson, Ala., 1949
RODDAM, Ronnie (C)
Birmingham, Ala., 1968-69
RODRIGUEZ, Mike (MG)
Melbourne, Fla., 1981-82-83
ROGERS, Eddie Bo (LB)
Bessemer, Ala., 1966-67
ROGERS, Isaac "Ike" (RT)
Vina, Ala., 1916-17-18-19
ROGERS, John David (OG) All-SEC
Montgomery, Ala., 1972-73-74
ROGERS, O'Neal (B)
Russellville, Ala., 1927
ROGERS, Richard (OG)
Boise, Idaho, 1973
ROHRDANZ, Clarence (FB)
Harvey, Ind., 1935
RONSONET, Norbie (E)
Biloxi, Miss., 1958-59-60
ROOT, Steve (LB)
Indio, Calif., 1971
ROPER, Todd (LB)
Snellville, Ga., 1983-84-85
•ROSE, Larry (OT) All-SEC
Gadsden, Ala., 1985-86-87-88
ROSENFIELD, David (HB)
Ensley, Ala., 1925-26
ROSENFIELD, Max (QB)
Birmingham, Ala., 1920-21
ROSSER, Jimmy Lynn (OT)
Birmingham, Ala., 1969-70-71
ROUZIE, Jefferson Carr (LB)
Jacksonville, Fla., 1970-71-73
ROWAN, Robert "Robby" (DB)
Huntsville, Ala., 1972
ROWE, Harry (RG)
Elba, Ala., 1919
ROWELL, Terry (DT)
Heidelberg, Miss., 1969-70-71
RUFFIN, Larry Joe (OG)
Fayette, Ala., 1973-74-75

RUMBLEY, Roy (OG)
Moss Point, Miss., 1981-82
RUSHTON, Derrick (DT)
Mobile, Ala., 1986-88-89
RUSSELL, Lamonde (TE-SE)
All SEC, Oneonta, Ala., 1987-88-89
RUSTIN, Nathan (DT)
Phenix City, Ala., 1966-67
RUTLEDGE, Gary (QB)
Birmingham, Ala., 1972-73-74
RUTLEDGE, Jack (G)
Birmingham, Ala., 1959-60-61
RUTLEDGE, Jeffery R. (QB)
Birmingham, Ala., 1975-76-77-78
•RYBA, Jim (T)
Cicero, Ill., 1937
RYLES, Willie (DT)
Phenix City, Ala., 1985
S
SABO, Al (QB)
Los Angeles, Calif., 1940-41-42
SADLER, David A. (OG)
Cadiz, Ky., 1975-76-77
•SALEM, Ed (HB) All-SEC
Birmingham, Ala., 1948-49-50
SALEM, George (HB)
Birmingham, Ala., 1956
SALEM, George (OG)
Birmingham, Ala., 1986
SALEM, Jimbo (LB)
Birmingham, Ala., 1988
SALLS, Don (FB)
White Plains, N.Y., 1940-41-42
SAMFORD, Conner (RG)
Montgomery, Ala., 1916
•SAMPLES, Alvin (OG) All-SEC
Tarrant, Ala., 1967-68-69
SANDERS, Terry (K)
Birmingham, Ala., 1981-82-83-84
SANDERSON, Craig (WR)
Hamilton, Ala., 1988
SANFORD, Donald (G)
Parrish, Ala., 1930-31-32
SANFORD, Hayward "Sandy" (E-K)
Adona, Ark., 1936-37
SANSING, Walter (FB)
West Blocton, Ala., 1958
SARTAIN, Harvey (T)
Tuscaloosa, Ala., 1904
SASSER, Mike (DB)
Brewton, Ala., 1966-69
SAUL, Calhoun "Sunbeam" (G)
Montgomery, Ala., 1916
SAVAGE, Frank (RT)
Centre, Ala., 1892-93
SAWYER, Bubba (SE)
Fairhope, Ala., 1969-71
SCALES, Lou (FB)
Gadsden, Ala., 1941-42-45
SCHAMUN, Russ (SE)
Napa, Calif., 1974-76
SCHMISSRAUTER, Kurr (OT)
Chattanooga, Tenn., 1981-82-83
SCHUMANN, Eric (DB)
Blue Island, Ill., 1977
SCISSUM, Willard (OG)
Huntsville, Ala., 1981-82-83-84
SCOTT, Authur (T)
Jasper, Ala., 1957
SCOTT, James Alfred (E)
Thomasville, Ala., 1910
SCOTT, Randy (LB) All-SEC
Decatur, Ga., 1978-79-80

SCROGGINS, Billy (SE)
Jacksonville, Fla., 1967-68
SEARCEY, Bill (OG)
Savannah, Ga., 1978-80
SEAY, Buddy (HB)
Dadeville, Ala., 1969-70
SEBASTIAN, Mike (DT)
Columbus, Ga., 1978
SECRIST, Troy (WR)
Pensacola, Fla., 1988
SELF, Hal (QB)
Decatur, Ala., 1944-45-46
SELMAN, Tom (T)
Rome, Ga., 1950
SESSIONS, Tram (C)
Birmingham, Ala., 1917-19-20
SEWELL, J. Luke (QB)
Titus, Ala., 1919-20
SEWELL, Joe (HB)
Titus, Ala., 1917-18-19
SEWELL, Ray (QB)
Breman, Ga., 1976
SEWELL, Toxey
Titus, Ala., 1913-14
SHANKLES, Don (E)
Fort Payne, Ala., 1967
SHARPE, Jimmy (OG)
Montgomery, Ala., 1960-61-62
SHARPE, Joe F. (C)
Mobile, Ala., 1929-30-31
SHARPE, Sam (E)
Birmingham, Ala., 1940-41-42
SHARPLESS, John Waylon, Jr. (SE)
Elba, Ala., 1972-73
SHAW, Wayne (FB)
Tullahoma, Tenn., 1987-88-89
SHEALY, Steadman (QB) All-SEC
Dothan, Ala., 1977-78-79
SHELBY, Willie (HB) All-SEC
Purvis, Miss., 1973-74-75
SHEPHARD, Willie (LB)
Prichard, Ala., 1985-86-87-88
SHEPHERD, Joe Ruffus (G)
Tuscaloosa, Ala., 1935-36
SHERRILL, Jackie (FB-LB)
Biloxi, Miss., 1963-64-65
SHERRILL, Wm. Swift (E)
Athens, Ala., 1901-02-03
SHINN, Richard (DT)
Columbiana, Ala., 1980-82
SHIPP, Billy (T)
Mobile, Ala., 1949-52-53
SHIRLEY, Patrick Kyle
Wetumpka, Ala., 1910
SHOEMAKER, Perron "Tex" (E)
Birmingham, Ala., 1937-38-39
SHULA, Mike (QB) All-SEC
Miami, Fla., 1984-85-86
SHULTZ, Roger (C) All-SEC
Atlanta, Ga., 1987-88-89
SIDES, John "Brownie" (DT)
Tuskegee, Ala., 1966-67
SIMON, Kenny (RB)
Montgomery, Ala., 1979-81
SIMMONS, Jim (T)
Piedmont, Ala., 1962-63-64
SIMMONS, Jim (TE)
Yazoo City, Miss., 1969-70-71
SIMMONS, Malcolm (P)
Montgomery, Ala., 1981-82-83
SIMS, T. S. (LG)
Birmingham, Ala., 1905-06

SIMS, Wayne (G)
Columbiana, Ala., 1958-59
SIMS, Williams Comer (G)
Searight, Ala., 1931-32
SINGTON, Dave (T)
Birmingham, Ala.,1956-57-58
•SINGTON, Fred (T) All-SC
Birmingham, Ala., 1928-29-30
SINGTON, Fred, Jr. (T)
Birmingham, Ala., 1958-59
SISIA, Joseph (T)
Clark, N.J., 1960
SKELTON, Robert "Bobby" (QB)
Pell City, Ala., 1957-59-60
SKIDMORE, Jim (G)
Winchester, Tenn., 1928
SLAUGHTER, Derrick (DT)
Birmingham, Ala., 1985-86
SLEMONS, Billy (HB)
Orlando, Fla., 1937-38
•SLOAN, Steve (QB) All-SEC
Cleveland, Tenn., 1963-64-65
SLONE, Samuel Byron (P)
Lebanon, Ala., 1893-94-95-96
SMALLEY, Jack (T)
Tuscaloosa, Ala., 1951-52-53
SMALLEY, Jack, Jr. (LB)
Douglasville, Ga., 1976-77
SMALLEY, Roy (G)
Birmingham, Ala., 1950
SMILEY, Anthony (DE)
Birmingham, Ala., 1981-82-83
SMITH, Anthony (DT)
Elizabeth City, N.J., 1985-86-87
SMITH, Barry S. (C)
Anniston, Ala., 1977-78-79
SMITH, Ben (E)
Haleyville, Ala., 1929-30-31
SMITH, Bill (P)
Russellville, Ala., 1989
SMITH, Bobby (DB)
Fairhope, Ala., 1978-79
SMITH, Bobby (QB)
Brewton, Ala., 1956-57-58
SMITH, Dan (P)
Hayden, Ala., 1984
SMITH, David (QB)
Gadsden, Ala., 1986-87-88
SMITH, D. H. (LH)
Anniston, Ala., 1892-93
SMITH, Earl (E)
Haleyville, Ala., 1926-27-28
SMITH, Jack (G)
Hueytown, Ala., 1949
SMITH, James Sidney (C)
Warner Robins, Ga., 1974-75-76
SMITH, Joe (WR)
Mobile, Ala., 1983-84-85
SMITH, Mike (S-SE)
Gainesville, Fla., 1987-88-89
SMITH, Molton (G-T)
Birmingham, Ala., 1928-29
•SMITH, Riley H. (QB) All-SEC
Columbus, Miss., 1934-35
SMITH, Sammy Wayne (G)
Talladega, Ala., 1957
SMITH, Truman A. (HB)
University, Ala., 1903-04
SNEED, Byron (DE)
Alexandria, Va., 1988-89
SNODERLY, John M. (C)
Montgomery, Ala., 1952-53-56

SOMERVILLE, Tom (OG)
  White Station, Tenn., 1965-66-67
SOWELL, Brent (DT)
  Clearwater, Fla., 1983-84-85
SPEED, Elliott (C)
  Selma, Ala., 1948-49-50
SPENCER, Paul (FB)
  Hampton, Va., 1939-40
SPENCER, Tom (DB)
  Fairfax, Va., 1979
SPIVEY, Paul Randall (FB)
  Montgomery, Ala., 1972-73
SPRAYBERRY, Steve (OT) All-SEC
  Sylacauga, Ala., 1972-73
SPRINKLE, Jerrill (DB)
  Chamblee, Ga., 1980-81-82
SPRUIELL, Jerry (E)
  Pell City, Ala., 1960
•STABLER, Ken "Snake" (QB)
  All-SEC, Foley, Ala., 1965-66-67
STACY, Siran (RB)
  Geneva, Ala., 1989
STAFFORD, Angelo (TE)
  Prichard, Ala., 1986-87
STANFORD, Robert "Bobby" (OT)
  Albany, Ga., 1969-72
STAPP, Charlie (HB)
  Birmingham, Ala., 1935
STAPP, Laurien "Goobie" (QB-K)
  Birmingham, Ala., 1958-59-60
STARLING, Hugh (E)
  Troy, Ala. 1928-29
STARR, Bryan Bartlett (QB)
  Montgomery, Ala., 1952-53-54-55
STAPLES, John (G)
  Owensboro, Ky., 1942-46
STEAKLEY, Rod (SE)
  Huntsville, Ala., 1971
STEINER, Rebel (E) All-SEC
  Ensley, Ala., 1945-47-48-49
STEPHENS, Bruce (G) All-SEC
  Thomasville, Ala., 1965-66-67
STEPHENS, Charles (E)
  Thomasville, Ala., 1962-63-64
STEPHENS, Gerald (C)
  Thomasville, Ala., 1962
•STEPHENSON, Dwight (C)
  All-SEC
  Hampton, Va., 1977-78-79
STEPHENSON, Lovick Leonidas
  (RE), Birmingham, Ala., 1915-16
STEPHENSON, Riggs (FB) All-SC
  Akron, Ala., 1917-19-20
STEVENS, Wayne (E)
  Gadsden, Ala., 1966
STEWART, Arthur Walter (HB)
  Marion, Ala., 1901
STEWART, Robert (LB-FB)
  Ashford, Ala., 1987-88
STEWART, Vaughn (C)
  Anniston, Ala., 1941
STICKNEY, Enoch Morgan (B)
  University, Ala., 1912
STICKNEY, Frederick Grist (E)
  Tuscaloosa, Ala., 1901-02
STICKNEY, Ravis "Red" (FB)
  Key West, Fla., 1957-59
STOCK, Mike (HB)
  Elkhart, Ind., 1973-74-75
STOKES, Ralph Anthony (HB)
  Montgomery, Ala., 1972-74
STONE, G. E. (C)
  Mobile, Ala., 1894

STONE, Rocky (G)
  Birmingham, Ala., 1969
STONE, William J. (FB)
  Yukon, W.Va., 1953-54-55
STOWERS, Max Frederick (QB)
  Attalla, Ala., 1916-17
STRICKLAND, Charles "Chuck"
  (LB) All-SEC
  East Ridge, Tenn., 1971-72-73
STRICKLAND, Lynwood (DE)
  Alexander City, Ala., 1965
STRICKLAND, Vince (OT)
  College Park, Ga., 1989
STRICKLAND, William Ross (T)
  Birmingham, Ala., 1970
STRUM, Richard (HB)
  Biloxi, Miss., 1957
STURDIVANT, Raymond (B)
  Dadeville, Ala., 1906-07
STUTSON, Brian (DB)
  Birmingham, Ala., 1988-89
SUGG, Joseph Cullen (G)
  Russellville, Ala., 1938-39
SULLINS, John (LB)
  Oxford, Miss., 1988-89
SULLIVAN, Johnny (DT)
  Nashville, Tenn., 1964-65-66
•SURLAS, Tom (LB) All-SEC
  Mt. Pleasant, Pa., 1970-71
•SUTHER, John Henry (HB) All-SC
  Tuscaloosa, Ala., 1928-29-30
SUTTON, Donnie (SE)
  Blountsville, Ala., 1966-67-68
SUTTON, Mike (DB)
  Brewton, Ala., 1978
SUTTON, Vince (QB)
  LaGrange, Ga., 1984-87-88
SWAFFORD, Bobby "Hawk" (SE)
  Heflin, Ala., 1967-68
SWAIM, R. M. (G)
  Tuscaloosa, Ala., 1931-32
SWANN, Gerald (DB)
  Ashville, Ala., 1982
T
TAYLOR, Archie (B)
  Savannah, Ga., 1926-27
TAYLOR, J. K. (RH)
  Adkinville, N.C., 1914-15
TAYLOR, James E. (HB)
  Citronelle, Ala., 1973-74-75
TAYLOR, Paul (FB)
  Hartford, Ala., 1948
TEAGUE, George (CB)
  Montgomery, Ala., 1989
TERLIZZI, Nicholas (T)
  Upper Montclair, N.J., 1945
TEW, Lowell (FB)
  Waynesboro, Miss., 1944-45-46-47
THARP, Thomas "Corky" (HB)
  All-SEC
  Birmingham, Ala., 1951-52-53-54
THERIS, Bill (T)
  Mobile, Ala., 1948
THOMAS, Cliff (NG)
  Pearl, Miss., 1984-86
THOMAS, Daniel Martin (C)
  Clinton, Tenn., 1970
•THOMAS, Derrick (LB) All-SEC
  Miami, Fla., 1985-86-87-88
THOMAS, Efrum (CB) All-SEC
  Long Beach, Calif., 1989
THOMAS, Lester (FB)
  Birmingham, Ala., 1921

THOMAS, Ricky (S)
  Eglin AFB, Fla., 1983-84-85-86
THOMASON, Frank Boyd (E)
  Albertville, Ala., 1919
THOMPSON, Louis (DT)
  Lebanon, Tenn., 1965-66
THOMPSON, Richard "Dickey"
  (DHB) All-SEC
  Thomasville, Ga., 1965-66-67
THOMPSON, Wesley (T)
  Decatur, Ala., 1951-55-56
THORNTON, George (DT)
  Montgomery, Ala., 1988-89
TIDWELL, Robert Earl (C)
  Blountsville, Ala., 1903-04
•TIFFIN, Van (PK) All-SEC
  Red Bay, Ala., 1983-84-85-86
TILLMANN, Homer Newton
  "Chip" (OT)
  Panama City, Fla., 1976-77
TILLMAN, Tommy (E)
  Haleyville, Ala., 1952-53-54
TIPTON, Jim (T)
  Blytheville, Ark., 1936-37
TODD, Richard (QB) All-SEC
  Mobile, Ala., 1973-74-75
TOLLESON, Tommy (SE) All-SEC
  Talladega, Ala., 1963-64-65
•TRAMMELL, Pat (QB) All-SEC
  Scottsboro, Ala., 1959-60-61
TRAVIS, Timothy Lee "Tim" (TE)
  Bessemer, Ala., 1976-77-78-79
TRIMBLE, Wayne (QB)
  Cullman, Ala., 1964-65-66
TRIPOLI, Paul (DB)
  Liverpool, N.Y., 1983-84
TRODD, Paul (PK)
  Eufaula, Ala., 1981-83
TUCK, Ed (SE)
  Sacramento, Calif., 1984
TUCK, Floyd (B)
  Decatur, Ala., 1927
TUCKER, John (QB)
  Russellville, Ark., 1930-31
TUCKER, Michael V. (DB)
  Alexandria, Ala., 1975-76-77
TUCKER, Richard Glenn "Ricky"
  (DB) All-SEC
  Florence, Ala., 1977-78-79-80
TURNER, Craig (FB)
  Gaithersburg, Md., 1982-83-85
TURNER, Kevin (FB)
  Prattville, Ala., 1988-89
TURNER, Rory (DB)
  Decatur, Ga., 1984-85-87
TURNER, Steve (DT)
  Bessemer, Ala., 1987-88
TURPIN, John R. (FB)
  Birmingham, Ala., 1977-78
TURPIN, Richard "Dick" (DE)
  Birmingham, Ala., 1973-74-75
TUTWILER, Edward McGruder (B)
  Birmingham, Ala., 1898
TYSON, Adrian (NG)
  Mobile, Ala., 1983
U
UMPHREY, Woody (P)
  Bourbonnais, Ill., 1978-79-80
V
VAGOTIS, Chris (OG)
  Canton, Ohio, 1966
VALLETTO, Carl (E)
  Oakmont, Pa., 1957-58

VALLETTO, David (DB)
  Gulf Breeze, Fla., 1983-84
VANDEGRAAFF, Adrian V. (B)
  Tuscaloosa, Ala., 1912
VANDEGRAAFF, Hargrove (LHB)
  Tuscaloosa, Ala., 1913
•VANDEGRAAFF, W. T. "Bully"
  (T-FB)
  Tuscaloosa, Ala., 1912-13-14-15
VARNADO, Carey Reid (C)
  Hattiesburg, Miss., 1970
VAUGHANS, Cedric (SE)
  Montgomery, Ala., 1984
VEAZY, Louis (G)
  Alexander City, Ala., 1955
VERSPRILLE, Eddie (FB)
  Norfolk, Va., 1961-62-63
VICKERS, Doug (OG)
  Enterprise, Ala., 1981-82-83
VICKERY, Roy Leon (T)
  Charlotte, N.C., 1956
VINES, Jay (OG)
  Birmingham, Ala., 1978
VINES, Melvin (E)
  Bessemer, Ala., 1926-28-29
W
WADE, Steve (DB)
  Dothan, Ala., 1971-72
WADE, Tommy (DB)
  Dothan, Ala., 1967-68-79
WAGNER, Richard (OLB)
  Ft. Payne, Ala., 1983
WAITES, W. L. (HB)
  Tuscaloosa, Ala., 1938
WALKER, Bland, Jr. (C)
  Eutaw, Ala., 1957
WALKER, Erskine "Bubba" (HB)
  Ensley, Ala., 1931-32-33
WALKER, Hardy (OT)
  Huntsville, Ala., 1981-83-85
WALKER, Hilmon (E)
  Hattiesburg, Miss., 1936
WALKER, James E. (E)
  Holt, Ala., 1935
WALKER, M. P. (E)
  Birmingham, Ala., 1892
WALKER, Noojin (FB)
  Falkville, Ala., 1955
WALKER, Wayne D. (T)
  Martha, Tenn., 1944
WALKER, William Mudd (QB)
  Birmingham, Ala., 1892-94
WALL, Jeff (H)
  Birmingham, Ala., 1989
WALL, Larry "Dink" (FB)
  Fairfax, Ala., 1961-62-64
WALLS, Clay (HB)
  Bessemer, Ala., 1955-56-57
WARD, Alan (PK)
  Pensacola, Fla., 1987-89
WARD, Lorenzo (S)
  Greensboro, Ala., 1987-88-89
WARD, Wm. LaFayette (HB)
  Greensboro, Ala., 1904-05
WARREN, Derrick (TE)
  Panama City, Fla., 1989
WARREN, Erin "Tut" (E) All-SEC
  Montgomery, Ala., 1937-38-39
WASHCO, Gerard George (DT)
  West Orange, N.J., 1973-74-75
•WASHINGTON, Mike (DB)
  All-SEC
  Montgomery, Ala., 1972-73-74

155

WATFORD, Jerry (G) All-SEC
   Gadsden, Ala., 1950-51-52
WATKINS, David (DE)
   Rome, Ga., 1971-72-73
WATSON, Rick, (FB)
   Birmingham, Ala., 1974-75-76
WATSON, William C. (E)
   New Decatur, Ala., 1908
WATTS, Jimmy (DE)
   Gulf Breeze, Fla., 1981-82-83
WEAVER, Sam (E)
   Birmingham, Ala., 1928-29
WEBB, Steve (DE)
   Holt, Ala., 1988-89
WEEKS, George (E)
   Dothan, Ala., 1940-41-42
WEIGAND, Tommy (HB)
   Enterprise, Ala., 1968
WEIST, T. J. (WR)
   Bay City, Mich., 1987
WELSH, Clem (HB)
   Winchester, Ill., 1948
WERT, Thomas William (RT-FB)
   Birmingham, Ala., 1899
WESLEY, L. O. (QB)
   Guin, Ala., 1922-23
WESLEY, Wm. Earl "Buddy" (FB)
   Talladega, Ala., 1958-59-60
WHALEY, Frank (DE)
   Lineville, Ala., 1965-66
WHATLEY, James W. (T) All-SEC
   Alexander City, Ala., 1933-34-35
WHATLEY, Seaborn Thornton (B)
   Havana, Ala., 1906
•WHEELER, Wayne (SE) All-SEC
   Orlando, Fla., 1971-72-73
WHETSTONE, Darryl (DT)
   Montgomery, Ala., 1987
WHITAKER, Hulet (E)
   Guntersville, Ala., 1925
•WHITE, Arthur P. "Tarzan" (G)
   All-SEC
   Atmore, Ala., 1934-35-36
WHITE, Darryl (SE)
   Tuscaloosa, Ala., 1981-82
WHITE, Ed (E)
   Anniston, Ala., 1947-48-49
WHITE, Frank S., Jr. (FB)
   Birmingham, Ala., 1897-98-99
WHITE, Gus (MG)
   Dothan, Ala., 1974-75-76
WHITE, Jack (OG)
   Louisville, Miss., 1971
WHITE, Mike (OG)
   Decatur, Ga., 1983-84
WHITE, Tommy (FB)
   West Blocton, Ala., 1958-59-60
WHITEHURST, Clay (SE)
   Nashville, Tenn., 1984-85-86
WHITLEY, Tom (T) All-SEC
   Birmingham, Ala., 1944-45-46-47
WHITLOCK, Darin (C)
   Orlando, Fla., 1985-86
WHITMAN, Steven K. (FB)
   Birmingham, Ala., 1977-78-79
WHITMIRE, Don (G) All-SEC
   Decatur, Ala., 1941-42
WHITTLESLEY, C. S. (LG)
   Opelika, Ala., 1916-17
WHITWORTH, J. B. "Ears" (T)
   Blytheville, Ark., 1930-31
WICKE, Dallas (QB)
   Pensacola, Fla., 1938-39

WIESEMAN, Bill (G)
   Louisville, Ky., 1962-63
WILBANKS, Danny (FB)
   Tallassee, Ala., 1957
WILCOX, George Spigener (E)
   Montgomery, Ala., 1903-04
•WILCOX, Tommy (DB) All-SEC
   Harahan, La., 1979-80-81-82
WILDER, Ken (OT)
   Columbiana, Ala., 1968-69
WILDER, Roosevelt (FB)
   Macon, Ga., 1982
WILGA, Bob (G)
   Webster, Mass., 1951-52-53
WILHITE, Al (T)
   Tuscumbia, ala., 1949-50-51
WILKINS, Red (E)
   Bay Minette, Ala., 1961
WILKINSON, Everett (B-K)
   Prattville, Ala., 1909-10-12-13
WILKINSON, Vernon (DB)
   Enterprise, Ala., 1984-85-87
WILLIAMS, Billy (T)
   Lincoln, Ala., 1951-52
WILLIAMS, Charlie (FB)
   Bessemer, Ala., 1980
WILLIAMS, John Byrd (G)
   Decatur, Ala., 1965-66
WILLIAMS, Steven Edward (DB)
   Moline, Ill., 1969-70-71
WILLIAMSON, Richard (SE)
   Fort Deposit, Ala., 1961-62
WILLIAMSON, Temple (QB)
   Tuscaloosa, Ala., 1935
WILLIS, Perry (SE)
   Dadeville, Ala., 1967
WILLIS, Virgil "Bud" (E)
   Tifton, Ga., 1951-52
WILSON, Bobby (QB)
   Bay Minette, Ala., 1950-51-52
WILSON, George "Butch" (HB)
   Hueytown, Ala., 1960-61-62
WILSON, Jimmy (OG)
   Haleyville, Ala., 1961-62
WILSON, Steve (DB)
   Brundidge, Ala., 1985-86-87
WILSON, Woody (LB)
   Shawnee, Okla., 1987-88-89
WIMBLEY, Prince (SE)
   Miami, Fla., 1988-89
WINDHAM, Edward Price (B)
   Stone, Ala., 1897
WINGO, Richard Allen "Rich" (LB)
   Elkhart, Ind., 1976-77-78
•WINSLETT, Hoyt "Wu" (E)
   All-SEC
   Dadeville, Ala., 1924-25-26
WISE, Mack (HB)
   Elba, Ala., 1958
WOFFORD, Curtis (DB)
   Atlanta, Ga., 1984
WOFFORD, Lloyd (DT)
   Atlanta, Ga., 1984
WOOD, Bobby (DT)
   McComb, Miss., 1937-38
WOOD, Russ (DE)
   Elba, Ala., 1980-81-82
WOOD, William B (E)
   Guntersville, Ala., 1957
WOOD, William Dexter (SE)
   Ozark, Ala., 1970-71-72
WOODRUFF, Glen (TE)
   Aliceville, Ala., 1971

WORLEY, Butch (PK)
   Huntsville, Ala., 1986
WOZNIAK, John (G) All-SEC
   Fairhope, Pa., 1944-45-46-47
WRIGHT, Bo (FB)
   Prichard, Ala., 1985-86-87
WRIGHT, Steve (T)
   Louisville, Ky., 1962-63
WYATT, Willie (NG) All-SEC
   Gardendale, Ala., 1986-87-88-89
WYATT, W. S. (QB)
   New Decatur, Ala., 1903-04
WYHONIC, John (G) All-SEC
   Connorville, Ohio 1939-40-41
Y
YATES, Ollie Porter (QB)
   Hattiesburg, Miss., 1954
YELVINGTON, Gary (DB)
   Daytona Beach, Fla., 1973-74
YOUNG, Cecil Hugh (HB)
   Anniston, Ala., 1902-03
YOUNG, William A. (T)
   Pine Bluff, Ark., 1936
YOUNGLEMAN, Sid (T)
   Brooklyn, N.Y., 1952-53-54
Z
ZIVICH, George (HB)
   East Chicago, Ind., 1937-38
ZUGA, Mike (C)
   Newnan, Ga., 1987-88-89

•All-America

University of Alabama All-Time Football Record
Won 651, Lost 228, Tied 43–72.9 PCT.
(1892-1990)

1892—WON 2, LOST 2

56	B'ham H. Sch...	0	Birmingham	Nov. 11
4	B'ham A.C....	5	Birmingham	Nov. 12
14	B'ham A.C....	0	Birmingham	Dec. 10
22	Auburn	32	B'ham	Feb. 22, 1893
96		37		

1893—WON 0, LOST 4

0	B'ham A.C....	4	Tuscaloosa	Oct. 14
8	B'ham A.C....	10	Birmingham	Nov. 4
0	Sewanee	20	Birmingham	Nov. 11
16	Auburn	40	Montgomery	Nov. 30
24		74		

1894—WON 3, LOST 1

0	Mississippi	6	Jackson, Miss.	Oct. 27
18	Tulane	6	New Orleans	Nov. 3
24	Sewanee	4	Birmingham	Nov. 15
18	Auburn	0	Montgomery	Nov. 29
60		16		

1895—WON 0, LOST 4

6	Georgia	30	Columbus, Ga.	Nov. 2
0	Tulane	22	New Orleans	Nov. 16
6	LSU	12	B. Rouge, La.	Nov. 18
0	Auburn	48	Tuscaloosa	Nov. 23
12		112		

1896—WON 2, LOST 1

30	B'ham A.C....	0	Tuscaloosa	Oct. 24
6	Sewanee	10	Tuscaloosa	Oct. 31
20	Miss. State	0	Tuscaloosa	Nov. 14
56		10		

1897—WON 1, LOST 0

6	Tuscaloosa A.C.	0	Tuscaloosa	Nov. 13

1898—(NO TEAM)

1899—WON 3, LOST 1

16	Tuscaloosa A.C.	5	Tuscaloosa	Oct. 21
16	Montgomery A.C.	0	Tuscaloosa	Nov. 11
7	Mississippi	5	Jackson, Miss.	Nov. 24
0	N. Orleans A.C.	21	New Orleans	Nov. 25
39		31		

1900—WON 2, LOST 3

35	Taylor School	0	Tuscaloosa	Oct. 21
12	Mississippi	5	Tuscaloosa	Oct. 26
0	Tulane	6	Tuscaloosa	Nov. 3
5	Auburn	53	Montgomery	Nov. 17
0	Clemson	35	Birmingham	Nov. 29
52		99		

1901—WON 2, LOST 1, TIED 2

41	Mississippi	0	Tuscaloosa	Oct. 19
0	Georgia	0	Montgomery	Nov. 9
0	Auburn	17	Tuscaloosa	Nov. 15
45	Miss. State	0	Tuscaloosa	Nov. 16
6	Tennessee	6	Birmingham	Nov. 28
92		23		

1902—WON 4, LOST 4

57	B'ham H.S.	0	Tuscaloosa	Oct. 10
81	Marion Inst.	0	Tuscaloosa	Oct. 13
0	Auburn	23	Tuscaloosa	Oct. 18
0	Georgia	5	Birmingham	Nov. 1
27	Miss. State	0	Tuscaloosa	Nov. 8
0	Texas	10	Tuscaloosa	Nov. 11
26	Georgia Tech.	0	Birmingham	Nov. 27
0	LSU	11	Tuscaloosa	Nov. 29
191		49		

1903—WON 4, LOST 4

0	Vanderbilt	30	Nashville	Oct. 10
0	Miss. State	11	Columbus, Miss.	Oct. 16
18	Auburn	6	Montgomery	Oct. 23
0	Sewanee	23	Birmingham	Nov. 2
18	LSU	0	Tuscaloosa	Nov. 9
0	Cumberland U.	44	Tuscaloosa	Nov. 14
24	Tennessee	0	Birmingham	Nov. 26
60		114		

1904—WON 7, LOST 3

29	Florida	0	Tuscaloosa	Oct. 3
0	Clemson	18	Birmingham	Oct. 8
6	Miss. State	0	Columbus, Miss.	Oct. 15
17	Nashville U.	0	Tuscaloosa	Oct. 24
16	Georgia	5	Tuscaloosa	Nov. 5
5	Auburn	29	Birmingham	Nov. 12
0	Tennessee	5	Birmingham	Nov. 24
11	LSU	0	B. Rouge	Dec. 2
6	Tulane	0	N. Orleans	Dec. 3
10	Pensacola A.C.	5	Pensacola, Fla.	Dec. 4
100		62		

1905—WON 6, LOST 4

17	Maryville	0	Tuscaloosa	Oct. 3
0	Vanderbilt	34	Nashville	Oct. 7
34	Miss. State	0	Tuscaloosa	Oct. 14
5	Georgia Tech.	12	Atlanta	Oct. 21
0	Clemson	25	Columbia, S.C.	Oct. 25
36	Georgia	0	Birmingham	Nov. 4
21	Centre	0	Tuscaloosa	Nov. 9
30	Auburn	0	Birmingham	Nov. 18
6	Sewanee	42	Birmingham	Nov. 23
29	Tennessee	0	Birmingham	Nov. 30
178		113		

1906—WON 5, LOST 1

6	Maryville	0	Tuscaloosa	Oct. 6
14	Howard	0	Tuscaloosa	Oct. 13
0	Vanderbilt	78	Nashville	Oct. 20
16	Miss. State	4	Starkville, Miss.	Nov. 3
10	Auburn	0	Birmingham	Nov. 17
51	Tennessee	0	Birmingham	Nov. 29
97		82		

1907—WON 5, LOST 1, TIED 2

17	Maryville	0	Tuscaloosa	Oct. 5
20	Mississippi	0	Columbus, Miss.	Oct. 12
4	Sewanee	54	Birmingham	Oct. 21
0	Georgia	0	Montgomery	Oct. 25
12	Centre	0	Birmingham	Nov. 2
6	Auburn	6	Birmingham	Nov. 16
6	LSU	4	Mobile	Nov. 23
5	Tennessee	0	Birmingham	Nov. 28
70		64		

1908—WON 6, LOST 1, TIED 1

27	Wetumpka	0	Tuscaloosa	Oct. 3
17	Howard	0	Birmingham	Oct. 10
16	Cincinnati	0	Birmingham	Oct. 17
6	Ga. Tech.	11	Atlanta	Oct. 24
23	Chattanooga	6	Tuscaloosa	Oct. 31
6	Georgia	6	Birmingham	Nov. 14
9	Haskell Inst.	8	Tuscaloosa	Nov. 20
4	Tennessee	0	Birmingham	Nov. 26
108		31		

1909—WON 5, LOST 1, TIED 2

16	Union	0	Tuscaloosa	Oct. 2
14	Howard	0	Tuscaloosa	Oct. 9
3	Clemson	0	Birmingham	Oct. 16
0	Mississippi	0	Jackson, Miss.	Oct. 23
14	Georgia	0	Atlanta	Oct. 30
10	Tennessee	0	Knoxville	Nov. 13
5	Tulane	5	N. Orleans	Nov. 20
6	LSU	12	Birmingham	Nov. 25
68		17		

1910—WON 4, LOST 4

25	B'ham Inst.	0	Tuscaloosa	Oct. 1
26	Marion Inst.	0	Tuscaloosa	Oct. 8
0	Georgia	22	Birmingham	Oct. 15
0	Georgia Tech.	36	Tuscaloosa	Oct. 22
0	Mississippi	16	Greenville, Miss.	Nov. 5
0	Sewanee	30	Birmingham	Nov. 12
5	Tulane	3	N. Orleans	Nov. 19
9	Wash. & Lee	0	Birmingham	Nov. 24
65		107		

1911—WON 5, LOST 2, TIED 2

24	Howard	0	Tuscaloosa	Sept. 30
47	B'ham Southern	5	Birmingham	Oct. 14
3	Georgia	11	Tuscaloosa	Oct. 7
6	Miss. State	6	Columbus, Miss.	Oct. 21
0	Ga. Tech.	0	Atlanta	Oct. 29
35	Marion Inst.	0	Marion, Ala.	Nov. 4
0	Sewanee	3	Tuscaloosa	Nov. 11
22	Tulane	0	Birmingham	Nov. 18
16	Davidson	6	Birmingham	Nov. 30
153		31		

1912—WON 5, LOST 3, TIED 1

52	Marion Inst.	0	Tuscaloosa	Sept. 28
62	B'ham Southern	0	Tuscaloosa	Oct. 5
3	Ga. Tech.	20	Atlanta	Oct. 12
0	Miss. State	7	Aberdeen, Miss.	Oct. 18
9	Georgia	13	Columbus, Ga.	Oct. 26
7	Tulane	0	N. Orleans	Nov. 2
10	Mississippi	9	Tuscaloosa	Nov. 9
6	Sewanee	6	Birmingham	Nov. 16
7	Tennessee	0	Birmingham	Nov. 28
156		55		

1913—WON 6, LOST 3

27	Howard	0	Tuscaloosa	Sept. 27
81	B'ham Southern	0	Tuscaloosa	Oct. 4
20	Clemson	0	Tuscaloosa	Oct. 11
0	Georgia	20	Tuscaloosa	Oct. 18
26	Tulane	0	N. Orleans	Oct. 25
21	Miss. College	3	Jackson, Miss.	Nov. 1
7	Sewanee	10	Birmingham	Nov. 9
6	Tennessee	0	Tuscaloosa	Nov. 14
0	Miss. State	7	Birmingham	Nov. 27
188		40		

1914—WON 5, LOST 4

13	Howard	0	Tuscaloosa	Oct. 3
54	B'ham Southern	0	Tuscaloosa	Oct. 10
13	Ga. Tech.	0	Birmingham	Oct. 17
7	Tennessee	17	Knoxville	Oct. 24
58	Tulane	0	Tuscaloosa	Oct. 31
0	Sewanee	18	Birmingham	Nov. 7
63	Chattanooga	0	Tuscaloosa	Nov. 13
0	Miss. State	9	Birmingham	Nov. 26
3	Carlisle	20	Birmingham	Dec. 2
211		64		

*First season games played on Denny Field

157

*1915—WON 6, LOST 2

44	Howard	0	Tuscaloosa	Oct. 2
67	B'ham Southern	0	Tuscaloosa	Oct. 9
40	Miss. College	0	Tuscaloosa	Oct. 16
16	Tulane	0	Tuscaloosa	Oct. 23
23	Sewanee	10	Birmingham	Oct. 30
7	Ga. Tech.	21	Atlanta	Nov. 6
0	Texas	20	Austin, Tex.	Nov. 13
53	Mississippi	0	Birmingham	Nov. 25
250		51		

1916—WON 6, LOST 3

13	B'ham Southern	0	Tuscaloosa	Sept. 30
80	Sou. Univ.	0	Tuscaloosa	Oct. 7
13	Miss. Col.	7	Tuscaloosa	Oct. 14
16	Florida	0	Jacksonville, Fla.	Oct. 21
27	Mississippi	0	Tuscaloosa	Oct. 28
7	Sewanee	6	Birmingham	Nov. 4
0	Georgia Tech.	13	Atlanta	Nov. 11
0	Tulane	33	N. Orleans	Nov. 18
0	Georgia	3	Birmingham	Nov. 30
156		62		

1917—WON 5, LOST 2, TIED 1

7	Ohio Am. Corp.	0	Montgomery	Oct. 3
13	Marion Inst.	0	Tuscaloosa	Oct. 12
46	Miss. College	0	Tuscaloosa	Oct. 20
64	Mississippi	0	Tuscaloosa	Oct. 26
3	Sewanee	3	Birmingham	Nov. 3
2	Vanderbilt	7	Birmingham	Nov. 10
27	Kentucky	0	Lexington	Nov. 17
6	Cp. Gordon	19	Birmingham	Nov. 29
168		29		

1918—(NO TEAM)

1919—WON 8, LOST 1

27	B'ham Southern	0	Tuscaloosa	Oct. 4
49	Mississippi	0	Tuscaloosa	Oct. 11
48	Howard	0	Tuscaloosa	Oct. 18
61	Marion Inst.	0	Tuscaloosa	Oct. 24
40	Sewanee	0	Birmingham	Nov. 1
12	Vanderbilt	16	Nashville	Nov. 8
23	LSU	0	B. Rouge	Nov. 15
6	Georgia	0	Atlanta	Nov. 22
14	Miss. State	6	Birmingham	Nov. 27
280		22		

1920—WON 10, LOST 1

59	Sou. Mil. Aca.	0	Tuscaloosa	Sept. 25
49	Marion Inst.	0	Tuscaloosa	Oct. 2
45	B'ham Southern	0	Tuscaloosa	Oct. 9
57	Miss. College	0	Tuscaloosa	Oct. 16
33	Howard	0	Tuscaloosa	Oct. 23
21	Sewanee	0	Birmingham	Oct. 30
14	Vanderbilt	7	Birmingham	Nov. 6
21	LSU	0	Tuscaloosa	Nov. 11
14	Georgia	21	Atlanta	Nov. 20
24	Miss. State	7	Birmingham	Nov. 25
40	Case College	14	Cleveland, Ohio	Nov. 27
377		35		

1921—WON 5, LOST 4, TIED 2

34	Howard	14	Tuscaloosa	Sept. 24
27	Spring Hill	7	Tuscaloosa	Oct. 1
55	Marion Inst.	0	Tuscaloosa	Oct. 8
95	Bryson Tenn.	0	Tuscaloosa	Oct. 15
0	Sewanee	17	Birmingham	Oct. 22
7	LSU	7	N. Orleans	Oct. 29
0	Vanderbilt	14	Birmingham	Nov. 5
2	Florida	9	Tuscaloosa	Nov. 11
0	Georgia	22	Atlanta	Nov. 19
7	Miss. State	7	Birmingham	Nov. 24
14	Tulane	7	N. Orleans	Dec. 3
241		104		

1922—WON 6, LOST 3, TIED 1

110	Marion Inst.	0	Tuscaloosa	Sept. 30
41	Oglethorpe	0	Tuscaloosa	Oct. 7
7	Georgia Tech.	33	Atlanta	Oct. 14
7	Sewanee	7	Birmingham	Oct. 21
10	Texas	19	Austin, Tex.	Oct. 28
9	Pennsylvania	7	Philadelphia	Nov. 4
47	LSU	3	Tuscaloosa	Nov. 10
0	Kentucky	6	Lexington	Nov. 18
10	Georgia	6	Montgomery	Nov. 25
59	Miss. State	0	Birmingham	Nov. 30
300		81		

1923—WON 7, LOST 2, TIED 1

12	Union	0	Tuscaloosa	Sept. 29
56	Mississippi	0	Tuscaloosa	Oct. 6
0	Syracuse	23	Syracuse, N.Y.	Oct. 13
7	Sewanee	0	Birmingham	Oct. 20
59	Spring Hill	0	Mobile	Oct. 27
0	Georgia Tech.	0	Atlanta	Nov. 3
16	Kentucky	8	Tuscaloosa	Nov. 10
30	LSU	3	Montgomery	Nov. 16
36	Georgia	0	Montgomery	Nov. 24
6	Florida	16	Birmingham	Nov. 29
222		50		

1924—WON 8, LOST 1
SOUTHERN CONFERENCE CHAMPIONS

55	Union	0	Tuscaloosa	Sept. 27
20	Furman	0	Greenville, S.C.	Oct. 4
51	Miss. College	0	Tuscaloosa	Oct. 11
14	Sewanee	0	Birmingham	Oct. 18
14	Ga. Tech.	0	Atlanta	Oct. 25
61	Mississippi	0	Montgomery	Nov. 1
42	Kentucky	7	Tuscaloosa	Nov. 8
0	Centre Col.	17	Birmingham	Nov. 15
33	Georgia	0	Birmingham	Nov. 27
290		24		

1925—WON 10, LOST 0
NATIONAL CHAMPIONS
SOUTHERN CONFERENCE CHAMPIONS

53	Union College	0	Tuscaloosa	Sept. 26
50	B'ham Southern	7	Tuscaloosa	Oct. 2
42	LSU	0	B. Rouge	Oct. 10
27	Sewanee	0	Birmingham	Oct. 17
7	Georgia Tech.	0	Atlanta	Oct. 24
6	Miss. State	0	Tuscaloosa	Oct. 31
31	Kentucky	0	Birmingham	Nov. 7
34	Florida	0	Montgomery	Nov. 14
27	Georgia	0	Birmingham	Nov. 26
*20	Washington	19	Rose Bowl	Jan. 1, 1926
297		26		

1926—WON 9, LOST 0, TIED 1
NATIONAL CHAMPIONS
SOUTHERN CONFERENCE CHAMPIONS

54	Millsaps	0	Tuscaloosa	Sept. 24
19	Vanderbilt	7	Nashville	Oct. 2
26	Miss. State	7	Meridian, Miss.	Oct. 9
21	Georgia Tech.	0	Atlanta	Oct. 16
2	Sewanee	0	Birmingham	Oct. 23
24	LSU	0	Tuscaloosa	Oct. 30
14	Kentucky	0	Birmingham	Nov. 6
49	Florida	0	Montgomery	Nov. 13
33	Georgia	6	Birmingham	Nov. 25
*7	Stanford	7	Rose Bowl	Jan. 1, 1927
249		27		

1927—WON 5, LOST 4, TIED 1

46	Millsaps	0	Tuscaloosa	Sept. 24
31	So. Pres. U.	0	Tuscaloosa	Sept. 30
0	LSU	0	Birmingham	Oct. 8
0	Georgia Tech.	13	Atlanta	Oct. 15
24	Sewanee	0	Birmingham	Oct. 22
13	Miss. State	7	Tuscaloosa	Oct. 29
21	Kentucky	6	Birmingham	Nov. 5
6	Florida	13	Montgomery	Nov. 12
†6	Georgia	20	Birmingham	Nov. 27
7	Vanderbilt	14	Birmingham	Dec. 3
154		73		

1928—WON 6, LOST 3

27	Mississippi	0	Tuscaloosa	Oct. 6
46	Miss. State	0	Starkville, Miss.	Oct. 13
13	Tennessee	15	Tuscaloosa	Oct. 20
42	Sewanee	12	Birmingham	Oct. 27
0	Wisconsin	15	Madison, Wisc.	Nov. 3
14	Kentucky	0	Montgomery	Nov. 10
13	Georgia Tech.	33	Atlanta	Nov. 17
19	Georgia	0	Birmingham	Nov. 29
13	LSU	0	Birmingham	Dec. 8
187		75		

1929—WON 6, LOST 3

55	Miss. College	0	Tuscaloosa	Sept. 28
22	Mississippi	7	Tuscaloosa	Oct. 5
46	Chattanooga	0	Tuscaloosa	Oct. 12
0	Tennessee	6	Knoxville	Oct. 19
35	Sewanee	7	Birmingham	Oct. 26
0	Vanderbilt	13	Nashville	Nov. 2
24	Kentucky	13	Montgomery	Nov. 9
13	Georgia Tech.	0	Atlanta	Nov. 16
0	Georgia	12	Birmingham	Nov. 28
196		58		

1930—WON 10, LOST 0
NATIONAL CHAMPIONS
SOUTHERN CONFERENCE CHAMPIONS

43	Howard	0	Tuscaloosa	Sept. 27
64	Mississippi	0	Tuscaloosa	Oct. 4
25	Sewanee	0	Birmingham	Oct. 11
18	Tennessee	6	Tuscaloosa	Oct. 18
12	Vanderbilt	7	Birmingham	Oct. 25
19	Kentucky	0	Lexington	Nov. 1
20	Florida	0	Gainesville	Nov. 8
33	LSU	0	Montgomery	Nov. 15
13	Georgia	0	Birmingham	Nov. 27
*24	Wash. State	0	Rose Bowl	Jan. 1, 1931
271		13		

1931—WON 9, LOST 1

42	Howard	0	Tuscaloosa	Sept. 28
55	Mississippi	6	Tuscaloosa	Oct. 3
53	Miss. State	0	Meridian, Miss.	Oct. 10
0	Tennessee	25	Knoxville	Oct. 17
33	Sewanee	0	Birmingham	Oct. 24
9	Kentucky	7	Tuscaloosa	Oct. 31
41	Florida	0	Birmingham	Nov. 7
74	Clemson	7	Montgomery	Nov. 14
14	Vanderbilt	6	Nashville	Nov. 26
49	Chattanooga	0	Chattanooga	Dec. 2
370		57		

1932—WON 8, LOST 2

45	Southwestern	6	Tuscaloosa	Sept. 24
53	Miss. State	0	Montgomery	Oct. 1
28	George Wash.	6	Wash, D.C.	Oct. 8
3	Tennessee	7	Birmingham	Oct. 15
24	Mississippi	13	Tuscaloosa	Oct. 22
12	Kentucky	7	Lexington	Oct. 29
9	Virginia Tech	6	Tuscaloosa	Nov. 5
0	Georgia Tech.	6	Atlanta	Nov. 12
20	Vanderbilt	0	Birmingham	Nov. 24
6	St. Mary's	0	San Francisco	Dec. 5
200		51		

1933—WON 7, LOST 1, TIED 1
SEC CHAMPIONS

34	Oglethorpe	0	Tuscaloosa	Sept. 30
0	Mississippi	0	Birmingham	Oct. 7
18	Miss. State	0	Tuscaloosa	Oct. 14
12	Tennessee	6	Knoxville	Oct. 21
0	Fordham	2	New York	Oct. 28
20	Kentucky	0	Birmingham	Nov. 4
27	Virginia Tech	0	Tuscaloosa	Nov. 11
12	Georgia Tech.	9	Atlanta	Nov. 18
7	Vanderbilt	0	Nashville	Nov. 30
130		17		

*Indicates Bowl games
†First game in B'ham Mun. Stad. (Legion Field)
‡Indicates first night game
(N) Night game

1934—WON 10, LOST 0
NATIONAL CHAMPIONS
SEC CHAMPIONS

4	Howard	0	Tuscaloosa	Sept. 29
5	Sewanee	6	Montgomery	Oct. 5
1	Miss. State	0	Tuscaloosa	Oct. 13
3	Tennessee	6	Birmingham	Oct. 20
6	Georgia	6	Birmingham	Oct. 27
4	Kentucky	14	Lexington	Nov. 3
0	Clemson	0	Tuscaloosa	Nov. 10
0	Georgia Tech.	0	Atlanta	Nov. 17
4	Vanderbilt	0	Birmingham	Nov. 29
9	Stanford	13	Rose Bowl	Jan. 1, 1935
6		45		

1935—WON 6, LOST 2, TIED 1

7	Howard	7	Tuscaloosa	Sept. 28
39	Geo. Wash.	0	Wash., D.C.	Oct. 5
7	Miss. State	20	Tuscaloosa	Oct. 12
25	Tennessee	0	Knoxville	Oct. 19
17	Georgia	7	Athens, Ga.	Oct. 26
13	Kentucky	0	Birmingham	Nov. 2
33	Clemson	0	Tuscaloosa	Nov. 9
38	Georgia Tech.	7	Birmingham	Nov. 16
6	Vanderbilt	14	Nashville	Nov. 28
35		55		

1936—WON 8, LOST 0, TIED 1

34	Howard	0	Tuscaloosa	Sept. 26
32	Clemson	0	Tuscaloosa	Oct. 3
7	Miss. State	0	Tuscaloosa	Oct. 10
0	Tennessee	0	Birmingham	Oct. 17
13	Loyola, N.O.	6	N. Orleans	Oct. 24
14	Kentucky	0	Lexington	Oct. 31
34	Tulane	7	Birmingham	Nov. 7
20	Georgia Tech.	16	Atlanta	Nov. 14
14	Vanderbilt	6	Birmingham	Nov. 25
68		35		

1937—WON 9, LOST 1*
SEC CHAMPIONS

41	Howard	0	Tuscaloosa	Sept. 25
65	Sewanee	0	Birmingham	Oct. 2
20	S. Carolina	0	Tuscaloosa	Oct. 9
14	Tennessee	7	Knoxville	Oct. 16
19	Geo. Wash.	0	Wash., D.C.	Oct. 23
41	Kentucky	0	Tuscaloosa	Oct. 30
9	Tulane	6	N. Orleans	Nov. 6
7	Georgia Tech.	0	Birmingham	Nov. 13
9	Vanderbilt	7	Nashville	Nov. 25
0	California	13	Rose Bowl	Jan. 1, 1938
25		33		

1938—WON 7, LOST 1, TIED 1

19	Southern Cal.	7	Los Angeles	Sept. 24
34	Howard	0	Tuscaloosa	Oct. 1
14	NC State	0	Tuscaloosa	Oct. 8
0	Tennessee	13	Birmingham	Oct. 15
32	Sewanee	0	Tuscaloosa	Oct. 22
26	Kentucky	6	Lexington	Oct. 29
3	Tulane	0	Birmingham	Nov. 5
14	Georgia Tech.	14	Atlanta	Nov. 12
7	Vanderbilt	0	Birmingham	Nov. 24
149		40		

1939—WON 5, LOST 3, TIED 1

21	Howard	0	Tuscaloosa	Sept. 30
7	Fordham	6	New York	Oct. 7
20	Mercer	0	Tuscaloosa	Oct. 14
0	Tennessee	21	Knoxville	Oct. 21
7	Miss. State	0	Tuscaloosa	Oct. 28
7	Kentucky	0	Birmingham	Nov. 4
0	Tulane	13	N. Orleans	Nov. 11
0	Georgia Tech.	6	Birmingham	Nov. 18
39	Vanderbilt	0	Nashville	Nov. 30
101		53		

1940—WON 7, LOST 2

‡26	Spring Hill	0	Mobile (N)	Sept. 27
20	Mercer	0	Tuscaloosa	Oct. 5
31	Howard	0	Tuscaloosa	Oct. 12
12	Tennessee	27	Birmingham	Oct. 19
25	Kentucky	0	Lexington	Nov. 2
13	Tulane	6	Birmingham	Nov. 9
14	Georgia Tech.	13	Atlanta	Nov. 16
25	Vanderbilt	21	Birmingham	Nov. 23
0	Miss. State	13	Tuscaloosa	Nov. 30
166		80		

1941—WON 9, LOST 2
NATIONAL CHAMPIONS

47	SW Louisiana	6	Tuscaloosa	Sept. 27
0	Miss. State	14	Tuscaloosa	Oct. 4
61	Howard	0	Birmingham	Oct. 11
9	Tennessee	2	Knoxville	Oct. 18
27	Georgia	14	Birmingham	Oct. 25
30	Kentucky	0	Tuscaloosa	Nov. 1
19	Tulane	14	N. Orleans	Nov. 8
20	Georgia Tech.	0	Birmingham	Nov. 15
0	Vanderbilt	7	Nashville	Nov. 22
21	Miami (Fla.)	7	Miami (N)	Nov. 28
*29	Texas A&M	21	Cotton Bowl	Jan. 1, 1942
263		85		

1942—WON 8, LOST 3

54	SW Louisiana	0	Montgomery (N)	Sept. 25
21	Miss. State	6	Tuscaloosa	Oct. 3
27	Pensacola N.A.S.	0	Mobile	Oct. 10
8	Tennessee	0	Birmingham	Oct. 17
14	Kentucky	0	Lexington	Oct. 24
10	Georgia	21	Atlanta	Oct. 31
29	South Carolina	0	Tuscaloosa	Nov. 7
0	Georgia Tech.	0	Atlanta	Nov. 14
27	Vanderbilt	7	Birmingham	Nov. 21
19	Ga. N. Pre-Fit	35	Birmingham	Nov. 28
*37	Boston College	21	Orange Bowl	Jan. 1, 1943
246		97		

1943—(NO TEAM)
1944—WON 5, LOST 2, TIED 2

27	LSU	27	B. Rouge (N)	Sept. 30
63	Howard	7	Birmingham	Oct. 7
55	Millsaps	0	Tuscaloosa	Oct. 14
0	Tennessee	0	Knoxville	Oct. 21
41	Kentucky	0	Montgomery (N)	Oct. 27
7	Georgia	14	Birmingham	Nov. 4
34	Mississippi	6	Mobile	Nov. 11
19	Miss. State	0	Tuscaloosa	Nov. 18
*26	Duke	29	Sugar Bowl	Jan. 1, 1945
272		83		

1945—WON 10, LOST 0
SEC CHAMPIONS

21	Keesler A.A.F.	0	Biloxi, Miss.	Sept. 29
26	LSU	7	B. Rouge (N)	Oct. 6
55	South Carolina	0	Montgomery	Oct. 13
25	Tennessee	7	Birmingham	Oct. 20
28	Georgia	14	Birmingham	Oct. 27
60	Kentucky	19	Louisville	Nov. 3
71	Vanderbilt	0	Nashville	Nov. 17
55	Pensacola N.A.S.	6	Tuscaloosa	Nov. 24
55	Miss. State	13	Tuscaloosa	Dec. 1
*34	Southern Cal.	14	Rose Bowl	Jan. 1, 1946
430		80		

1946—WON 7, LOST 4

26	Furman	7	Birmingham	Sept. 20
7	Tulane	6	N. Orleans	Sept. 28
14	South Carolina	6	Columbia, S.C.	Oct. 5
54	SW Louisiana	0	Tuscaloosa	Oct. 12
0	Tennessee	12	Knoxville	Oct. 19
21	Kentucky	7	Montgomery	Oct. 27
0	Georgia	14	Athens, Ga.	Nov. 2
21	LSU	31	Baton Rouge	Nov. 9
12	Vanderbilt	7	Birmingham	Nov. 16
7	Boston College	13	Boston	Nov. 23
24	Miss. State	7	Tuscaloosa	Nov. 30
186		110		

1947—WON 8, LOST 3

34	Miss. Southern	7	Birmingham (N)	Sept. 20
20	Tulane	21	New Orleans	Sept. 27
7	Vanderbilt	14	Nashville	Oct. 4
26	Duquesne	0	Tuscaloosa	Oct. 11
10	Tennessee	0	Birmingham	Oct. 18
17	Georgia	7	Athens, Ga.	Oct. 25
13	Kentucky	0	Lexington	Nov. 1
14	Georgia Tech.	7	Birmingham	Nov. 15
41	LSU	12	Tuscaloosa	Nov. 22
21	Miami (Fla.)	6	Miami	Nov. 29
* 7	Texas	27	Sugar Bowl	Jan. 1, 1948
210		101		

1948—WON 6, LOST 4, TIED 1

14	Tulane	21	New Orleans	Sept. 25
14	Vanderbilt	14	Mobile	Oct. 2
48	Duquesne	6	Tuscaloosa (N)	Oct. 8
6	Tennessee	21	Knoxville	Oct. 16
10	Miss. State	7	Starkville	Oct. 23
0	Georgia	35	Birmingham	Oct. 30
27	Miss. Southern	0	Tuscaloosa	Nov. 6
14	Georgia Tech.	12	Atlanta	Nov. 13
6	LSU	26	Baton Rouge	Nov. 20
34	Florida	28	Tuscaloosa	Nov. 27
55	Auburn	0	Birmingham	Dec. 4
228		170		

1949—WON 6, LOST 3, TIED 1

14	Tulane	28	Mobile	Sept. 24
7	Vanderbilt	14	Nashville	Oct. 1
48	Duquesne	8	Tuscaloosa (N)	Oct. 7
7	Tennessee	7	Birmingham	Oct. 15
35	Miss. State	6	Tuscaloosa	Oct. 22
14	Georgia	7	Athens	Oct. 29
20	Georgia Tech.	7	Birmingham	Nov. 12
34	Miss. Southern	26	Tuscaloosa	Nov. 19
35	Florida	13	Gainesville	Nov. 26
13	Auburn	14	Birmingham	Dec. 3
227		130		

1950—WON 9, LOST 2

27	Chattanooga	0	Birmingham	Sept. 23
26	Tulane	14	New Orleans	Sept. 30
22	Vanderbilt	27	Mobile	Oct. 1
34	Furman	6	Tuscaloosa (N)	Oct. 13
9	Tennessee	14	Knoxville	Oct. 21
14	Miss. State	7	Tuscaloosa	Oct. 28
14	Georgia	7	Birmingham	Nov. 4
53	Miss. Southern	0	Tuscaloosa	Nov. 11
54	Georgia Tech.	19	Atlanta	Nov. 18
41	Florida	13	Jacksonville	Nov. 25
34	Auburn	0	Birmingham	Dec. 2
328		107		

1951—WON 5, LOST 6

89	Delta State	0	Montgomery (N)	Sept. 21
7	LSU	13	Mobile (N)	Sept. 29
20	Vanderbilt	22	Nashville (N)	Oct. 6
18	Villanova	41	Tuscaloosa (N)	Oct. 12
13	Tennessee	27	Birmingham (TV)	Oct. 20
7	Miss. State	0	Starkville	Oct. 27
16	Georgia	14	Athens	Nov. 3
40	Miss. Southern	7	Tuscaloosa	Nov. 10
7	Georgia Tech.	27	Birmingham	Nov. 17
21	Florida	30	Tuscaloosa	Nov. 24
25	Auburn	7	Birmingham	Dec. 1
263		188		

1952—WON 10, LOST 2

20	Miss. Southern	6	Montgomery (N)	Sept. 19
21	LSU	20	Baton Rouge (N)	Sept. 27
21	Miami	7	Miami (N)	Oct. 3
33	Virginia Tech.	0	Tuscaloosa	Oct. 11
0	Tennessee	20	Knoxville	Oct. 18
42	Miss. State	19	Tuscaloosa	Oct. 25
34	Georgia	19	Birmingham	Nov. 1
42	Chattanooga	28	Tuscaloosa	Nov. 8
3	Georgia Tech.	7	Atlanta (TV)	Nov. 15
27	Maryland	7	Mobile	Nov. 22
21	Auburn	0	Birmingham	Nov. 29
*61	Syracuse	6	Orange Bowl	Jan. 1, 1953
325		139		

*Indicates Bowl game
(N) Night game

1953—WON 6, LOST 3, TIED 3
SEC CHAMPIONS

19	Miss. Southern	25	Montgomery (N)	Sept. 18
7	LSU	7	Mobile (N)	Sept. 26
21	Vanderbilt	12	Nashville (N)	Oct. 3
41	Tulsa	13	Tuscaloosa	Oct. 10
0	Tennessee	0	Birmingham (TV)	Oct. 17
7	Miss. State	7	Tuscaloosa	Oct. 24
33	Georgia	12	Athens	Oct. 31
21	Chattanooga	14	Tuscaloosa	Nov. 7
13	Georgia Tech.	6	Birmingham	Nov. 14
0	Maryland	21	College Park	Nov. 21
10	Auburn	7	Birmingham	Nov. 28
*6	Rice	28	Cotton Bowl	Jan. 1, 1954
178		152		

1954—WON 4, LOST 5, TIED 2

2	Miss. Southern	7	Montgomery (N)	Sept. 17
12	LSU	0	Baton Rouge (N)	Sept. 25
28	Vanderbilt	14	Mobile (N)	Oct. 2
40	Tulsa	0	Tuscaloosa	Oct. 9
27	Tennessee	0	Knoxville	Oct. 16
7	Miss. State	12	Tuscaloosa	Oct. 23
0	Georgia	0	Birmingham	Oct. 30
0	Tulane	0	New Orleans	Nov. 6
0	Georgia Tech.	20	Atlanta (TV)	Nov. 13
7	Miami	23	Miami (N)	Nov. 19
0	Auburn	28	Birmingham	Nov. 27
123		104		

1955—WON 0, LOST 10

0	Rice	20	Houston (N)	Sept. 24
6	Vanderbilt	21	Nashville (N)	Oct. 1
0	TCU	21	Tuscaloosa	Oct. 8
0	Tennessee	20	Birmingham	Oct. 15
7	Miss. State	26	Tuscaloosa	Oct. 22
14	Georgia	35	Athens	Oct. 29
7	Tulane	27	Mobile	Nov. 5
2	Georgia Tech.	26	Birmingham	Nov. 12
12	Miami	34	Miami (N)	Nov. 18
0	Auburn	26	Birmingham	Nov. 26
48		256		

1956—WON 2, LOST 7, TIED 1

13	Rice	20	Houston (N)	Sept. 22
7	Vanderbilt	32	Mobile (N)	Oct. 6
6	TCU	23	Tuscaloosa	Oct. 13
0	Tennessee	24	Knoxville	Oct. 20
13	Miss. State	12	Tuscaloosa	Oct. 27
13	Georgia	16	Birmingham	Nov. 3
13	Tulane	7	New Orleans	Nov. 10
0	Georgia Tech.	27	Atlanta	Nov. 17
13	Miss. Southern	13	Tuscaloosa	Nov. 24
7	Auburn	34	Birmingham	Dec. 1
85		208		

1957—WON 2, LOST 7, TIED 1

0	LSU	28	Baton Rouge (N)	Sept. 28
6	Vanderbilt	6	Nashville (N)	Oct. 5
0	TCU	28	Ft. Worth (N)	Oct. 12
0	Tennessee	14	Birmingham	Oct. 19
13	Miss. State	25	Tuscaloosa	Oct. 26
14	Georgia	13	Athens	Nov. 2
0	Tulane	7	Mobile	Nov. 9
7	Georgia Tech.	10	Birmingham	Nov. 16
29	Miss. Southern	2	Tuscaloosa	Nov. 23
0	Auburn	40	Birmingham	Nov. 30
69		173		

1958—WON 5, LOST 4, TIED 1

3	LSU	13	Mobile (N)	Sept. 27
0	Vanderbilt	0	Birmingham (N)	Oct. 4
29	Furman	6	Tuscaloosa (N)	Oct. 11
7	Tennessee	14	Knoxville	Oct. 18
9	Miss. State	7	Starkville	Oct. 25
12	Georgia	0	Tuscaloosa	Nov. 1
7	Tulane	13	New Orleans (N)	Nov. 8
17	Georgia Tech.	8	Atlanta	Nov. 15
14	Memphis State	0	Tuscaloosa	Nov. 22
8	Auburn	14	Birmingham	Nov. 29
106		75		

1959—WON 7, LOST 2, TIED 2

3	Georgia	17	Athens	Sept. 19
3	Houston	0	Houston (N)	Sept. 26
7	Vanderbilt	7	Nashville (N)	Oct. 3
13	Chattanooga	0	Tuscaloosa	Oct. 10
7	Tennessee	7	Birmingham	Oct. 17
10	Miss. State	0	Tuscaloosa	Oct. 31
19	Tulane	7	Mobile (N)	Nov. 7
9	Georgia Tech.	7	Birmingham	Nov. 14
14	Memphis State	7	Tuscaloosa	Nov. 21
10	Auburn	0	Birmingham	Nov. 28
*0	Penn State	7	Liberty Bowl	Dec. 19
95		59		

1960—WON 8, LOST 1, TIED 2

21	Georgia	6	Birmingham (TV)	Sept. 17
6	Tulane	6	New Orleans (N)	Sept. 24
21	Vanderbilt	0	Birmingham (N)	Oct. 1
7	Tennessee	20	Knoxville	Oct. 15
14	Houston	0	Tuscaloosa	Oct. 22
7	Miss. State	0	Starkville	Oct. 29
51	Furman	0	Tuscaloosa	Nov. 5
16	Georgia Tech.	15	Atlanta	Nov. 12
34	Tampa	6	Tuscaloosa	Nov. 19
3	Auburn	0	Birmingham	Nov. 26
*3	Texas	3	Bluebonnet Bowl	Dec. 17
183		56		

1961—WON 11, LOST 0
NATIONAL CHAMPIONS
SEC CHAMPIONS

32	Georgia	6	Athens	Sept. 23
9	Tulane	0	Mobile (N)	Sept. 30
35	Vanderbilt	6	Nashville (N)	Oct. 7
26	N.C. State	7	Tuscaloosa	Oct. 14
34	Tennessee	3	Birmingham (TV)	Oct. 21
17	Houston	0	Houston (N)	Oct. 28
24	Miss. State	0	Tuscaloosa	Nov. 4
66	Richmond	0	Tuscaloosa	Nov. 11
10	Georgia Tech.	0	Birmingham	Nov. 18
34	Auburn	0	Birmingham	Dec. 2
*10	Arkansas	3	Sugar Bowl	Jan. 1, 1962
297		25		

1962—WON 10, LOST 1

35	Georgia	0	Birmingham (N)	Sept. 22
44	Tulane	6	New Orleans (N)	Sept. 28
17	Vanderbilt	7	Birmingham (N)	Oct. 6
14	Houston	3	Tuscaloosa	Oct. 13
27	Tennessee	7	Knoxville (TV)	Oct. 20
35	Tulsa	6	Tuscaloosa	Oct. 27
20	Miss. State	0	Starkville	Nov. 3
36	Miami	3	Tuscaloosa	Nov. 10
6	Georgia Tech.	7	Atlanta	Nov. 17
38	Auburn	0	Birmingham	Dec. 1
*17	Oklahoma	0	Orange Bowl	Jan. 1, 1963
289		39		

1963—WON 9, LOST 2

32	Georgia	7	Athens	Sept. 21
28	Tulane	0	Mobile (N)	Sept. 28
21	Vanderbilt	6	Nashville (N)	Oct. 5
6	Florida	10	Tuscaloosa	Oct. 12
35	Tennessee	0	Birmingham	Oct. 19
21	Houston	13	Tuscaloosa	Oct. 26
20	Miss. State	19	Tuscaloosa	Nov. 2
27	Georgia Tech.	11	Birmingham	Nov. 16
8	Auburn	10	Birmingham	Nov. 30
17	Miami	12	Miami (TV)	Dec. 14
*12	Mississippi	7	Sugar Bowl	Jan. 1, 1964
227		95		

1964—WON 10, LOST 1
NATIONAL CHAMPIONS
SEC CHAMPIONS

31	Georgia	3	Tuscaloosa (N)	Sept. 19
36	Tulane	6	Mobile (N)	Sept. 26
24	Vanderbilt	0	Birmingham (N)	Oct. 3
21	N.C. State	0	Tuscaloosa	Oct. 10
19	Tennessee	8	Knoxville	Oct. 17
17	Florida	14	Tuscaloosa	Oct. 24
23	Miss. State	6	Jackson (N)	Oct. 31
17	LSU	9	Birmingham	Nov. 7
24	Georgia Tech.	7	Atlanta	Nov. 14
21	Auburn	14	Birmingham (TV)	Nov. 26
*17	Texas	21	Orange Bowl (N)	Jan. 1
250		88		

1965—WON 9, LOST 1, TIED 1
AP NATIONAL CHAMPIONS
SEC CHAMPIONS

17	Georgia	18	Athens (TV)	Sept. 18
27	Tulane	0	Mobile (N)	Sept. 25
17	Mississippi	16	Birmingham (N)	Oct. 2
22	Vanderbilt	7	Nashville (N)	Oct. 9
7	Tennessee	7	Birmingham	Oct. 16
21	Florida State	0	Tuscaloosa	Oct. 23
10	Miss. State	7	Jackson (N)	Oct. 30
31	LSU	7	Baton Rouge (TV)	Nov. 6
35	South Carolina	14	Tuscaloosa	Nov. 13
30	Auburn	3	Birmingham	Nov. 27
*39	Nebraska	28	Orange Bowl (N)	Jan. 1
256		107		

1966—WON 11, LOST 0
SEC CHAMPIONS

34	La. Tech.	0	Birmingham (N)	Sept. 24
17	Mississippi	7	Jackson (N)	Oct. 1
26	Clemson	0	Tuscaloosa	Oct. 8
11	Tennessee	10	Knoxville	Oct. 15
42	Vanderbilt	6	Birmingham	Oct. 22
27	Miss. State	14	Tuscaloosa	Oct. 29
21	LSU	0	Birmingham	Nov. 5
24	South Carolina	0	Tuscaloosa	Nov. 12
34	Southern Miss.	0	Mobile	Nov. 26
31	Auburn	0	Birmingham (TV)	Dec. 3
*34	Nebraska	7	Sugar Bowl	Jan. 2, 1967
301		44		

1967—WON 8, LOST 2, TIED 1

37	Florida State	37	Birmingham (N)	Sept. 23
25	Southern Miss.	3	Mobile (N)	Sept. 30
21	Mississippi	7	Birmingham (TV)	Oct. 7
35	Vanderbilt	21	Nashville (N)	Oct. 14
13	Tennessee	24	Birmingham	Oct. 21
13	Clemson	10	Clemson	Oct. 28
13	Miss. State	0	Tuscaloosa	Nov. 4
7	LSU	6	Baton Rouge (N)	Nov. 11
17	So. Carolina	0	Tuscaloosa	Nov. 18
7	Auburn	3	Birmingham	Dec. 2
*16	Texas A&M	20	Cotton Bowl	Jan. 1, 1968
204		131		

1968—WON 8, LOST 3

14	Virginia Tech.	7	Birmingham (N)	Sept. 21
17	Southern Miss.	14	Mobile	Sept. 28
8	Mississippi	10	Jackson	Oct. 5
31	Vanderbilt	7	Tuscaloosa	Oct. 12
9	Tennessee	10	Knoxville (TV)	Oct. 19
21	Clemson	14	Tuscaloosa	Oct. 26
20	Miss. State	13	Tuscaloosa	Nov. 2
16	LSU	7	Birmingham	Nov. 9
14	Miami	6	Miami (N) (TV)	Nov. 16
24	Auburn	16	Birmingham	Nov. 30
*10	Missouri	35	Gator Bowl	Dec. 28
184		139		

1969—WON 6, LOST 5

17	Virginia Tech.	13	Blacksburg	Sept. 20
63	Southern Miss.	14	Tuscaloosa (N)	Sept. 27
33	Mississippi	32	Birmingham (N)	Oct. 4
10	Vanderbilt	14	Nashville (N)	Oct. 11
14	Tennessee	41	Birmingham	Oct. 18
38	Clemson	13	Clemson	Oct. 25
23	Miss. State	19	Jackson (N)	Nov. 1
15	LSU	20	Baton Rouge (N)	Nov. 6
42	Miami	6	Tuscaloosa	Nov. 15
26	Auburn	49	Birmingham	Nov. 29
*33	Colorado	47	Liberty Bowl	Dec. 13
314		268		

1970—WON 6, LOST 5, TIED 1

21	Southern Cal.	42	Birmingham (N)	Sept. 12
51	Virginia Tech.	18	Birmingham (N)	Sept. 19
46	Florida	15	Tuscaloosa	Sept. 26
23	Mississippi	48	Jackson (N) (TV)	Oct. 3
35	Vanderbilt	11	Tuscaloosa	Oct. 10
0	Tennessee	24	Knoxville	Oct. 17
30	Houston	21	Houston	Oct. 24
35	Miss. State	6	Tuscaloosa	Oct. 31
9	LSU	14	Birmingham (TV)	Nov. 7
32	Miami	8	Miami (N)	Nov. 14
28	Auburn	33	Birmingham (TV)	Nov. 28
*24	Oklahoma	24	Astro-Bluebonnet Bowl (N)	Dec. 31
334		264		

*Indicates Bowl game
(N) Night game

1971—WON 11, LOST 1
SEC CHAMPIONS

```
17  Southern Cal...  10  Los Angeles (N) ..Sept. 10
42  Southern Miss..   6  Tuscaloosa ......Sept. 18
38  Florida ........   0  Gainesville .....Sept. 25
40  Mississippi ....   6  Birmingham ......Oct. 2
42  Vanderbilt ....   0  Nashville (N) ....Oct. 9
32  Tennessee ....  15  Birmingham ......Oct. 16
34  Houston ......  20  Tuscaloosa ......Oct. 23
41  Miss. State ....  10  Jackson (N) ......Oct. 30
14  LSU ..........   7  Baton Rouge (N) (TV) ...Nov. 6
31  Miami ........   3  Tuscaloosa ......Nov. 13
31  Auburn .......   7  Birmingham (TV) Nov. 27
 6  Nebraska ......  38  Orange Bowl (N) ...Jan. 1
368                122
```

1972—WON 10, LOST 2
SEC CHAMPIONS

```
35  Duke .........  12  Birmingham (N) ..Sept. 9
35  Kentucky .....   0  Birmingham (N) .Sept. 23
48  Vanderbilt ....  21  Tuscaloosa (N) ...Sept. 30
25  Georgia .......   7  Athens ..........Oct. 7
24  Florida ........   7  Gainesville ......Oct. 14
17  Tennessee ....  10  Knoxville ......Oct. 21
48  Southern Miss..  11  Birmingham (N) ..Oct. 28
58  Miss. State ....  14  Tuscaloosa .....Nov. 4
35  LSU ..........  21  Birmingham (TV) Nov. 11
52  Virginia Tech..  13  Tuscaloosa ......Nov. 18
16  Auburn .......  17  Birmingham ....Dec. 2
13  Texas ........  17  Cotton Bowl .Jan. 1, 1973
406                150
```

1973—WON 11, LOST 1
UPI NATIONAL CHAMPIONS
SEC CHAMPIONS

```
66  California .....   0  Birmingham (N) .Sept. 15
28  Kentucky .....  14  Lexington ......Sept. 22
44  Vanderbilt ....   0  Nashville (N) ...Sept. 29
28  Georgia .......  14  Tuscaloosa ......Oct. 6
35  Florida .......  14  Gainesville .....Oct. 13
42  Tennessee ....  21  Birmingham (TV) .Oct. 20
77  Virginia Tech..   6  Tuscaloosa (N) ...Oct. 27
35  Miss. State ....   0  Jackson (N) .....Nov. 3
43  Miami ........  13  Tuscaloosa ......Nov. 17
21  LSU ..........   7  Baton Rouge (N) (TV) ...Nov. 22
35  Auburn .......   0  Birmingham (N) .Dec. 1
23  Notre Dame ....  24  Sugar Bowl (N) ...Dec. 31
477                113
```

1974—WON 11, LOST 1
SEC CHAMPIONS

```
21  Maryland .....  16  College Park ....Sept. 14
52  Southern Miss..   0  Birmingham (N) .Sept. 21
23  Vanderbilt ....  10  Tuscaloosa .....Sept. 28
35  Mississippi ....  21  Jackson (TV) ......Oct. 5
 8  Florida State ...   7  Tuscaloosa ......Oct. 12
28  Tennessee ....   6  Knoxville ......Oct. 19
41  TCU .........   3  Birmingham ....Oct. 26
35  Miss. State ....   0  Tuscaloosa .....Nov. 2
30  LSU ..........   0  Birmingham (TV) .Nov. 9
28  Miami ........   7  Miami (N) .....Nov. 16
17  Auburn .......  13  Birmingham (TV) Nov. 29
11  Notre Dame ....  13  Miami (N) ...Jan. 1, 1975
329                 96
```

1975—WON 11, LOST 1
SEC CHAMPIONS

```
 7  Missouri ......  20  Birmingham (N) ..Sept. 8
56  Clemson .....   0  Tuscaloosa (N) ...Sept. 20
40  Vanderbilt ....   7  Nashville ......Sept. 27
32  Mississippi ....   6  Birmingham .....Oct. 4
52  Washington ...   0  Tuscaloosa .....Oct. 11
30  Tennessee ....   7  Birmingham ....Oct. 18
45  TCU .........   0  Tuscaloosa .....Oct. 25
21  Miss. State ....  10  Jackson (N) .....Nov. 1
23  LSU ..........  10  Baton Rouge (N) ...Nov. 8
27  Southern Miss..   6  Tuscaloosa .....Nov. 15
28  Auburn .......   0  Birmingham (TV) Nov. 29
13  Penn. State ....   6  Sugar Bowl (N) ...Dec. 31
374                 72
```

1976—WON 9, LOST 3

```
 7  Mississippi ....  10  Jackson (N) .....Sept. 11
56  SMU ........   3  Birmingham ....Sept. 18
42  Vanderbilt ....  14  Tuscaloosa .....Sept. 25
 0  Georgia .......  21  Athens ..........Oct. 2
24  Southern Miss..   8  Birmingham .....Oct. 9
20  Tennessee ....  13  Knoxville (TV) ...Oct. 16
24  Louisville .....   3  Tuscaloosa .....Oct. 23
34  Miss. State ....  17  Tuscaloosa .....Oct. 30
28  LSU ..........  17  Birmingham ....Nov. 6
18  Notre Dame ....  21  South Bend (TV) .Nov. 13
38  Auburn .......   7  Birmingham ....Nov. 27
*36  UCLA ........   6  Liberty Bowl (N) .Dec. 20
327                140
```

1977—WON 11, LOST 1
SEC CHAMPIONS

```
34  Mississippi ....  13  Birmingham (N) .Sept. 10
24  Nebraska ......  31  Lincoln (TV) ....Sept. 17
24  Vanderbilt ....  12  Nashville ......Sept. 24
18  Georgia .......  10  Tuscaloosa .......Oct. 1
21  Southern Cal..  20  Los Angeles (TV) .Oct. 8
24  Tennessee ....  10  Birmingham ....Oct. 15
55  Louisville .....   6  Tuscaloosa .....Oct. 22
37  Miss. State ....   7  Jackson (N) .....Oct. 29
24  LSU ..........   3  Baton Rouge (TV) Nov. 5
36  Miami ........   0  Tuscaloosa .....Nov. 12
48  Auburn .......  21  Birmingham ....Nov. 26
*35  Ohio State ....   6  Sugar Bowl ...Jan. 2, 1978
380                139
```

1978—WON 11, LOST 1
AP NATIONAL CHAMPIONS
SEC CHAMPIONS

```
20  Nebraska ......   3  Birmingham (N) ..Sept. 2
38  Missouri ......  20  Columbia ......Sept. 16
14  Southern Cal..  24  Birmingham (TV) Sept. 23
51  Vanderbilt ....  28  Tuscaloosa ......Sept. 30
20  Washington ...  17  Seattle ..........Oct. 7
23  Florida .......  12  Tuscaloosa ......Oct. 14
30  Tennessee ....  17  Knoxville ......Oct. 21
35  Virginia Tech..   0  Tuscaloosa ......Oct. 28
35  Miss. State ....  14  Birmingham ....Nov. 4
31  LSU ..........  10  Birmingham (TV) Nov. 11
34  Auburn .......  16  Birmingham ....Dec. 2
*14  Penn. State ....   7  Sugar Bowl ...Jan. 1, 1979
345                168
```

1979—WON 12, LOST 0
AP & UPI NATIONAL CHAMPIONS
SEC CHAMPIONS

```
30  Georgia Tech...   6  Atlanta (TV) .....Sept. 8
45  Baylor ........   0  Birmingham (N) .Sept. 22
66  Vanderbilt ....   3  Nashville .....Sept. 29
38  Wichita State ..   0  Tuscaloosa .....Oct. 6
40  Florida ........   0  Gainesville .....Oct. 13
27  Tennessee ....  17  Birmingham ....Oct. 20
31  Virginia Tech..   7  Tuscaloosa .....Oct. 27
24  Miss. State ....   7  Tuscaloosa .....Nov. 3
 3  LSU ..........   0  Baton Rouge (N) .Nov. 10
30  Miami (Fla.) ...   0  Tuscaloosa (TV) .Nov. 17
25  Auburn .......  18  Birmingham ....Dec. 1
*24  Arkansas ......   9  Sugar Bowl ...Jan. 1, 1980
383                 67
```

1980—WON 10, LOST 2

```
26  Georgia Tech...   3  Birmingham .....Sept. 6
59  Mississippi ....  35  Jackson ........Sept. 20
41  Vanderbilt ....   0  Tuscaloosa .....Sept. 27
45  Kentucky .....   0  Birmingham ....Oct. 4
17  Rutgers .......  13  Meadowlands ....Oct. 11
27  Tennessee ....   0  Knoxville (TV) ...Oct. 18
42  Southern Miss..   7  Tuscaloosa .....Oct. 25
 3  Miss. State ....   6  Jackson .......Nov. 1
28  LSU ..........   7  Tuscaloosa .....Nov. 8
 0  Notre Dame ....   7  Birmingham (TV)) Nov. 15
34  Auburn .......  18  Birmingham ....Nov. 29
*30  Baylor ........   2  Cotton Bowl ..Jan. 1, 1981
352                 98
```

1981—WON 9, LOST 2, TIED 1
SEC CHAMPIONS

```
24  LSU ..........   7  Baton Rouge (TV) ..Sept. 5
21  Georgia Tech..  24  Birmingham ....Sept. 12
19  Kentucky .....  10  Lexington ......Sept. 19
28  Vanderbilt ....   7  Nashville ......Sept. 26
38  Mississippi ....   7  Tuscaloosa .......Oct. 3
13  Southern Miss..  13  Birmingham ....Oct. 10
38  Tennessee ....  19  Birmingham ....Oct. 17
31  Rutgers .......   7  Tuscaloosa .....Oct. 24
13  Miss. State ....  10  Tuscaloosa ......Oct. 31
31  Penn. State ....  16  University.Pk. (TV)Nov. 14
28  Auburn .......  17  Birmingham (TV) Nov. 28
*12  Texas ........  14  Cotton Bowl .Jan. 1, 1982
296                151
```

1982—WON 8, LOST 4

```
45  Georgia Tech..   7  Atlanta ........Sept. 11
42  Mississippi ....  14  Jackson .........Sept. 18
24  Vanderbilt ....  21  Tuscaloosa ......Sept. 25
34  Arkansas State .   7  Birmingham (N) ...Oct. 2
42  Penn. State ....  21  Birmingham (TV) ..Oct. 9
28  Tennessee ....  35  Knoxville ......Oct. 16
21  Cincinnati ....   3  Tuscaloosa .....Oct. 23
20  Miss. State ....  12  Jackson .......Oct. 30
10  LSU ..........  20  Birmingham ....Nov. 6
29  Southern Miss..  38  Tuscaloosa .....Nov. 13
22  Auburn .......  23  Birmingham (TV) Nov. 27
*21  Illinois ........  15  Liberty Bowl (N) .Dec. 29
338                216
```

1983—WON 8, LOST 4

```
20  Georgia Tech..   7  Birmingham .....Sept. 10
40  Mississippi ....   0  Tuscaloosa .....Sept. 17
44  Vanderbilt .....  24  Nashville (N) ....Sept. 24
44  Memphis State .  13  Tuscaloosa ......Oct. 1
28  Penn. State ....  34  State College (TV) .Oct. 8
34  Tennessee ....  41  Birmingham ......Oct. 15
35  Miss. State ....  18  Tuscaloosa ......Oct. 29
32  LSU ..........  26  Baton Rouge (TV) .Nov. 5
28  Southern Miss .  16  Birmingham ....Nov. 12
13  Boston College .  20  Foxboro (TV) ....Nov. 19
20  Auburn .......  23  Birmingham (TV) .Dec. 3
*28  SMU ........   7  Sun Bowl (TV) .Dec. 24
366                229
```

1984—WON 5, LOST 6

```
31  Boston College .  38  Birmingham (TV) .Sept. 8
 6  Georgia Tech ...  16  Atlanta (TV) ....Sept. 15
37  SW Louisiana ..  14  Tuscaloosa .....Sept. 22
21  Vanderbilt .....  30  Tuscaloosa .....Sept. 29
14  Georgia .......  24  Birmingham (TV) ..Oct. 6
 6  Penn State ....   0  Tuscaloosa ......Oct. 13
27  Tennessee ....  28  Knoxville .......Oct. 20
24  Miss. State ....  20  Jackson .......Nov. 3
14  LSU ..........  16  Birmingham ....Nov. 10
29  Cincinnati ....   7  Cincinnati ......Nov. 17
17  Auburn .......  15  Birmingham (TV) .Dec. 1
226                208
```

1985—WON 9, LOST 2, TIED 1

```
20  Georgia .......  16  Athens (TV) ....Sept. 2
23  Texas A&M ....  10  Birmingham (TV) Sept. 14
45  Cincinnati ....  10  Tuscaloosa .....Sept. 21
40  Vanderbilt ....  20  Nashville (TV) ...Sept. 28
17  Penn State ....  19  State College (TV) .Oct. 12
14  Tennessee ....  16  Birmingham (TV) .Oct. 19
28  Memphis State .   9  Memphis ......Oct. 26
44  Miss. State ....  28  Tuscaloosa .......Nov. 2
14  LSU ..........  14  Baton Rouge (TV) .Nov. 9
24  Southern Miss .  13  Tuscaloosa .....Nov. 16
25  Auburn .......  23  Birmingham (TV) Nov. 30
*24  Southern Cal..   3  Aloha Bowl (TV) .Dec. 28
226                208
```

*Indicates Bowl game

1986—WON 10, LOST 3

16	Ohio State	10	East Rutherford (N) (TV)
			.... Aug. 27
42	Vanderbilt	10	Tuscaloosa (TV) . . . Sept. 6
31	Southern Miss .	17	Birmingham . . . . Sept. 13
21	Florida	7	Gainesville . . . . . Sept. 20
28	Notre Dame	10	Birmingham (TV) . . Oct. 4
37	Memphis St.	0	Tuscaloosa . . . . . . Oct. 11
56	Tennessee	28	Knoxville (TV) . . . Oct. 18
3	Penn State	23	Tuscaloosa (TV) . . Oct. 25
38	Miss. State	3	Starkville (TV) . . . . Nov. 1
10	LSU	14	Birmingham (N) (TV)
			.... Nov. 8
24	Temple	14	Tuscaloosa . . . . . . Nov. 15
17	Auburn	21	Birmingham (TV)
			.... Nov. 29
*28	Washington	6	Sun Bowl (TV) . . . . . Dec. 25

1987—WON 7, LOST 5

38	Southern Miss	6	Birmingham . . . . Sept. 5
24	Penn State	13	State College (N) (TV)
			...................Sept. 12
14	Florida	23	Birmingham (TV).. Sept. 19
30	Vanderbilt	23	Nashville (N) . . . . . . Sept. 26
38	SW Louisiana	10	Birmingham . . . . Oct. 3
10	Memphis State	13	Memphis . . . . Oct. 10
41	Tennessee	22	Birmingham (N) (TV)
			...................Oct. 17
21	Miss. State	18	Birmingham (N) . . . Oct. 31
22	LSU	10	Baton Rouge (N) (TV)
			...................Nov. 7
6	Notre Dame	37	South Bend (TV) . . . Nov. 14
0	Auburn	10	Birmingham (TV).. Nov. 25
*24	Michigan	28	Hall of Fame (TV) . . . Jan. 2
268		213	

1988—WON 9, LOST 3

37	Temple	0	Philadelphia (N) . . . Sept. 10
44	Vanderbilt	10	Tuscaloosa . . . . Sept. 24
31	Kentucky	27	Lexington (TV) . . . . . . Oct. 1
12	Ole Miss	22	Tuscaloosa (TV) . . . . . . Oct. 8
28	Tennessee	20	Knoxville . . . . Oct. 15
8	Penn State	3	Birmingham (TV) . . . Oct. 22
53	Miss. State	34	Starkville . . . . Oct. 29
18	LSU	19	Tuscaloosa (TV) . . . . . Nov. 5
17	SW Louisiana	0	Birmingham . . . . Nov. 12
10	Auburn	15	Birmingham (TV) . Nov. 25
30	Texas A&M	10	College Station (N)(TV)
			...........................Dec. 1
*29	Army	28	Sun Bowl (TV) . . . . . . Dec. 24
297		188	

1989—WON 10, LOST 2

35	Memphis State	7	Birmingham . . . . Sept. 16
15	Kentucky	3	Tuscaloosa (TV) . . . Sept. 23
20	Vanderbilt	14	Nashville (TV) . . . . . . Sept. 30
62	Ole Miss	27	Jackson . . . . Oct. 7
24	SW Louisiana	17	Tuscaloosa . . . . Oct. 14
47	Tennessee	30	Birmingham (TV) . . . Oct. 21
17	Penn State	16	State College (TV) . . . Oct. 28
23	Miss. State	10	Birmingham (TV) . . . Nov. 4
32	LSU	16	Baton Rouge (N)(TV)
			........................Nov. 11
37	Southern Miss	14	Tuscaloosa . . . . Nov. 18
20	Auburn	30	Auburn (TV) . . . . Dec. 2
*25	Miami	33	Sugar Bowl (N)(TV) . . . Jan. 1
357		217	

1990–WON 7, LOST 5

24	Southern Miss	27	Birmingham . . . Sept. 8
13	Florida	17	Tuscaloosa . . . . Sept. 15
16	Georgia	17	Athens . . . . . . Sept. 22
59	Vanderbilt	28	Tuscaloosa . . . . Sept. 29
25	USL	6	Lafayette . . . . Oct. 6
9	Tennessee	6	Knoxville . . . . . . Oct. 20
0	Penn State	9	Tuscaloosa . . . . . Oct. 27
22	Miss State	0	Starkville . . . . Nov. 3
24	LSU	3	Tuscaloosa . . . . . Nov. 10
45	Cincinnati	7	Birmingham . . . Nov. 17
16	Auburn	7	Birmingham . . . . Dec. 1
7	Louisville	34	Tempe . . . . Jan. 1
260		161	

*Indicates Bowl game

162